Briefs of Leading Cases in Corrections

Second Edition

Rolando V. del Carmen

Sam Houston State University

Susan E. Ritter

University of Texas at Brownsville

Betsy A. Witt

Sam Houston State University

anderson publishing co.
2035 Reading Rd.
Cincinnati, OH 45202
1-800-582-7295

Briefs of Leading Cases in Corrections

ISBN 0-87084-116-5
Library of Congress Catalog Number 97-75146

Elisabeth Roszmann Ebben *Editor*
Elizabeth A. Shipp *Assistant Editor*

Preface

Many new cases have been added to *Briefs of Leading Cases in Corrections*. It is current as of September 1997. Some cases have been deleted from the earlier edition to make room for new and more important cases.

As in the previous edition, cases briefed are divided into: FACTS, ISSUE, DECISION, REASON, and CASE SIGNIFICANCE. In addition, a new feature, the CAPSULE, is added at the beginning of every case after the case title and citation. The CAPSULE summarizes the court's decision and is included to facilitate understanding of the case.

The cases briefed are taken from several legal sources. For readers unfamiliar with legal citation, the following provides guidance to the citations used in this text:

U.S. *United States Reports.* This is the official source of U.S. Supreme Court decisions. It is published by the United States government.

S. Ct. *Supreme Court Reporter.* This reports U.S. Supreme Court cases and is published by the West Publishing Company, a private publisher.

Cr. L. *Criminal Law Reporter.* This reports U.S. Supreme Court decisions, and is published by the Bureau of National Affairs, Inc., a private publisher.

L.W. *United States Law Week.* This reports U.S. Supreme Court decisions, and is also published by the Bureau of National Affairs, Inc., a private publisher.

The first case in this book is *Turner v. Safley*, 107 S. Ct. 2254 (1987). For those unfamiliar with legal citation, 107 S. Ct. 2254 (1987) means that this case is found in Volume 107 of the *Supreme Court Reporter*, starting on page 2254, and was decided in 1987. The same case may also be found, however, in different volumes and pages of the *United States Reports* **(U.S.)**, *the Criminal Law Reporter* **(Cr. L.)**, and *United States Law Week* **(L.W.)**.

The authors hope that this book contributes to a better understanding of the various aspects of corrections law.

Rolando V. del Carmen
College of Criminal Justice
Sam Houston State University

Contents

Chapter 3—Parole 141

Chapter 4—Death Penalty 165

Chapter 5—Juvenile Justice 209

Table of Cases

List of Cases with "Capsule"

Prisons and Jails—Prisons and Jails Introductory Case: Current Standard Set by the United States Supreme Court to Determine Whether Prison Regulations and Laws Violate the Constitutional Rights of Inmates

Turner v. Safley, 482 U.S. 78 (1987): A prison regulation that impinges on inmates' constitutional rights is valid if it is reasonably related to legitimate penological interests.

A. Conditions of Confinement—In General

Bell v. Wolfish, 441 U.S. 520 (1979): "Double bunking," the "publisher only rule," body cavity searches of pretrial detainees after contact visits, and searches of a pretrial detainee's quarters in his absence are constitutional.

Wilson v. Seiter, 59 L.W. 4671 (1991): "Deliberate indifference" is required for liability in conditions of confinement cases. In conditions of confinement cases under Section 1983, "deliberate indifference" means a "culpable state of mind" on the part of prison officials.

Helling v. McKinney, 53 Cr. L. 2230 (1993): Prison conditions that pose an alleged risk of harm to a prisoner's health, both in the future and in the present, can be actionable under the Eighth Amendment's prohibition against cruel and unusual punishment.

B. Conditions of Confinement—Double Celling

Rhodes v. Chapman, 452 U.S. 337 (1981): Double celling of prisoners does not, in itself, constitute cruel and unusual punishment.

C. Consent Decree—Modification

Griffin v. Illinois, 351 U.S. 12 (1956): Indigent inmates in noncapital cases are entitled to adequate and effective appellate review, including a stenographic transcript of the trial proceeding.

Burns v. Ohio, 360 U.S. 252 (1959): Indigent inmates are constitutionally entitled to have their motions to appeal a felony conviction considered without paying a filing fee.

Rufo v. Inmates of Suffolk County Jail, 60 L.W. 4100 (1992): Modification of a consent decree may be allowed by federal law under certain circumstances.

D.   Court Access

Johnson v. Avery, 393 U.S. 483 (1969): Prison authorities cannot prohibit prisoners from helping other prisoners prepare legal writs unless they provide reasonable alternatives whereby inmates can have access to the courts.

Bounds v. Smith, 430 U.S. 817 (1977): Prison authorities are required to assist inmates by providing meaningful access to the courts.

Murray v. Giarratano, 109 S. Ct. 2765 (1989): States are not required by the Constitution to provide inmates with a lawyer in post-conviction (meaning after appeal, as in habeas corpus) proceedings even in death penalty cases.

Lewis v. Casey, 64 L.W. 4587 (1996): The constitutional right of court access is violated only if a prisoner's attempt to pursue a legal claim is hindered by prison officials. Inadequacies in a state's delivery of legal services to inmates is insufficient as a basis for such claim.

E.   Counsel

United States v. Gouveia, 104 S. Ct. 2292 (1984): Inmates in administrative segregation (as distinguished from those in punitive segregation) are not entitled to counsel prior to the initiation of judicial proceedings.

McFarland v. Scott, 114 S. Ct. 2568 (1994): Federal law requires that an indigent capital offender be given a lawyer even before a habeas petition is filed. Under that law, a federal district court has the authority to stay an execution as soon as the inmate asks for a lawyer to be able to file a habeas petition.

F.   Damages

Smith v. Wade, 33 Cr. L. 3021 (1983): Punitive damages may be awarded in addition to compensatory damages if a correctional officer acts with reckless or callous disregard of, or indifference to, the rights and safety of inmates.

G.   Disciplinary Hearings

Wolff v. McDonnell, 418 U.S. 539 (1974): Inmates are entitled to due process in prison disciplinary proceedings that can result in the loss of good-time credits or in punitive segregation.

Baxter v. Palmigiano, 425 U.S. 308 (1976): Inmates are not entitled to counsel or cross-examination in prison disciplinary hearings. In addition, silence by the inmate in a disciplinary proceeding may be given adverse evidentiary significance.

Cleavinger v. Saxner, 106 S. Ct. 496 (1985): Prison disciplinary board members are entitled to qualified immunity, not absolute immunity.

Ponte v. Real, 37 Cr. L. 3051 (1985): Reasons for refusing to call witnesses requested by an inmate in a disciplinary hearing need not be placed in writing or made part of the disciplinary record.

Superintendent, Walpole v. Hill, 37 Cr. L. 3107 (1985): Disciplinary board findings that result in loss of good-time credits must be supported by a "modicum" of evidence to satisfy due process requirements.

H.   Discrimination—Indigents

Smith v. Bennett, 365 U.S. 708 (1961): A $4 filing fee violates the constitutional rights of indigent inmates.

I.   Discrimination—Racial

Lee v. Washington, 390 U.S. 333 (1968): Racial segregation in prisons is unconstitutional, except when a compelling state interest justifies it.

J.   Due Process

Estelle v. Williams, 425 U.S. 501 (1976): An accused cannot be compelled to stand trial before a jury while dressed in identifiable prison clothes.

Hughes v. Rowe, 449 U.S. 5 (1980): Placing a prisoner in segregation without a hearing is unconstitutional, unless justified by emergency conditions. The award of attorney's fees against the prisoner in this case was not proper.

Parratt v. Taylor, 451 U.S. 527 (1981): Loss of inmate hobby materials because a correctional officer failed to follow prison regulations does not amount to a violation of an inmate's due process rights under the Constitution.

Daniels v. Williams, 474 U.S. 327 (1986): A negligent act of a prison official (such as leaving a pillow on the stairs) does not violate the due process rights of inmates.

K.   Use of Force

Whitley v. Albers, 475 U.S. 312 (1986): The shooting of a prisoner, without prior verbal warning, to suppress a prison riot did not violate the prisoner's right against cruel and unusual punishment. Liability arises only if such deadly force was used with "obduracy and wantonness."

Hudson v. McMillian, 60 L.W. 4151 (1992): Use of excessive physical force against a prisoner may constitute cruel and unusual punishment, even though no serious injury results, if that force was used "maliciously and sadistically" to cause harm.

L.   Good Faith Defense

Harlow v. Fitzgerald, 457 U.S. 800 (1982): Government officials performing discretionary functions are civilly liable only if their conduct violates a clearly established statutory or constitutional right of which a reasonable person would have known.

M.   Good-Time Reduction

Weaver v. Graham, 450 U.S. 24 (1981): A state statute that repeals an earlier statute and reduces the amount of good time deducted from a convicted inmate's sentence is unconstitutional if applied to an inmate whose offenses were committed before the law took effect.

N.   Habeas Corpus

Ex parte Hull, 61 S. Ct. 640 (1941): A state and its officers cannot abridge or impair a prisoner's right, given by federal law, to apply for a federal writ of habeas corpus.

Rose v. Lundy, 455 U.S. 509 (1982): Under federal law, state prisoners must exhaust state court remedies before filing for a writ of habeas corpus in federal court.

McCleskey v. Zant, 59 L.W. 4288 (1991): Failure to claim violation of a constitutional right in a first federal habeas corpus petition constitutes an abuse of the writ and precludes a claim in a second habeas corpus petition.

O.   Mail

Turner v. Safley, 482 U.S. 78 (1987): A prison regulation that impinges on inmates' constitutional rights (in this case the freedom to send and receive mail) is valid if it is reasonably related to legitimate penological interests.

Thornburgh v. Abbott, 109 S. Ct. 1874 (1989): Prison regulations regarding receipt of publications by inmates are valid if reasonably related to a legitimate penological interest.

P.   Medical Care

Estelle v. Gamble, 429 U.S. 97 (1976): "Deliberate indifference" to inmate medical needs constitutes cruel and unusual punishment.

West v. Atkins, 108 S. Ct. 2250 (1988): Private physicians under contract with the state are "acting under color of state law" when treating prisoners.

Washington v. Harper, 58 L.W. 4249 (1990): A prisoner with a serious mental illness may be treated with antipsychotic drugs against his will. There must be a hearing prior to such treatment, but the hearing does not have to be before a judge; a hearing before a special committee (in this case composed of a psychiatrist, a psychologist, and a correctional official) is sufficient.

Q.   Freedom of the Press

Pell v. Procunier, 417 U.S. 817 (1974): A state prison regulation prohibiting media interviews with specific inmates does not violate the constitutional rights of the media or the inmates as long as alternative means of communication are available.

Houchins v. KQED, Inc., 438 U.S. 1 (1978): The media have no right of access to inmates and prisons beyond that given to the general public.

R.   Protection of Inmates from Injury

DeShaney v. Winnebago County Department of Social Services, 57 L.W. 4218 (1989): The state has no duty to protect individuals who are not in state custody from harm by private persons. (This implies that the state may be held liable if the individual is under its custody, as when in prison.)

Farmer v. Brennan, 55 Cr. L. 2135 (1994): A prison official is not liable under the Eighth Amendment for injury inflicted on an inmate by other inmates "unless the official knows of and disregards an excessive risk of harm to an inmate." It is not enough for liability that "the risk was so obvious that a reasonable person should have noticed it."

S.   Freedom of Religion

Cruz v. Beto, 405 U.S. 319 (1972): Inmates must be given reasonable opportunities to exercise their religious beliefs.

O'Lone v. Estate of Shabazz, 482 U.S. 342 (1987): Prison policies that in effect prevented inmates from exercising freedom of religion are constitutional because they are reasonably related to legitimate penological interests.

T.   Searches and Seizures

Stone v. Powell, 428 U.S. 465 (1976): A habeas corpus petition in federal court will not be granted based on an alleged violation of the Fourth Amendment right if the same allegation was raised and rejected earlier in state court during the criminal trial.

Hudson v. Palmer, 468 U.S. 517 (1984): A prison cell may be searched without a warrant or probable cause because a prison cell is not protected by the Fourth Amendment.

U.   Administrative Segregation

Hewitt v. Helms, 459 U.S. 460 (1983): A formal hearing is not required to place an inmate in administrative segregation; an informal evidentiary review is sufficient.

V.   Punitive Segregation

Hutto v. Finney, 437 U.S. 678 (1978): Courts can set time limitations on solitary confinement (punitive segregation); they can also order that plaintiff's attorney's fees be paid from Department of Corrections funds.

W.   Transfer

Meachum v. Fano, 427 U.S. 215 (1976): Inmates are not entitled to due process when transferred intrastate (meaning from one prison to another within the state), even if conditions in one prison are less favorable than in another.

Montanye v. Haymes, 427 U.S. 236 (1976): A prisoner is not entitled to a hearing before being transferred to another prison facility within the state even if the reason for the transfer was disciplinary or punitive.

Vitek v. Jones, 445 U.S. 480 (1980): Inmates are entitled to due process in involuntary transfers from prison to a mental hospital.

X.   Union Membership and Activities

Jones v. North Carolina Prisoners' Labor Union Inc., 433 U.S. 119 (1977): A ban on prison union membership and activities is valid. Prisoners do not retain First Amendment rights that are inconsistent with their prison status or with the legitimate objectives of the corrections system.

Y.   Visitation

Block v. Rutherford, 468 U.S. 576 (1984): Prisoners have no constitutional right to contact visits or to observe shakedown searches of their cells.

Chapter 2—Probation

Ex parte United States (Killits), 37 S. Ct. 72 (1916): A federal district court does not have the legal authority to place a convicted felon on probation.

Mempa v. Rhay, 389 U.S. 128 (1967): A defendant has a constitutional right to a lawyer during probation revocation that is followed by sentencing (as opposed to probation revocation after the probationer has been sentenced).

Gagnon v. Scarpelli, 411 U.S. 778 (1973): Probationers are entitled to certain due process rights before probation can be revoked.

Cabell v. Chavez-Salido, 454 U.S. 432 (1982): Requiring American citizenship to become a probation officer is constitutional.

Bearden v. Georgia, 461 U.S. 660 (1983): It is unconstitutional to revoke probation based on failure to pay a fine or restitution if the probationer is indigent.

Minnesota v. Murphy, 465 U.S. 420 (1984): Statements made by a probationer to his probation officer during interrogation while not in custody are admissible in a subsequent criminal trial.

Black v. Romano, 471 U.S. 606 (1985): A sentencing judge does not have to indicate that he or she considered alternatives to incarceration before revoking probation.

Griffin v. Wisconsin, 483 U.S. 868 (1987): The search of a probationer's home without a warrant and based on reasonable grounds (which is a lower standard than probable cause) is valid.

Forrester v. White, 108 S. Ct. 538 (1988): Judges do not enjoy absolute immunity when not performing judicial or adjudicative acts. The act performed by the judge in this case was administrative, not judicial or adjudicative.

Chapter 3—Parole

Morrissey v. Brewer, 408 U.S. 471 (1972): A parolee must be given six basic due process rights prior to parole revocation.

Moody v. Daggett, 429 U.S. 78 (1976): An incarcerated parolee has no constitutional right to a prompt judicial hearing after a detainer is issued against him.

Greenholtz v. Nebraska Penal Inmates, 442 U.S. 1 (1979): Inmates are not entitled to due process rights under the Constitution in discretionary parole release determinations.

Martinez v. California, 444 U.S. 275 (1980): A state law exempting parole officers from civil liability under state law is valid. The Court did not decide, however, whether that state law can be used to defeat a civil liability claim under Section 1983 (a federal law) against the same state officials.

Jago v. Van Curen, 454 U.S. 14 (1981): An inmate does not have a due process right in the decision by a parole board to withdraw parole prior to the inmate's release.

Connecticut Board of Pardons v. Dumschat, 452 U.S. 458 (1981): Prior actions of the Board of Pardons in granting commutation of life sentences created no right nor entitlement to commutation. Inmates are not constitutionally entitled to reasons from the Board for rejecting their application for parole or commutation.

California Department of Corrections v. Morales, 57 Cr. L. 2021 (1995): A law decreasing the frequency of parole hearings for certain prisoners does not change the punishment for crimes already committed and, therefore, may be applied retrospectively without violating the ex post facto clause of the Constitution.

Lynce v. Mathis, No. 95-7452 (1997): A Florida statute canceling an inmate's provisional release is ex post facto if applied to a prisoner who was convicted before the law was in effect.

Young v. Harper, No. 95-1598 (1997): Oklahoma's pre-parole release program was equivalent to parole and therefore released prisoners under pre-parole were entitled to due process rights prior to being brought back to prison.

Chapter 4—Death Penalty

Louisiana ex rel. Francis v. Resweber, 329 U.S. 459 (1947): The carrying out of an execution after a failed first attempt does not violate the Constitution.

Furman v. Georgia, 408 U.S. 238 (1972): The death penalty violates the equal protection clause of the Fourteenth Amendment and the prohibition against cruel and unusual punishment and is therefore unconstitutional.

Gregg v. Georgia, 428 U.S. 153 (1976): Death penalty statutes that contain sufficient safeguards against arbitrary and capricious imposition are constitutional.

Pulley v. Harris, 465 U.S. 37 (1984): Proportionality review is not required in death penalty cases.

Ford v. Wainright, 106 S. Ct. 2595 (1986): An insane prisoner may not be executed.

Lockhart v. McCree, 476 U.S. 162 (1986): Prospective jurors opposed to the death penalty may be disqualified.

Tison v. Arizona, 481 U.S. 137 (1987): The death penalty may be imposed on defendants who did not specifically intend to kill their victims.

McCleskey v. Kemp, 481 U.S. 279 (1987): A statistical study suggesting racial discrimination in the imposition of death sentences does not make the sentence unconstitutional.

Sumner v. Shuman, 483 U.S. 66 (1987): A mandatory death penalty for inmates convicted of murder while in prison is unconstitutional.

Penry v. Lynaugh, 109 S. Ct. 2934 (1989): A mentally retarded defendant may be given the death penalty.

Whitmore v. Arkansas, 58 L.W. 4495 (1990): A third party cannot challenge the validity of a death sentence.

Lankford v. Idaho, 59 L.W. 4434 (1991): Lack of adequate notice during the sentencing hearing that the defendant might be given the death penalty violates due process if the judge later imposes the death penalty.

Payne v. Tennessee, 59 L.W. 4814 (1991): A victim impact statement is admissible in the sentencing phase of death penalty cases.

Morgan v. Illinois, 60 L.W. 4541 (1992): The defendant in death penalty cases must be allowed to ask a juror whether he or she would automatically vote to impose the death penalty upon conviction.

Graham v. Collins, 52 Cr. L. 2114 (1993): The relief sought by the prisoner could not be granted because it would require the announcement of a new rule of constitutional law that could not be done in habeas corpus cases. Also, the Texas statute is constitutional because it adequately narrowed the class of murder defendants eligible for the death penalty and permitted the sentencing authority to consider the mitigating circumstances raised by the defendant.

Arave v. Creech, 52 Cr. L. 2373 (1993): A capital sentencing provision that singles out first-degree murders committed with "utter disregard for human life" satisfies constitutional standards.

Johnson v. Texas, 53 Cr. L. 2257 (1993): A special instruction advising a death penalty jury that it could consider age as a mitigating factor is not required.

Simmons v. South Carolina, 114 S. Ct. 2187 (1994): Death penalty defendants are entitled to a jury instruction informing the jury that a "life" sentence means life imprisonment without parole.

Tuilaepa v. California, 55 Cr. L. 2244 (1994): Circumstances of the crime, the defendant's history of violent crimes, and the age of the defendant are constitutional as sentencing factors in death penalty cases.

Harris v. Alabama, 56 Cr. L. 2152 (1995): A capital sentencing law that calls for the sentencing judge to consider an advisory jury verdict is not constitutionally required to specify the weight the judge must give the advisory verdicts.

Chapter 5—Juvenile Justice

Haley v. Ohio, 68 S. Ct. 302 (1948): Coerced confessions are not admissible as evidence in a juvenile proceeding.

Kent v. United States, 383 U.S. 541 (1966): A juvenile must be given due process before being transferred from a juvenile court to an adult court.

In re Gault, 387 U.S. 1 (1967): Juveniles must be given four basic due process rights in adjudication proceedings that can result in confinement in an institution.

In re Winship, 397 U.S. 358 (1970): Proof beyond a reasonable doubt, not simply a preponderance of the evidence, is required in juvenile adjudication hearings in cases in which the act would have been a crime if it had been committed by an adult.

McKeiver v. Pennsylvania, 403 U.S. 528 (1971): Juveniles have no constitutional right to trial by jury in a delinquency proceeding.

Davis v. Alaska, 415 U.S. 308 (1974): Despite state confidentiality laws, the probation status of a juvenile witness may be brought out by the opposing lawyer on cross-examination.

Breed v. Jones, 421 U.S. 517 (1975): Juveniles are entitled to the constitutional right against double jeopardy.

Fare v. Michael C., 442 U.S. 707 (1979): A request by a juvenile to see his probation officer is not equivalent to asking for a lawyer.

Smith v. Daily Publishing Co., 443 U.S. 97 (1979): A state law making it a crime to publish the name of a juvenile charged with a crime is unconstitutional.

Schall v. Martin, 104 S. Ct. 2403 (1984): Preventive detention of juveniles is constitutional.

New Jersey v. T.L.O., 469 U.S. 325 (1985): Public school officials need only have "reasonable grounds" to search; they do not need a warrant or probable cause.

Thompson v. Oklahoma, 487 U.S. 815 (1988): It is cruel and unusual punishment to impose the death penalty on a juvenile who commits an offense at age 15 or younger.

Stanford v. Kentucky, 109 S. Ct. 2969 (1989): It is not cruel and unusual punishment to impose the death penalty on a juvenile who commits an offense at age 16 or older.

Coy v. Iowa, 487 U.S. 1012 (1988): Placing a screen between the complaining witnesses and the defendant during a criminal trial violates a defendant's right to confront witnesses and is unconstitutional.

Maryland v. Craig, 497 U.S. 836 (1990): A criminal defendant does not have an absolute right to face-to-face confrontation of witnesses.

Chapter 6—Sentencing

Weems v. United States, 217 U.S. 349 (1910): A sentence that is disproportionate to the offense constitutes cruel and unusual punishment.

Trop v. Dulles, 356 U.S. 86 (1958): Loss of American citizenship constitutes cruel and unusual punishment.

North Carolina v. Pearce, 395 U.S. 711 (1969): Full credit must be given upon reconviction to time already served in prison for the same offense. Judges may impose a higher sentence on reconviction.

Williams v. Illinois, 399 U.S. 235 (1970): A state law that requires "work off" for indigents beyond the maximum sentence is unconstitutional.

Tate v. Short, 401 U.S. 395 (1971): A state law that automatically converts a fine to imprisonment if an indigent defendant cannot pay is unconstitutional.

Harmelin v. Michigan, 59 L.W. 4839 (1991): Mandatory and disproportionate sentences are not necessarily unconstitutional.

Nichols v. United States, 114 S. Ct. 1921 (1994): Because an uncounseled misdemeanor conviction is valid as long as no term of imprisonment is imposed, a prior misdemeanor conviction obtained in the absence of counsel may be used for sentence enhancement for another offense.

Koon v. United States, 64 L.W. 4512 (1996): An appellate court should not review *de novo* (meaning afresh or anew) a decision to depart from the Federal Sentencing Guidelines. Instead, the question to be asked is whether the sentencing court abused its discretion.

Chapter 1—Prisons and Jails

Turner v. Safley, 482 U.S. 78 (1987)
Bell v. Wolfish, 441 U.S. 520 (1979)
Wilson v. Seiter, 59 L.W. 4671 (1991)
Helling v. McKinney, 53 Cr. L. 2230 (1993)
Rhodes v. Chapman, 452 U.S. 337 (1981)
Griffin v. Illinois, 351 U.S. 12 (1956)
Burns v. Ohio, 360 U.S. 252 (1959)
Rufo v. Inmates of Suffolk County Jail, 60 L.W. 4100 (1992)
Johnson v. Avery, 393 U.S. 483 (1969)
Bounds v. Smith, 430 U.S. 817 (1977)
Murray v. Giarratano, 109 S. Ct. 2765 (1989)
Lewis v. Casey, 64 L.W. 4587 (1996)
United States v. Gouveia, 104 S. Ct. 2292 (1984)
McFarland v. Scott, 114 S. Ct. 2568 (1994)
Smith v. Wade, 33 Cr. L. 3021 (1983)
Wolff v. McDonnell, 418 U.S. 539 (1974)
Baxter v. Palmigiano, 425 U.S. 308 (1976)
Cleavinger v. Saxner, 106 S. Ct. 496 (1985)
Ponte v. Real, 37 Cr. L. 3051 (1985)
Superintendent, Walpole v. Hill, 37 Cr. L. 3107 (1985)
Smith v. Bennett, 365 U.S. 708 (1961)

1

Lee v. Washington, 390 U.S. 333 (1968)
Estelle v. Williams, 425 U.S. 501 (1976)
Hughes v. Rowe, 449 U.S. 5 (1980)
Parratt v. Taylor, 451 U.S. 527 (1981)
Daniels v. Williams, 474 U.S. 327 (1986)
Whitley v. Albers, 475 U.S. 312 (1986)
Hudson v. McMillian, 60 L.W. 4151 (1992)
Harlow v. Fitzgerald, 457 U.S. 800 (1982)
Weaver v. Graham, 450 U.S. 24 (1981)
Ex parte Hull, 61 S. Ct. 640 (1941)
Rose v. Lundy, 455 U.S. 509 (1982)
McCleskey v. Zant, 59 L.W. 4288 (1991)
Turner v. Safley, 482 U.S. 78 (1987)
Thornburgh v. Abbott, 109 S. Ct. 1874 (1989)
Estelle v. Gamble, 429 U.S. 97 (1976)
West v. Atkins, 108 S. Ct. 2250 (1988)
Washington v. Harper, 58 L.W. 4249 (1990)
Pell v. Procunier, 417 U.S. 817 (1974)
Houchins v. KQED, Inc., 438 U.S. 1 (1978)
DeShaney v. Winnebago County Department of Social Services,
  57 L.W. 4218 (1989)
Farmer v. Brennan, 55 Cr. L. 2135 (1994)
Cruz v. Beto, 405 U.S. 319 (1972)
O'Lone v. Estate of Shabazz, 482 U.S. 342 (1987)
Stone v. Powell, 428 U.S. 465 (1976)
Hudson v. Palmer, 468 U.S. 517 (1984)
Hewitt v. Helms, 459 U.S. 460 (1983)
Hutto v. Finney, 437 U.S. 678 (1978)
Meachum v. Fano, 427 U.S. 215 (1976)
Montanye v. Haymes, 427 U.S. 236 (1976)
Vitek v. Jones, 445 U.S. 480 (1980)
Jones v. North Carolina Prisoners' Labor Union Inc., 433 U.S. 119 (1977)
Block v. Rutherford, 468 U.S. 576 (1984)

Introductory Case: Current Standard Set by the United States Supreme Court to Determine Whether Prison Regulations and Laws Violate the Constitutional Rights of Inmates

NOTE: The cases under Prisons and Jails are divided into topics and are arranged chronologically within each topic. Despite this, the case of *Turner v. Safley*, although decided comparatively recently, is the first case briefed in Prisons and Jails because it is arguably the most significant case ever to be decided by the Court in prison law. It is significant because it sets the legal standard by which prison regulations and state law allegedly infringing on prisoners' rights are judged. It says that prison regulations and state laws are valid as long as they are "reasonably related to legitimate penological interests," such interests being prison security, inmate rehabilitation, and the orderly running of the institution.

The case was decided in 1987 and the standard set has been applied by most courts to prison cases decided since then. It is likely that some cases briefed in this book involving the constitutionality of prison regulations and state law before this case was decided would perhaps be decided differently today using the *Turner* standard.

Turner v. Safley
482 U.S. 78 (1987)

CAPSULE: A prison regulation that impinges on inmates' constitutional rights is valid if it is reasonably related to legitimate penological interests.

FACTS: State prison inmates brought a class action challenging regulations of the Missouri Division of Corrections that (1) permit correspondence between immediate family members who are inmates at different institutions and between inmates concerning legal matters, but allows other inmate correspondence only if each inmate's classification/treatment deems it in the best interest of the parties (this had the effect of prohibiting inmate-to-inmate correspondence); and (2) permit an inmate to marry only with the prison superintendent's permission, which can only be given when there are "compelling" reasons to do so. Testimony indicated that generally only a pregnancy or the birth of an illegitimate child would be considered "compelling."

ISSUES: (1) Does a regulation that permits correspondence between immediate family members who are inmates at different institutions and between inmates concerning legal matters, but allows other correspondence only if it is in the best interests of the parties violate the constitutional rights of inmates? NO.

(2) Does a regulation permitting an inmate to marry only when there are compelling reasons violate an inmate's constitutional right? YES.

DECISION: A prison regulation that impinges on inmates' constitutional rights is valid if it is reasonably related to legitimate penological interests. The factors to be considered in making the reasonableness determination include:

1. whether there is a valid, rational connection between the regulation and the legitimate government interest put forward to justify it;
2. whether there are alternative means of exercising the right that remain open to prisoners;
3. the impact that accommodation of the asserted right will have on correctional officers and inmates, and on the allocation of prison resources generally; and
4. the existence of ready alternatives to the regulation.

Under the above factors, (1) the inmate-to-inmate correspondence rule is reasonably related to legitimate security concerns of prison officials and (2) the inmate marriage regulation is not reasonably related to any legitimate penological objective and is therefore a denial of inmates' constitutional rights under the First Amendment.

REASON: "The prohibition on correspondence between institutions is logically connected to these legitimate security concerns . . . The rule is content neutral, it logically advances the goals of institutional security and safety identified by Missouri prison officials, and it is not an exaggerated response to these objectives. On that basis, we conclude that the regulation does not unconstitutionally abridge the First Amendment rights of prison inmates.

"The right to marry, like many other rights, is subject to substantial restrictions as a result of incarceration. Many important attributes of marriage remain, however, after taking into account the limitations imposed by prison life. First, inmate marriages, like others, are expressions of emotional support and public commitment . . . In addition, many religions recognize marriage as having spiritual significance; . . . Third, most inmates eventually will be released by parole or commutation, and therefore most inmate marriages are formed in the expectation that they ultimately will be fully consummated. Finally, marital status often is a precondition to the receipt of government benefits, property rights, and other, less tangible benefits . . . Taken together, we conclude that these remaining elements are sufficient to form a constitutionally protected marital relationship in the prison context."

CASE SIGNIFICANCE: The effect of this decision is twofold. First, it dispels the confusion as to the proper standard courts should use when balancing inmates' rights and prison authority. In previous cases, the Court used various tests, such as "compelling state interest," "least restrictive means," and "rational relationship," to decide prison cases. No single test was prescribed, hence lower courts adopted the test they wanted to use—depending upon the constitutional right invoked. For example, some courts gave better protection to violations of First Amendment rights than to others. This case does not make such a distinction, saying instead that the "reasonable relationship" test is to be used every time there is an alleged violation of a constitutional right. Second, this decision gives prison authorities more power and authority in prison administration. All they must do is prove that a prison regulation is reasonably related to a legitimate penological interest in order for that regulation to be valid even if a constitutional right is infringed. That standard is easier to establish than the "compelling state interest" or the "least restrictive means" tests. It is therefore a conservative decision that limits constitutional rights and expands state power.

The Court laid out four factors to be considered when determining reasonableness, giving lower courts better guidance when deciding cases. It is obvious from reading these factors, however, that they are far from clear and can be interpreted in various ways. Although precision in standards has yet to be attained, this decision draws a bright line rule by which prison cases alleging violations of constitutional rights are judged. This is an improvement over the unguided past. Note, however, that this standard does not apply to state tort cases filed by prisoners.

A. Conditions of Confinement—In General

Bell v. Wolfish
441 U.S. 520 (1979)

CAPSULE: **"Double bunking," the "publisher only rule," body cavity searches of pretrial detainees after contact visits, and searches of a pretrial detainee's quarters in his absence are constitutional.**

FACTS: Pretrial detainees at the New York City Metropolitan Correctional Center (MCC) filed a lawsuit alleging violation of their constitutional rights. The Center had opened less than four months before and had been described as "the architectural embodiment of the best and most progressive penological planning" and "unquestionably a top-flight, first-class facility." However, within a short time after opening, the facility became filled above its planned capacity and correctional officials began replacing single bunks in the cells and dormitories with double bunks. The inmates filed a lawsuit alleging violations of statutory and constitutional rights arising from overcrowded conditions, undue length of confinement, improper searches, inadequate recreational facilities, lack of educational and employment opportunities, insufficient staff, and restrictions on the purchase and receipt of personal items and books. The restriction on books and publications prohibited the receipt of all books and magazines mailed from outside the MCC except those sent directly from a publisher or a book club.

ISSUE: Are pretrial detainees' conditions of confinement that include double bunking, post-contact visit body cavity searches, searches of detainees' quarters, and prohibit the receipt of books and magazines from sources other than the publisher unconstitutional?   NO.

DECISION:
1.   "Double bunking" did not deprive the pretrial detainees of liberty without due process of law;
2.   The "publisher only" rule did not violate inmates' First Amendment rights;
3.   The policy on body cavity searches of pretrial detainees after contact visits did not violate their Fourth Amendment rights; and
4.   The rule permitting searches of a pretrial detainee's quarters in his absence did not violate his constitutional rights under the Fourth Amendment.

REASON: "In evaluating the constitutionality of conditions or restrictions of pretrial detention that implicate only the protection against deprivation of liberty without due process of law, we think that the proper inquiry is whether those conditions amount to punishment of the detainee. For under the Due Process Clause, a detainee may not be punished prior to an adjudication of guilt in accordance with the due process of law. Not every disability imposed during pretrial detention amounts to 'punishment' in the constitutional sense, however. Once the Government has exercised its conceded authority to detain a person pending trial, it obviously is entitled to employ devices that are calculated to effectuate this detention. Traditionally, this has meant confinement in a facility which, no matter how modern or how antiquated, results in restricting the movement of a detainee in a manner in which he would not be restricted if he simply were free to walk the streets pending trial.

"Absent a showing of an expressed intent to punish on the part of detention facility officials, the determination generally will turn on '[w]hether an alternative purpose to which [the restriction] may rationally be connected is assignable for it, and whether it appears excessive in relation to the alternative purpose assigned [to it].' Thus, if a particular condition or restriction of pretrial detention is reasonably related to a legitimate governmental objective, it does not, without more, amount to 'punishment.' Judged by this analysis, respondents' claim that double-bunking violated their due process rights fails. Neither the District Court nor the Court of Appeals intimated that it considered double-bunking to constitute punishment: instead, they found that it contravened the compelling necessity test, which today we reject. On this record, we are convinced as a matter of law that double-bunking as practiced at the MCC did not amount to punishment and did not, therefore, violate respondents' rights under the Due Process Clause of the Fifth Amendment.

"A fortiori, pretrial detainees, who have not been convicted of any crimes, retain at least those constitutional rights that we have held are enjoyed by convicted prisoners. But our cases also have insisted on a second proposition: simply because prison inmates retain certain constitutional rights does not mean that these rights are not subject to restrictions and limitations. We conclude that a prohibition against receipt of hardback books unless mailed directly from publishers, book clubs or bookstores does not violate the First Amendment rights of MCC inmates. That limit restriction is a rational response by prison officials to an obvious security problem . . . Corrections officials concluded that permitting the introduction of packages of personal property and food would increase the risk of gambling, theft and inmate fights over that which the institution already experienced by permitting certain items to be purchased from its commissary. It is also all too obvious that such packages are handy devices for the smuggling of contraband. There is simply no basis in this record for concluding that MCC officials have exaggerated their response to these serious problems or that this restriction is irrational. It does not therefore deprive the convicted inmates or pretrial detainees of the MCC of their property without due process of law in contravention of the Fifth Amendment

"Inmates at all Bureau of Prison facilities, including the MCC, are required to expose their body cavities for visual inspection as a part of a strip search conducted after every contact visit with a person from outside the institution. The searches must be conducted in a reasonable manner. But we deal here with the question whether visual body cavity inspections as contemplated by the MCC rules can ever be conducted on less than probable cause. Balancing the significant and legitimate security interests of the institution against the privacy interest of the inmates, we conclude that they can.

"Judges, after all, are human. They, no less than others in our society, have a natural tendency to believe that their individual solutions to often intractable problems are better and more workable than those of the persons who are actually charged with and trained in the running of the particular institution under examination. But under the Constitution, the first question to be answered is not whose plan is best, but in what branch of the Government is lodged the authority to initially devise the plan. This does not mean that constitutional rights are not to be scrupulously observed. It does mean, however, that the inquiry of federal courts into prison management must be limited to the issue of whether a particular system violates any prohibition of the Constitution, or in the case of a federal prison, a statute."

CASE SIGNIFICANCE: This is one of the few cases decided by the Court on the rights of pretrial detainees who are housed in jails. In essence, the Court rejected the concept of the presumption of innocence for pretrial detainees in favor of the need for jail authorities to run the institution in a secure and orderly manner. The Court said, however, that confinement conditions will constitute a violation of due process if: (1) the detainees are subjected to "genuine privation and hardships over an extended period of time" or (2) if detainees are subjected to conditions that are "not reasonably related to a legitimate goal." These two conditions, however, are not much different from those that would also make unconstitutional the confinement of those already convicted. In effect, the Court gave the go-ahead signal for jail officials to run the institution the way prisons are managed, although jails hold both convicts and pretrial detainees. This case implies that although jails and prisons are different in a number of ways, they are treated by the Court for purposes of inmates' rights as though they are the same. This is because the problems of institutional order and security are similar whether an institution houses pretrial detainees or convicts.

Wilson v. Seiter
59 L.W. 4671 (1991)

CAPSULE: "Deliberate indifference" is required for liability in conditions of confinement cases. In conditions of confinement cases under Section 1983, "deliberate indifference" means a "culpable state of mind" on the part of prison officials.

FACTS: Petitioner Pearly Wilson, a felon incarcerated at the Hocking Correctional Facility (HCF) in Nelsonville, Ohio, filed suit under 42 U.S.C. §1983, alleging that the conditions of his confinement constituted cruel and unusual punishment in violation of the Eighth and Fourteenth Amendments. These conditions of confinement included the following: overcrowding, excessive noise, insufficient locker storage space, inadequate heating and cooling, improper ventilation, unclean and inadequate rest rooms, unsanitary dining facilities and food preparation, and housing with mentally and physically ill inmates. Wilson sought declaratory and injunctive relief in addition to $900,000 in compensatory and punitive damages.

Motions for summary judgment with supporting affidavits were filed by both parties. Wilson's affidavits described the challenged conditions and charged that the authorities failed to take remedial action after notification. Seiter's affidavits denied the existence of some of the alleged conditions and described efforts by prison officials to improve the others.

ISSUE: Does a lawsuit alleging that conditions of confinement constitute cruel and unusual punishment require a showing of "deliberate indifference" on the part of prison officials? YES.

DECISION:
1. The "deliberate indifference" standard applies generally to inmate challenges to conditions of confinement.
2. An inmate making the claim that conditions of confinement violate the Eighth Amendment must show a "culpable state of mind" (meaning intent) on the part of prison officials.

REASON: "*Estelle v. Gamble, Rhodes v. Chapman, Whitley v. Albers* . . . These cases mandate inquiry into a prison official's state of mind when it is claimed that the official has inflicted cruel and unusual punishment . . . The source of the intent requirement is not the predilections of this Court, but the Eighth Amendment itself, which bans only cruel and unusual punishment. If the pain inflicted is not formally meted out as punishment by the statute or the sentencing judge, some mental element must be attributed to the inflicting officer before it can qualify . . . The long duration of a cruel prison condition may make it easier to establish knowledge and hence some form of intent, cf. *Canton v. Harris*, 489 U.S. 378, 390, n. 10 (1989); but there is no logical reason why it should cause the requirement of intent to evaporate.

"As described above, our cases say that the offending conduct must be wanton . . . *Whitley* makes clear, however, that in this context wantonness does not have a fixed meaning but must be determined with 'due regard for differences in the kind of conduct against which an Eighth Amendment objection is lodged.' 475 U.S., at 320 . . . The parties agree that the very high state of mind prescribed by *Whitley* does not apply to prison conditions cases. Petitioner argues that, to the extent officials' state of mind is relevant at all, there is no justification for a standard more demanding than *Estelle*'s 'deliberate indifference.'

"There is no indication that, as a general matter, the actions of prison officials with respect to these nonmedical conditions are taken under materially different constraints than their actions with respect to medical conditions. Thus, as retired Justice Powell has concluded: 'Whether one characterizes the treatment received by [the prisoner] as inhumane conditions of confinement, failure to attend to his medical needs, or a combination of both, it is appropriate to apply the "deliberate indifference" standard articulated in *Estelle*.'

"The Court of Appeals proceeded to uphold the District Court's dismissal of petitioner's remaining claims on the ground that his affidavits failed to establish the requisite culpable state of mind . . . It appears from this, and from the consistent reference to 'the *Whitley* standard' elsewhere in this opinion, that the court believed that the criterion of liability was whether the respondents acted 'maliciously and sadistically for the very purpose of causing harm,' *Whitley*, 475 U.S., at 320-321. To be sure, mere negligence would satisfy neither that nor the more lenient 'deliberate indifference' standard, so that any error on the point may have been harmless. Conceivably, however, the court would have given further thought to its finding of '[a]t best . . . negligence' if it realized that that was not merely an argument of a fortiori, but a determination almost essential to the judgment. Out of an abundance of caution, we vacate the judgment of the Sixth Circuit and remand the case for reconsideration under the appropriate standard."

CASE SIGNIFICANCE: This case is significant because it makes it difficult for inmates to recover damages from prison officials in conditions of confinement cases. The Court in this case said that the "deliberate indifference" standard used in *Estelle v. Gamble*, 429 U.S. 97 (1976) applies to these types of cases. The Court added that "a prisoner claiming that the conditions of his confinement violate the Eighth Amendment must show a culpable state of mind on the part of prison officials," stating further that, "an intent requirement is implicit in that Amendment's [Eighth] ban on cruel and unusual punishment." It will be difficult for inmates, alleging cruel and unusual punishment stemming from prison conditions, to establish that prison authorities allowed conditions to exist because of a "culpable state of mind," meaning that there was intent on their part that deplorable prison conditions should be allowed to continue. In most cases, poor conditions of confinement are mainly attributable to old facilities or lack of funds, both of which are outside the control of prison administrators. Since prison officials themselves work in the facility, a great majority of them want prison conditions to improve, but they may not have the resources or the authority to do it, hence a "culpable state of mind" is hard to prove.

While this case represents good news for prison administrators, it has the opposite effect for prisoners, who will now find it more difficult to seek improvement in prison conditions by filing cases against prison administrators. Prisoners may now have to seek relief primarily through the political process, an avenue that has traditionally been inhospitable to prisoners.

Helling v. McKinney
53 Cr. L. 2230 (1993)

CAPSULE: Prison conditions that pose an alleged risk of harm to a prisoner's health, both in the future and in the present, can be actionable under the Eighth Amendment's prohibition against cruel and unusual punishment.

FACTS: McKinney, a Nevada state prisoner, filed a claim under 42 U.S.C. §1983, stating that he was subjected to environmental tobacco smoke (ETS). The cause of this exposure was a cellmate who smoked five packs of cigarettes a day. The inmate alleged that he experienced health problems as a result of this exposure, which was cruel and unusual punishment, in violation of the Eighth Amendment. Both parties agreed to a jury trial before a magistrate. The magistrate held that the two issues to be considered were whether the inmate had a constitutional right to be housed in a smoke-free environment and whether prison officials showed deliberate indifference to the inmate's serious medical needs. He found that there was no constitutional right to be housed in a smoke-free environment, but that the inmate could state a claim for deliberate indifference if the underlying facts could be proven. However, the magistrate held that the inmate had failed to present evidence which indicated that his medical problems were the result of environmental tobacco smoke or the result of deliberate indifference on the part of prison officials.

ISSUE: Can the health risk posed by a prison inmate's involuntary exposure to environmental tobacco smoke (ETS) form the basis of a claim for relief under the Eighth Amendment? YES.

DECISION: The inmate has a cause of action under the Eighth Amendment by his allegations that prison officials, with deliberate indifference, exposed him to levels of ETS that pose an unreasonable risk of serious damage to his future health. The prisoner does not need to show that the condition he challenges has caused a current health problem; conditions that pose serious threats to his future health are also actionable.

REASON: "We have great difficulty agreeing that prison authorities may not be deliberately indifferent to an inmate's current health problems but may ignore a condition of confinement that is sure or very likely to cause serious illness and needless suffering the next week or month or year. In *Hutto v. Finney*, 437 U.S. 678, 682 (1978), we noted that inmates in punitive isolation were crowded into cells and some of them had infectious maladies such as hepatitis and venereal disease . . . It is 'cruel and unusual punishment to hold convicted criminals in unsafe conditions.' *Youngberg v. Romeo*, 457 U.S. 307, 315-316 (1982). It would be odd to deny an injunction to inmates who plainly proved an unsafe, life-threatening condition in their prison on the ground that nothing yet had happened to them . . . We thus reject petitioner's central thesis that only deliberate indifference to current serious health problems of inmates is actionable under the Eighth Amendment.

"With respect to the objective factor, McKinney must show that he himself is being exposed to unreasonably high levels of ETS. Plainly relevant to this determination is the fact that McKinney has been moved from Carson City to Ely State Prison and is no longer the cellmate of a five-pack-a-day smoker . . . Moreover, the Director of the Nevada State Prisons adopted a formal smoking policy on January 10, 1992 . . . It is possible that the new policy will be administered in a way that will minimize the risk to McKinney and make it impossible for him to prove that he will be exposed to unreasonable risk with respect to his future health or that he is now entitled to an injunction.

"Also with respect to the objective factor, determining whether McKinney's conditions of confinement violate the Eighth Amendment requires more than a scientific and statistical inquiry into the seriousness of the potential harm and the likelihood that such injury to health will actually be caused by exposure to ETS. It also requires a court to assess whether society considers the risk that the prisoner complains of to be so grave that it violates contemporary standards of decency to expose *anyone* unwillingly to such a risk.

"On remand, the subjective factor, deliberate indifference, should be determined in light of the prison authorities' current attitudes and conduct, which may have changed considerably since the judgment of the Court of Appeals. Indeed, the adoption of the smoking policy mentioned above will bear heavily on the inquiry into deliberate indifference."

CASE SIGNIFICANCE: This case is significant because it: (1) holds that the condition an inmate challenges need not cause a current health problem for the condition to be actionable, and (2) gives officials a great deal of authority to control or prohibit smoking in jails and prisons.

In this case, the inmate could not prove a current health damage resulting from excessive smoking by his cellmate. Prison officials therefore said that the allegation of injury to the inmate was "speculative" and "not sufficiently grave" as to be actionable under the cruel and unusual punishment clause. The Court disagreed, saying that "an unreasonable risk of serious damage to his future health states an Eighth Amendment cause of action" against the prison system.

This is the only case decided by the Court thus far on the controversial issue of controlling smoking in prisons. The Court in effect agreed that smoking is a health hazard for inmates and may therefore be curtailed. This decision gives prison officials authority to control or even completely prohibit smoking in prisons, justifying a no-smoking policy on the ground of possible lawsuit emanating from inmates who do not smoke. Many jails and prisons have already banned smoking in their facilities. Challenges in court by inmates who smoke are unlikely to succeed.

B. Conditions of Confinement—Double Celling

Rhodes v. Chapman
452 U.S. 337 (1981)

CAPSULE: Double celling of prisoners does not, in itself, constitute cruel and unusual punishment.

FACTS: State prisoners in the Southern Ohio Correctional Facility brought a class action suit against state officials in federal district court under 42 U.S.C. §1983, alleging that double celling (the housing of two inmates in a single cell) in itself violated the Constitution, and claiming they were entitled to injunctive relief. The prisoners alleged that double celling confined cellmates too closely and was a source of overcrowding. The inmates sought injunctive relief to bar prison officials from housing more than one inmate in a cell, except as a temporary measure. The District Court decided that double celling was cruel and unusual punishment in violation of the Eighth Amendment. The decision was based on five factors: (1) inmates at the prison were serving long terms of imprisonment; (2) the prison housed 38 percent more inmates than it was designed to hold; (3) several studies recommended that each inmate have at least 50 to 55 feet of living quarters while two double-celled inmates at the institution shared 63 feet; (4) the suggestion that double-celled inmates spend most of their time in their cells with their cellmates; and (5) the fact that the policy of double celling was not a temporary condition.

Prison officials appealed to the Court of Appeals for the Sixth Circuit, which affirmed the decision. The Court of Appeals viewed the District Court's opinion as holding that double celling was cruel and unusual punishment under the circumstances at the Southern Ohio Correctional Facility, not that double celling was unconstitutional per se. The U.S. Supreme Court granted certiorari "because of the importance of the question to prison administration."

ISSUE: Is the housing of two inmates in a single cell cruel and unusual punishment, prohibited by the Eighth and Fourteenth Amendments? NO.

DECISION: "Double celling" of inmates in prison is not, in and of itself, cruel and unusual punishment. There may be some instances, however, when because of deprivation of food, medical care, crowding, sanitation, and other factors, the conditions may be so poor as to constitute a violation of the Eighth Amendment's cruel and unusual punishment clause. The conditions at the Southern Ohio Correctional Facility did not constitute cruel and unusual punishment.

REASON: "Conditions that cannot be said to be cruel and unusual under contemporary standards are not unconstitutional. To the extent that such conditions are restrictive and even harsh, they are part of the penalty that criminal offenders pay for their offenses against society . . . The double celling made necessary by the unanticipated increase in prison population did not lead to deprivations of essential food, medical care, or sanitation. Nor did it increase violence among inmates or create other conditions intolerable for prison confinement. Although job and educational opportunities diminished marginally as a result of double celling, limited work hours and delay before receiving education do not inflict pain, much less unnecessary and wanton pain; deprivations of this kind simply are not punishments.

"The five considerations on which the District Court relied also are insufficient to support its constitutional conclusion . . . These general considerations fall far short in themselves of proving cruel and unusual punishment, for there is no evidence that double celling under these circumstances either inflicts unnecessary or wanton pain or is grossly disproportionate to the severity of crimes warranting imprisonment."

CASE SIGNIFICANCE: Although this case said that double celling in itself is not cruel and unusual punishment, there are instances in which it can be. The key to understanding how the Court ruled in this case is to realize that, as the District Court said, the physical plant at the Southern Ohio Correctional Facility was "unquestionably a top-flight, first-class facility." Among other things, the court found that each cell measures approximately 63 square feet, each contains a bed measuring 36 by 80 inches, has a cabinet-type night stand, a wall-mounted sink with hot and cold running water, and every cell has a heating and air circulation vent near the ceiling, and 960 of the cells have a window that inmates can open and close. The day rooms are located adjacent to the cell blocks and are open to the inmates between 6:30 a.m. and 9:30 p.m. Each day room contains a wall-mounted television, card tables, and chairs. The facility was built in the early 1970s and is therefore relatively modern.

Given the "top-flight, first-class" nature of the facility, this was not a difficult case for the Court to decide. The decision would have been different had conditions in the particular facility been bad. The Court said: "Courts certainly have a responsibility to scrutinize claims of cruel and unusual confinement, and conditions in a number of prisons, especially older ones, have justly been described as 'deplorable' and 'sordid.' " Double celling, therefore, becomes cruel and unusual punishment if the conditions are bad. How bad must the conditions be? That becomes a question of fact that must be decided by the courts on a case-by-case basis.

C. Consent Decree—Modification

Griffin v. Illinois
351 U.S. 12 (1956)

CAPSULE: Indigent inmates in noncapital cases are entitled to adequate and effective appellate review, including a stenographic transcript of the trial proceeding.

FACTS: Griffin and Crenshaw were tried and convicted of armed robbery. In order to appeal, they requested that a certified copy of their entire court record, including a stenographic transcript of the proceedings, be furnished to them without cost due to their indigent status. Illinois statute allowed that trial transcripts be furnished free of charge only to indigent death row inmates. The inmates filed suit, alleging that the failure of the court to provide them with a transcript violated the due process and equal protection clauses of the Fourteenth Amendment. The trial court denied the motion without a hearing.

ISSUE: Is it a violation of the due process or equal protection clauses of the Fourteenth Amendment to deny indigent inmates in noncapital cases a stenographic transcript of the trial proceeding? YES.

DECISION: Although not constitutionally required to do so, a state that does grant appellate review cannot discriminate against indigent convicted felons. Adequate appellate review includes furnishing trial transcripts to indigent inmates free of charge.

REASON: "In this tradition, our own constitutional guaranties of due process and equal protection both call for procedures in criminal trials which allow no invidious discriminations between persons and different groups of persons. Both equal protection and due process emphasize the central aim of our entire judicial system—all people charged with a crime must, so far as the law is concerned, 'stand on an equality before the bar of justice in every American court.' *Chambers v. Florida*, 309 U.S. 227, 241.

"In criminal trials a State can no more discriminate on account of poverty than on account of religion, race, or color. Plainly the ability to pay cost in advance bears no rational relationship to a defendant's guilt or innocence and could not be used as an excuse to deprive a defendant of a fair trial.

"There is no meaningful distinction between a rule which would deny the poor the right to defend themselves in a trial court and the one which effectively denies the poor an adequate appellate review accorded to all who have money enough to pay the costs in advance . . . Appellate review has now become an integral part of the Illinois trial system for finally adjudicating the guilt or innocence of a defendant. Consequently, at all stages of the proceedings the due process and equal protection clauses protect persons like the petitioners from invidious discriminations."

CASE SIGNIFICANCE: This case, decided in 1956, holds that although states are not constitutionally required to give inmates a stenographic transcript of trial proceedings, it is required to do so if that right is given by state law to one group of inmates. The Court's decision was based primarily on equal protection, meaning that individuals cannot be treated differently, particularly if the effect of the different treatment is discrimination based on financial status. The Illinois law discriminated against inmates who could not afford to pay for their own transcript. The case holds that discrimination against inmates based on economics is unconstitutional.

It is not clear whether this case would have been decided the same way if it were heard today. This is because over the last few decades the Court has consistently implied that death penalty cases are different from other types of offenses and therefore may be treated differently. There is still no constitutional right to a transcript of the criminal trial, but whether this case, based on equal protection, is still authoritative, is debatable.

Burns v. Ohio
360 U.S. 252 (1959)

CAPSULE: Indigent inmates are constitutionally entitled to have their motions to appeal a felony conviction considered without paying a filing fee.

FACTS: Burns was convicted of burglary and sentenced to life imprisonment. This conviction was affirmed without opinion by the Ohio Court of Appeals. The inmate filed notice of appeal immediately with this court but he did not actually appeal the case until four years later. At that time, he attached an affidavit of poverty to his notice of appeal and motion for leave to appeal before the Ohio Supreme Court. The Clerk of the Supreme Court refused to file the papers and sent a letter to the inmate stating that the Rules of Practice of the Supreme

Court, which required a docket fee of $20, took precedence over any other stat-
ute that may have allowed a pauper's affidavit in lieu of the docket fee. This
letter was considered to be the judgment of the Ohio Supreme Court. The inmate filed suit, alleging that the Court's refusal to consider his appeal without
the $20 docket fee was in violation of the Fourteenth Amendment.

ISSUE: Does the denial of an indigent inmate's application to appeal a felony
conviction based solely on his inability to pay a filing fee violate the Fourteenth
Amendment? YES.

DECISION: Denial of the inmate's right to appeal based solely on his inability
to pay a filing fee violates the Fourteenth Amendment. The state chose to allow
appellate review; it cannot foreclose indigent inmates from access to that procedure.

REASON: "Although the State admits that petitioner 'in truth and in fact' is a
pauper, it presses several arguments which it claims distinguish *Griffin v. Illinois*, 351 U.S. 12, and justify the Ohio practice. First, the State argues that petitioner received one appellate review of his conviction in Ohio, while in *Griffin*,
Illinois had left the defendant without any judicial review of his conviction.
This is one distinction without a difference for, as *Griffin* holds, once the State
chooses to establish appellate review in criminal cases, it may not foreclose indigents from access to any phase of that procedure because of their poverty.
    ". . . Ohio seeks to distinguish *Griffin* on the further ground that leave to
appeal to the Supreme Court of Ohio is a matter of discretion. But this argument misses the crucial significance of *Griffin*. In Ohio, the defendant who is
not indigent may have the Supreme Court consider on the merits of his application for leave to appeal from a felony conviction. But . . . an indigent defendant
is denied that opportunity. There is no rational basis for assuming that indigents' motions for leave to appeal will be less meritorious than those of other
defendants. Indigents must, therefore, have the same opportunities to invoke the
discretion of the Supreme Court of Ohio.
    "Here, the action of the State has completely barred the petitioner from
obtaining any review at all in the Supreme Court of Ohio. The imposition by
the State of financial barriers restricting the availability of appellate review for
indigent criminal defendants has no place in our heritage of Equal Justice."

CASE SIGNIFICANCE: This case reiterates the principle that no offender
should be discriminated against based on financial status, because such would
be a violation of the equal protection clause. Burns' appeal of a felony conviction here was refused because he could not pay the docket fee of $20. The
Court held that the Ohio law was discriminatory and therefore unconstitutional.

This case does not hold that docket fees for appeals are unconstitutional. What it holds is that if a defendant is too poor to pay a docket fee, the defendant should be exempt from payment and allowed to appeal the conviction.

Rufo v. Inmates of Suffolk County Jail
60 L.W. 4100 (1992)

CAPSULE: Modification of a consent decree is allowed by federal law under certain circumstances.

FACTS: After conditions in the Suffolk County Jail were held unconstitutional, the inmates and county officials entered into a consent decree that provided for the construction of a new jail that was to have single-occupancy cells for pretrial detainees. There was a delay in the construction, during which time the inmate population increased beyond projections. While construction was still under way, the sheriff moved to modify the consent decree to allow double bunking so the jail's capacity could be increased. The sheriff relied on Federal Rule of Civil Procedure 60(b), which provides that "upon such terms as are just, the court may relieve a party (from compliance with a consent decree) for the following reasons: . . . (5) . . . it is no longer equitable that the judgment should have prospective operation." The District Court denied relief, saying that "nothing less than a clear showing of grievous wrong evoked by new and unforeseen conditions should lead . . . to change in what was decreed after years of litigation with the consent of all concerned." This decision was affirmed by the Court of Appeals; the sheriff and the county appealed.

ISSUE: Did the District Court apply the correct standard in denying the sheriff's motion for relief from the provisions of the consent decree? NO.

DECISION: Modification of a consent decree is allowed by federal law "when changed factual conditions make compliance with the decree substantially more onerous, when the decree proves to be unworkable because of unforeseen obstacles, or when enforcement of the decree without modification would be detrimental to the public interest." The stricter "grievous wrong" standard used by the District Court does not apply to requests to modify consent decrees stemming from institutional reform litigation.

REASON: "Although we hold that a district court should exercise flexibility in considering requests for modification of an institutional reform consent decree, it does not follow that a modification will be warranted in all circumstances. Rule 60(b)(5) provides that a party may obtain relief from a court order when 'it is no longer equitable that the judgment should have prospective application,' not when it is no longer convenient to live with the terms of a consent decree. Accordingly, a party seeking modification of a consent decree bears the burden of establishing that a significant change in circumstances warrants revision of the decree. If the moving party meets this standard, the court should consider whether the proposed modification is suitably tailored to the changed circumstances.

"A party seeking modification of a consent decree may meet its initial burden by showing either a significant change in factual conditions or in law.

"Modification of a consent decree may be warranted when changed factual conditions make compliance with the decree substantially more onerous. Such a modification was approved by the District Court in this litigation in 1985 when it became apparent that plans for the new jail did not provide sufficient cell space. Modification is also appropriate when a decree proves to be unworkable because of unforeseen obstacles, *New York State Assn. for Retarded Children, Inc. v. Carey*, 706 F.2d at 969 (modification allowed where State could not find appropriate housing facilities for transfer patients); *Philadelphia Welfare Rights Organization v. Shapp*, 602 F.2d at 1120-1121 (modification allowed where State could not find sufficient clients to meet decree targets); or when enforcement of the decree without modification would be detrimental to the public interest, *Duran v. Elrod*, 760 F.2d 756, 759-761 (modification allowed to avoid pretrial release of accused violent felons).

"Respondents urge that modification should be allowed only when a change in facts is both 'unforeseen and unforeseeable.' Such a standard would provide even less flexibility than the exacting *Swift* test; we decline to adopt it. Litigants are not required to anticipate every exigency that could conceivably arise during the life of a consent decree.

"Ordinarily, however, modification should not be granted where a party relies upon events that actually were anticipated at the time it entered into a decree . . . If it is clear that a party anticipated changing conditions that would make performance of the decree more onerous but nevertheless agreed to the decree, that party would have to satisfy a heavy burden to convince a court that it agreed to the decree in good faith, made a reasonable effort to comply with the decree and should be relieved of the undertaking under Rule 60(b)."

CASE SIGNIFICANCE: This is a significant case in prison litigation because it addresses an issue that faces many jurisdictions: May a consent decree (a consent decree is an agreement arrived at by the two sides in a case and presented to the judge for approval), once entered, be modified by the parties and, if so, under what conditions?

A consent decree is an approach used by numerous courts to settle disputes in litigation involving prisons and jails. It allows the parties to come together and agree among themselves on conditions for settlement, after which the agreement is presented as a document to the court for approval. Consent decrees have the advantage of arriving at the solution after negotiation by both parties, instead of the solution being imposed on one or both parties by the judge. As the term implies, a consent decree is an agreement acceptable to both parties.

There are instances, however, in which one of the parties desires changes for various reasons. In this case, the sheriff sought modification of the consent decree while construction was still under way to allow double bunking so as to raise the jail's capacity. His reason was that the inmate population had outpaced population projections, hence the single-occupancy cell requirement for pretrial detainees under the consent decree became difficult for the county to meet. The District Court denied modification, saying that the county failed to demonstrate a "grievous wrong evoked by new or unforeseen conditions." This standard was enunciated by the Court in *United States v. Swift & Co.*, 286 U.S. 106 (1932) and, according to the Court, was codified by Rule 60(b)(5) of the Federal Rules of Civil Procedure, the section of law relied upon by the sheriff. The Court disagreed with this strict standard set by the District Court, holding that the "grievous wrong" test does not apply to consent decrees involving institutional reform litigation, such as prison cases. The Court opted for a less stringent and more flexible standard (easier for the government to establish), which states that modification may be allowed under the following conditions: (1) when changed factual conditions make compliance with the decree substantially more onerous; (2) when the decree proves to be unworkable because of unforeseen obstacles; or (3) when enforcement of the decree without modification would be detrimental to the public interest. Under this standard, "the party seeking modification of the consent decree (in this case the sheriff of Suffolk County) bears the burden of establishing that a significant change in facts or law warrants revision of the decree and that the proposed modification is suitably tailored to the changed circumstances."

The new standard set by the Court in this case makes it easier for prison and jail authorities to modify consent decrees as long as any of the three conditions set by the Court above are present. The effect of this decision on prison cases may be two-edged. On the one hand, prison authorities may be more willing to settle cases through consent decrees, knowing that the agreement entered into may be modified later. Conversely, however, they may be tempted to enter into a consent decree without much serious thought given to the consequences, knowing that the institution can later go back to the court for modification. It makes the provisions of a consent decree more flexible, but less certain.

D. Court Access

Johnson v. Avery
393 U.S. 483 (1969)

CAPSULE: Prison authorities cannot prohibit prisoners from helping other prisoners prepare legal writs unless they provide reasonable alternatives whereby inmates can have access to the courts.

FACTS: Johnson, a Tennessee state prisoner, was transferred to the maximum-security building in the state prison because he assisted other prisoners in preparing writs, in violation of a prison regulation that provided: "no inmate will advise, assist or otherwise contract to aid another, either with or without a fee, to prepare writs or other legal matters." He filed a motion for relief from confinement in the maximum security building. The District Court held the prison regulation void because it effectively barred illiterate prisoners from access to federal habeas corpus. The prisoner was released from maximum security but was not given regular prison privileges or restored to normal prison conditions until he promised to refrain from assisting other inmates. Another hearing was held before the District Court concerning compliance with the conditions of the original order and this same order was reaffirmed. The Court of Appeals reversed, holding that the State's interest in preserving discipline and limiting the practice of law to attorneys justified any burden the regulation could place on access to federal habeas corpus.

ISSUE: May the state validly enforce a regulation that prohibits prisoners from assisting other prisoners in preparing writs? NO, but with exception.

DECISION: The State of Tennessee cannot enforce a regulation that absolutely bars inmates from furnishing assistance to other prisoners in the preparation of petitions for post-conviction relief in the absence of some provision by the state for a reasonable alternative to assist illiterate or poorly educated inmates in such preparation.

REASON: "It is indisputable that prison 'writ writers' like petitioner are sometimes a menace to prison discipline and that their petitions are often so unskillful as to be a burden on the courts which receive them. But, as this Court held in *Ex parte Hull*, in declaring invalid a state prison regulation which required that prisoners' legal pleadings be screened by state officials:

The considerations that prompted [the regulation's] formulation are not without merit, but the state and its officers may not abridge or impair petitioner's right to apply to a federal court for a writ of habeas corpus. 312 U.S., at 549.

"Tennessee does not provide an available alternative to the assistance provided by other inmates. The warden of the prison in which petitioner was confined stated that the prison provided free notarization of prisoners' petitions. That obviously meets only a formal requirement. He also indicated that he sometimes allowed prisoners to examine the listing of attorneys in the Nashville telephone directory so they could select one to write to in an effort to interest him in taking the case, and that 'on several occasions' he had contacted the public defender on the request of an inmate. There is no contention, however, that there is any regular system of assistance by public defenders. In its brief the State contends that '[t]here is absolutely no reason to believe that prison officials would fail to notify the court should an inmate advise them of a complete inability, either mental or physical, to prepare a habeas application on his own behalf,' but there is no contention that they have in fact ever done so.

"This is obviously far short of the showing required to demonstrate that, in depriving prisoners of the assistance of fellow inmates, Tennessee has not, in substance, deprived those unable themselves, with reasonable adequacy, to prepare their petitions, of access to the constitutionally and statutorily protected availability of the writ of habeas corpus."

CASE SIGNIFICANCE: Decided on February 24, 1969, this was one of the first major prison cases to be decided by the Court involving an alleged violation of a constitutional right—the right of access to the courts. The State of Tennessee prohibited inmates from helping other inmates in legal matters for fear that doing so would jeopardize prison security and order. Because the offending inmate was placed in solitary confinement as a result of rule violation, the trial court treated the case as a petition for a writ of habeas corpus instead of a §1983 case.

The Court agreed that prison "writ writers" sometimes constitute a menace to prison discipline and impose a burden on the courts because of their unskillful petitions. The Court declared the regulation invalid anyway because Tennessee did not provide an alternative to the assistance provided by prison "writ writers." Stated conversely, prison authorities may prohibit inmates from helping other inmates on legal matters as long as the prison authorities provide reasonable alternative assistance. The question then arises: what types of assistance are reasonable to the Court so as to justify the prohibition against inmate writ writers?

In this decision, the Court enumerated several systems used in other states, including: (1) a public defender system supplying trained attorneys, paid from public funds, who are available to consult with prisoners regarding their habeas corpus petitions; (2) employing senior law students to interview and advise inmates in state prisons; and (3) voluntary programs whereby members of the local bar association make periodic visits to the prison to consult with prisoners concerning their cases. Significantly, however, the Court then added that: "We express no judgment concerning these plans, but their existence indicates that techniques are available to provide alternatives if the State elects to prohibit mutual assistance among inmates." The Court made clear, however, that Tennessee's system of free notarization of prisoners' petitions, allowing prisoners to examine the listing of attorneys in the Nashville telephone directory so they could select one to write to in an effort to interest him to take the case, and occasionally contacting the public defender at the request of the inmate did not constitute a reasonable alternative.

Subsequent cases have shown that courts have not done a good job of defining what a "reasonable alternative" means. In some cases, even a combination of services to inmates is not enough to comply with the requirement of inmate access to courts. The bottom line is that it is difficult for prison systems to prohibit writ writers from practicing their craft in prison, but that practice can be regulated in the interest of prison order and security.

Bounds v. Smith
430 U.S. 817 (1977)

CAPSULE: Prison authorities are required to assist inmates by providing meaningful access to the courts.

FACTS: State prison inmates brought actions in federal court alleging that the state of North Carolina denied them reasonable access to the courts and equal protection as guaranteed by the First and Fourteenth Amendments, by failing to provide them with adequate legal library facilities. The actions were consolidated and the District Court granted the inmates' motion for summary judgment, which was modified and affirmed by the Court of Appeals. The court found that the sole prison library in the state was inadequate, especially in view of the decentralized prison system in which 13,000 inmates were housed in 77 prison units in 67 counties. The state proposed a plan to establish seven libraries in the institutions to which the inmates could request appointments where they would be given transportation and housing for a full day's library work. The inmates sought establishment of a library at every prison.

ISSUE: Does the constitutional right of access to the courts require prison authorities to assist inmates in the preparation and filing of meaningful legal papers by providing prisoners with adequate law libraries or adequate assistance from persons trained in the law? YES.

DECISION: The constitutional right of access to the courts requires prison authorities to assist inmates in the preparation and filing of meaningful legal papers by providing prisoners with adequate law libraries or adequate assistance from persons trained in the law. Adequate law libraries in prisons are one constitutionally acceptable method of assuring meaningful access to the courts, but they are not the only acceptable alternative for providing such access. Any alternatives used, however, must comply with constitutional standards.

REASON: "It is now established beyond doubt that prisoners have a constitutional right of access to the courts . . . While applications for discretionary review need only apprise an appellate court of a case's possible relevance to the development of the law, the prisoner petitions here are the first line of defense against constitutional violations. The need for new legal research or advice to make a meaningful initial presentation to a trial court in such a case is far greater than is required to file an adequate petition for discretionary review. We hold, therefore, that the fundamental constitutional right of access to the courts requires prison authorities to assist inmates in the preparation and filing of meaningful legal papers by providing prisoners with adequate law libraries or adequate assistance from persons trained in law.

"It should be noted that while adequate law libraries are one constitutionally acceptable method to assure meaningful access to the courts, our decision here, as in *Gilmore*, does not foreclose alternative means to achieve that goal . . . Among the alternatives are the training of inmates as paralegal assistants to work under lawyers' supervision, the use of paraprofessionals and law students, either as volunteers or in formal clinical programs, the organization of volunteer attorneys through bar associations or other groups, the hiring of lawyers on a part-time basis, and the use of full-time staff attorneys, working either in new prison legal assistance organizations or as part of public defender or legal services offices."

CASE SIGNIFICANCE: This case is important because it reaffirms the constitutional right of prisoners to meaningful access to the courts. This is in accordance with the previous cases of prisoners' access to the courts, including *Johnson v. Avery* (393 U.S. 483 [1969]) and *Younger v. Gilmore* (404 U.S. 15 [1971]). The *Avery* case concerned access to the courts through legal assistance from other inmates. The *Gilmore* case also dealt with the state's responsibility to furnish inmates with extensive law libraries or to provide them with professional or quasi-professional legal assistance.

The *Bounds* case lists possible alternatives that prisons can use for complying with the duty to provide access to the courts. These are: (1) training inmates as paralegal assistants to work under lawyers' supervision; (2) using paraprofessionals and law students as volunteers or in formal clinical programs; (3) organizing volunteer attorneys through bar associations or in other groups; (4) hiring lawyers on a part-time consultant basis; and (5) using full-time staff attorneys in new prison legal assistance organizations or as part of the public defender or legal services offices. Moreover, the Court said that indigent inmates must be provided, at state expense, with writing materials (paper and pen) to draft legal documents, with notarial services to authenticate them, and with stamps to mail them. This case expands the list of possible alternatives to court access mentioned in *Johnson v. Avery*, but goes beyond that by requiring prisons to provide items, such as paper and pen, to ensure that inmates can have access to the courts.

It must be noted by the reader, however, that the *Bounds* case, decided in 1977, has recently been reinterpreted by the Court in the case of *Lewis v. Casey*, 64 L.W. 4587 (1996).

Murray v. Giarratano
109 S. Ct. 2765 (1989)

CAPSULE: **States are not required by the Constitution to provide inmates with a lawyer in post-conviction (meaning after appeal, as in habeas corpus) proceedings even in death penalty cases.**

FACTS: Giarratano was a Virginia prisoner under sentence of death. He brought suit under 42 U.S.C. §1983 against various state officials, including Edward W. Murray, the Director of the Virginia Department of Corrections. Inmate Giarratano claimed that the Constitution required that he be provided with counsel, at state expense, to pursue collateral proceedings (meaning proceedings taken after the appeal on the conviction has been exhausted, such as a habeas corpus) related to his conviction and death sentence.

ISSUE: Does the Eighth Amendment or the due process clause of the Fourteenth Amendment require states to appoint counsel for indigent death row inmates seeking post-conviction relief? NO.

DECISION: The rule in *Pennsylvania v. Finley*, 481 U.S. 551 (1987), which states that the Constitution does not require states to provide counsel in post-conviction proceedings, applies to capital as well as non-capital cases.

REASON: "In *Finley* we ruled that neither the due process clause of the Fourteenth Amendment nor the equal protection guarantee of 'meaningful access' required the State to appoint counsel for indigent prisoners seeking state postconviction relief. The Sixth and Fourteenth Amendments to the Constitution assure the right of an indigent defendant to counsel at the trial stage of a criminal proceeding, *Gideon v. Wainwright*, 372 U.S. 335, 83 S. Ct. 792, 9 L. Ed. 2d 799 (1963), and an indigent defendant is similarly entitled as a matter of right to counsel for an initial appeal from the judgment and sentence of the trial court. But we held in *Ross v. Moffitt, supra*, 417 U.S., at 610, 94 S. Ct., at 2443, that the right to counsel at these earlier stages of a criminal procedure did not carry over to a discretionary appeal provided by North Carolina law from the intermediate appellate court to the Supreme Court of North Carolina.

"We think that these cases require the conclusion that the rule of *Pennsylvania v. Finley* should apply no differently in capital cases than noncapital cases. State collateral proceedings are not constitutionally required as an adjunct to the state criminal proceedings and serve a different and more limited purpose than either the trial or appeal. The additional safeguards imposed by the Eighth Amendment at the trial stage of a capital case are, we think, sufficient to assure the reliability of the process by which the death penalty is imposed. We therefore decline to read either the Eighth Amendment or the due process clause to require yet another distinction between the rights of capital case defendants and those in non-capital cases."

CASE SIGNIFICANCE: The significance of this case lays in the Court's holding that an indigent death-row inmate is not entitled to appointed counsel when seeking post-conviction relief even in death penalty cases. The decision is in accordance with the *Finley* decision of 1987, which held that neither the due process clause nor the equal protection clause of the Fourteenth Amendment requires the state to appoint counsel for indigent prisoners seeking postconviction relief. The Supreme Court noted, however, that death row inmates are entitled to adequate and timely access to a law library during the final weeks before their execution dates. Note that while a death row inmate is not entitled under the Constitution to a court-appointed lawyer in post-conviction proceedings, a lawyer is in fact often provided in these cases by state or federal law. It must also be noted that defendants in death penalty cases are constitutionally entitled to a lawyer during trial and during the appeal of a conviction.

Lewis v. Casey
64 L.W. 4587 (1996)

CAPSULE: The constitutional right of court access is violated only if a prisoner's attempt to pursue a legal claim is hindered by prison officials. Inadequacies in a state's delivery of legal services to inmates is insufficient as a basis for such claim.

FACTS: Casey and other inmates of various prisons operated by the Arizona Department of Corrections (ADOC) brought a class action suit against prison officials in Arizona. The lawsuit alleged violation of the First, Sixth, and Fourteenth Amendments by the officials, depriving the inmates of their rights of access to the courts and counsel through inadequate legal research facilities. The inmates alleged that this deprivation violated the ruling in *Bounds v. Smith*, which was decided 19 years before this case. The *Bounds* case held that the right of access to the courts requires that prison authorities assist inmates in the preparation and filing of meaningful legal papers by providing them with adequate law libraries or adequate assistance from persons trained in the law.

ISSUE: Did the inadequacies in the legal research facilities and the legal services provided by Arizona violate the constitutional rights of inmates in the absence of proof of actual injury? NO

DECISION:
1. Theoretical deficiencies in the prison's law library or legal assistance programs are not sufficient to establish a violation of the right of access to court. What is needed is a showing of widespread actual injury.

2. *Bounds v. Smith* did not create a right to a law library or legal assistance; instead, it merely acknowledged a right to court access.

REASON: "Because *Bounds* did not create an abstract, free-standing right to a law library or legal assistance, an inmate cannot establish relevant actual injury simply by establishing that his prison's law library or legal assistance program is sub-par in some theoretical sense . . . the inmate therefore must go one step further and demonstrate that the alleged shortcomings in the library or legal assistance program hindered his efforts to pursue a legal claim . . . Although *Bounds* itself made no mention of an actual-injury requirement, it can hardly be thought to have eliminated that constitutional prerequisite.

"After the trial in this case, the court found actual injury on the part of only one named plaintiff, Bartholic; and the cause of that injury—the inadequacy which the suit empowered the court to remedy—was failure of the prison to provide the special services that Bartholic would have needed, in light of his illiteracy, to avoid dismissal of his case. At the outset, therefore, we can eliminate from the proper scope of this injunction provisions directed at special services or special facilities required by non-English-speakers, by prisoners in lockdown, and by the inmate population at large.

"The District Court here failed to accord adequate deference to the judgment of the prison authorities in at least three significant respects. First, in concluding that ADOC's restrictions on lockdown prisoners' access to law libraries was unjustified . . . Second, the injunction imposed by the District Court was inordinately—indeed, wildly—intrusive . . . Finally, the order was developed through a process that failed to give adequate consideration to the views of state prison authorities."

CASE SIGNIFICANCE: This is a significant case because it clarifies the extent of an inmate's right of access to court. The inmates in this case alleged constitutional violations because the Arizona system of providing legal help to inmates disadvantaged some inmates, particularly non-English speaking inmates or those confined in segregation units. The trial court agreed with the inmates and issued an order, applicable throughout the Arizona prison system, mandating that segregated inmates be allowed library access and that legal assistance be provided to inmates lacking reading or English language skills. This order was made despite the absence of a finding by the trial court that the plaintiffs suffered actual injury.

The Court overturned the trial court's system-wide order for relief, saying that there must be proof that the prison officials actually hindered a prisoner's access to court, hence actually injuring that inmate, before relief can be granted. General inadequacies in a state's system of delivery of legal services are insufficient for such claim and cannot be the basis for system-wide relief. Neither are they a violation of constitutional rights.

The Court made clear that *Bounds v. Smith*, decided 19 years earlier, "did not create an abstract, free-standing right to a law library or legal assistance; rather the right that *Bounds* acknowledged was the right of access to the courts." This is significant because prior to *Lewis*, courts throughout the country interpreted *Bounds* to mean that prisons were constitutionally obliged to have law libraries as part of their prisoners' right of access to court. This involved huge expenses for the acquisition and maintenance of law libraries in jails and prisons. This case rejects that interpretation and plainly states that what *Bounds* created was merely the right of access to the courts. Whether prison systems will now discontinue the practice of having prison libraries remains to be seen. What is clear is that in this decision the Court has held that access to court is a constitutional right in prisons, but that the right to a law library is not.

E. Counsel

United States v. Gouveia
104 S. Ct. 2292 (1984)

CAPSULE: Inmates in administrative segregation (as distinguished from those in punitive segregation) are not entitled to counsel prior to the initiation of judicial proceedings.

FACTS: Four inmates, including Gouveia, were suspected of murdering a fellow inmate at a federal prison in Lompoc, California. They were placed in the Administrative Detention Unit (ADU) in early December, 1978. Later that month, prison officials held disciplinary hearings and determined that all four of the inmates had participated in the murder. Officials ordered their continued confinement in ADU, where the inmates were separated from the general prison population and confined to individual cells. However, they were allowed regular visitation rights, exercise periods, unmonitored phone calls, and access to legal materials.

The inmates remained in the ADU without appointed counsel for approximately 19 months. In June, 1980, a federal grand jury returned indictments against them on charges of first-degree murder and conspiracy to commit murder. They were arraigned in federal court in July, 1980, at which time counsel was appointed for them. All four of the inmates were subsequently convicted of both counts and were sentenced to consecutive life and 99-year terms of imprisonment.

Before the trial began, the inmates filed a motion to have their indictments dismissed, claiming that their confinement in the ADU without appointed counsel violated their Sixth Amendment right to counsel.

ISSUE: Does the Sixth Amendment require the appointment of counsel before indictment for indigent inmates confined in administrative detention while being investigated for criminal activities? NO.

DECISION: Inmates are not constitutionally entitled to the appointment of counsel while in administrative segregation and before any adversary judicial proceedings have been initiated against them. The right to counsel attaches only at or after the initiation of judicial proceedings against the defendant.

REASON: "The Court of Appeals majority held that each respondent had been denied his Sixth Amendment right to counsel . . . Five judges dissented from the en banc majority's Sixth Amendment holding. Relying on *Kirby v. Illinois, supra*, the dissent concluded that the Sixth Amendment right to counsel is triggered by the initiation of formal criminal proceedings even in the prison context, and that the majority's conclusion to the contrary shows a misunderstanding of the purpose of the counsel guarantee. We agree with the dissenting judges' application of our precedents to this situation, and, accordingly, we reverse the en banc majority's holding that respondents had a Sixth Amendment right to the appointment of counsel during their preindictment segregation.

"The view that the right to counsel does not attach until the initiation of adversary judicial proceedings has been confirmed by this court in cases subsequent to *Kirby* . . . that interpretation of the Sixth Amendment right to counsel is consistent not only with the literal language of the Amendment, which requires the existence of both a 'criminal prosecutio[n]' and an 'accused,' but also with the purposes which we have recognized that the right to counsel serves. We have recognized that the 'core purpose' of the counsel guarantee is to assure aid at trial, 'when the accused [is] confronted with both the intricacies of the law and the advocacy of the public prosecutor.'

"Thus, the majority's [Court of Appeal's] attempt to draw an analogy between an arrest and an inmate's administrative detention pending investigation may have some relevance in analyzing when the speedy trial right attaches in this context, but it is not relevant to a proper determination of when the right to counsel attaches."

CASE SIGNIFICANCE: In this case, the Court clarified the limits of the right to counsel for incarcerated prisoners. The Court interpreted the Sixth Amendment to mean that the right to counsel should be invoked only after an indictment and not while a criminal investigation is being conducted, even if the inmate is in administrative segregation at that time. This decision was expected; in fact, a different decision would have been surprising. This is because in an earlier case, *Kirby v. Illinois*, 406 U.S. 682 (1972), the Court held that a suspect has no right to counsel at police lineups or identification procedures prior to the time the suspect is formally charged with a crime. Certainly, inmates do not have more rights than people in the free world, including the right to counsel.

McFarland v. Scott
114 S. Ct. 2568 (1994)

CAPSULE: Federal law requires that an indigent capital offender be given a lawyer even before a habeas petition is filed. Under that law, a federal district court has the authority to stay an execution as soon as the inmate asks for a lawyer to be able to file a habeas petition.

FACTS: McFarland was convicted of capital murder and sentenced to death. His conviction and sentence were affirmed by the Texas Court of Criminal Appeals. The inmate filed a *pro se* (on his own) motion requesting the trial court stay or withdraw his execution date to allow the Texas Resource Center an opportunity to recruit volunteer counsel for his state habeas corpus proceeding. The trial court declined to appoint counsel but did change the inmate's execution date to a later date. Upon learning that the Resource Center could not find volunteer counsel, the court concluded that Texas law did not authorize the appointment of counsel for state habeas corpus proceedings and it did not do so. McFarland then filed a *pro se* motion in the Texas Court of Criminal Appeals requesting a stay of execution and a remand for counsel. The motion was denied. The inmate then filed a *pro se* motion in the U.S. District Court challenging his conviction and sentence under federal law and requesting appointment of counsel, also under federal law.

ISSUE: Does federal law authorize the federal court to appoint counsel and stay state execution proceedings as soon as the inmate seeks appointment of counsel and even before a formal application for federal habeas corpus relief has been filed? YES.

DECISION: Federal law provides that an indigent death row inmate be given counsel before a habeas corpus petition is filed and as soon as the inmate seeks appointment of counsel. This should be done even before a formal application for federal habeas corpus relief has been filed. Moreover, a federal district court has the authority to stay an execution date as soon as the inmate asks for counsel to be able to file a habeas corpus petition.

REASON: "Construing Section 848(q)(4)(B) in light of its related provisions, however, indicates that the right to appointed counsel adheres prior to the filing of a formal, legally sufficient habeas corpus petition. Section 848(q)(4)(B) expressly incorporates 21 U.S.C. Section 848(q)(9), which entitles capital defendants to a variety of expert and investigative services upon a showing of necessity . . . Section 848(q)(9) clearly anticipates that capital defense counsel will have been appointed under Section 848(q)(4)(B) before the need for such technical assistance arises, since the statute requires 'the defendant's attorneys to obtain such services' from the court . . . Congress thus established a right to preapplication legal assistance for capital defendants in federal habeas corpus proceedings . . . This interpretation is the only one that gives meaning to the statute as a practical matter.

"We thus conclude that the two statutes [federal statutes] must be read *in pari materia* to provide that once a capital defendant invokes his right to appointed counsel, a federal court also has jurisdiction under Section 2251 to enter a stay of execution. Because Section 2251 expressly authorizes federal courts to stay state court proceedings 'for any matter involved in the habeas corpus proceeding,' the exercise of this authority is not barred by the Anti-Injunction Act.

"We conclude that a capital defendant may invoke this right to counseled federal habeas corpus proceeding by filing a motion requesting the appointment of habeas counsel, and that a district court has jurisdiction to enter a stay of execution where necessary to give effect to the statutory right. McFarland filed a motion for appointment of counsel and for stay of execution in this case, and the District Court had authority to grant the relief he sought."

CASE SIGNIFICANCE: This decision is based on the provisions of federal law rather than on the Constitution. Relying on federal law, the inmate sought the appointment of counsel to help him file a habeas corpus petition. Such filing, the Court said, qualifies as the initiation of a habeas corpus proceeding and therefore entitled the inmate to counsel. Moreover, the filing of such request authorized the court to stay the prisoner's execution.

Inmates do not have a *constitutional* right to a lawyer in post-conviction (such as habeas corpus) proceedings. Title 21 U.S.C. §848(q)(4)(B), however, entitles capital defendants to "qualified legal representation in any post-conviction proceeding." This was the law used by the inmate in this case.

Although inmates do not have a constitutional right to counsel in post-conviction proceedings, such right has been given by federal law and, in some cases, also by state law. The realization is that a lawyer is necessary not only during appeal, but also during the filing of a post-conviction case after an appeal has been exhausted. This is particularly true in death penalty cases such as this one.

F. Damages

Smith v. Wade
33 Cr. L. 3021 (1983)

CAPSULE: Punitive damages may be awarded in addition to compensatory damages if a correctional officer acts with reckless or callous disregard of, or indifference to, the rights and safety of inmates.

FACTS: Daniel Wade voluntarily checked into a protective custody unit in a reformatory for youthful first offenders because of prior incidents of violence against him. Due to disciplinary violations, he received a short term in punitive segregation before being transferred to administrative segregation. On the first day that he was in administrative segregation, he was placed in a cell with another inmate. Later, William Smith, a correctional officer in the reformatory, placed another inmate in the cell. This third inmate was in administrative segregation for fighting, and Smith made no effort to determine whether another cell was available. Wade was harassed, beaten, and sexually assaulted. He brought suit under 42 U.S.C. §1983 in federal district court against Smith, four other correctional officers, and correctional officials, alleging that his Eighth Amendment rights had been violated. The prisoner was awarded compensatory damages in the amount of $25,000, and $5,000 in punitive damages.

Smith appealed the award of punitive damages, but not the compensatory damage award, claiming that the trial court judge erred in giving instructions to the jury as to when punitive damages can be awarded to a plaintiff.

ISSUE: Did the federal district court apply the correct legal standard in instructing the jury that it may award punitive damages if the defendant acted with reckless or callous disregard of, or indifference to, the rights and safety of others? YES.

DECISION: A jury may be permitted to assess punitive damages in a civil rights case if the defendant's conduct (1) is motivated by actual or malicious intent, and also (2) if the defendant acted with reckless or callous disregard of or indifference to the rights and safety of others.

REASON: "The large majority of state and lower federal courts were in agreement that punitive damage awards did not require a showing of actual malicious intent; they permitted punitive awards on variously stated standards of negligence, recklessness, or other culpable conduct short of actual malicious intent.

"The same rule applies today. The Restatement (Second) of Torts (1977), for example, states: 'Punitive damages may be awarded for conduct that is outrageous, because of the defendant's evil motive or his reckless indifference to the rights of others.' Most cases under common law, although varying in their precise terminology, have adopted more or less the same rule, recognizing that punitive damages in tort cases may be awarded not only for actual intent to injure or evil motive, but also for recklessness, serious indifference to or disregard for the rights of others, or even gross negligence."

CASE SIGNIFICANCE: There are generally three kinds of negligence for which a person may be held liable: (1) simple; (2) reckless; or (3) callous disregard of, or indifference to, the rights and safety of others, and actual or malicious intent. There are also three kinds of damages: (1) nominal, (2) compensatory, and (3) punitive. Nominal damages are acknowledgments by the court that plaintiff proved his or her allegations but suffered no actual injury, hence the amount awarded is small. Compensatory damages are those given for actual injuries or loss suffered, such as medical bills or lost wages. Punitive damages are those awarded to punish the wrongdoer and are typically awarded when the conduct is reckless, gross, or malicious. The issue in this case involved the award of punitive damages by the jury in accordance with the judge's instructions.

The jury awarded the prisoner, Daniel Wade, $25,000 in compensatory damages. Smith, the correctional officer, did not appeal the award. The compensatory damage award was based on the jury's finding that Smith acted with "reckless or callous disregard of or indifference to the rights and safety of others." Smith, however, objected to the punitive damage award of $5,000, saying that the judge erred in telling the jury that it could also impose a punitive damage award using the same standard as that for the compensatory award, namely: if Smith acted with "reckless or callous disregard of or indifference to the rights and safety of others." Smith maintained that punitive damages could be awarded only if the jury found that he (Smith) acted with "actual or malicious intent." Under this standard, Smith could not have been liable for punitive damages because there was no proof that he acted with actual or malicious intent.

The Court rejected Smith's appeal, saying that the judge could instruct the jury to assess punitive damages in a civil rights case if the defendant's conduct (1) is motivated by actual or malicious intent, and also (2) if the defendant acted with reckless or callous disregard of, or indifference to, the rights and safety of others. In sum, actual or malicious intent is not needed for punitive damages to be imposed; acting with reckless or callous disregard of, or indifference to, the rights and safety of others (as Smith did here) suffices. This makes it easier for plaintiffs in civil rights cases to recover punitive damages. This is important because many jury awards are high because of punitive damages. Compensatory damages are quantifiable and easy to determine (hospital expenses, lost wages, etc.), but punitive damages are difficult to quantify and hence are often excessive.

G. Disciplinary Hearings

Wolff v. McDonnell
418 U.S. 539 (1974)

CAPSULE: Inmates are entitled to due process in prison disciplinary proceedings that can result in the loss of good-time credits or in punitive segregation.

FACTS: Inmates at a Nebraska prison filed a complaint for damages and an injunction under 42 U.S.C. §1983 in which they alleged, among other complaints, that the Nebraska prison disciplinary proceedings violated their constitutional right to due process.

Under Nebraska's disciplinary procedure, forfeiture or withholding of good-time credits or confinement in a disciplinary cell is the penalty imposed for serious misconduct. To establish misconduct: (1) a preliminary conference is held with the chief corrections supervisor and the charging party, in which the prisoner is orally informed of the charge and the merits are preliminarily discussed; (2) a conduct report is prepared and a hearing held before the prison's disciplinary body, which is composed of three prison officials; and (3) the inmate may ask questions of the charging party.

ISSUE: Is due process required in prison disciplinary proceedings? YES.

DECISION: In prison disciplinary proceedings involving serious misconduct that can result in loss of good-time credits or punitive segregation, the inmate must be given the following due process rights:

1. Advance written notice of the charges must be given to the inmate no less than 24 hours prior to his or her appearance before the committee;
2. There must be a written statement by the factfinders as to the evidence relied on and reasons for the disciplinary action;
3. The inmate should be allowed to call witnesses and present documentary evidence in his or her defense, if permitting him or her to do so will not jeopardize institutional safety or correctional goals;
4. Counsel substitute (either a fellow inmate or staff member) will be permitted when the inmate is illiterate or when the complexity of the issues make it unlikely that the inmate will be able to collect and present the evidence for an adequate comprehension of the case; and
5. The prison disciplinary board must be impartial. The state may constitutionally require that mail from an attorney to a prisoner be identified as such, and that his or her name and address appear on the communication, and—as a protection against contraband—that the authorities may open such mail in the inmates' presence. A lawyer desiring to correspond with a prisoner may also be required first to identify him- or herself and his or her client to the prison officials to ensure that letters marked "privileged" are actually from members of the bar.

REASON: "We hold that written notice of the charges must be given to the disciplinary-action defendant in order to inform him of the charges and to enable him to marshal the facts and prepare a defense. At least a brief period of time after the notice, no less than 24 hours, should be allowed the inmate to pre-pare for the appearance before the Adjustment Committee . . . Written records of proceedings will thus protect the inmate against collateral consequences based on a misunderstanding of the nature of the original proceeding. Further, as to the disciplinary action itself, the provision for a written record helps to insure that administrators, faced with possible scrutiny by state officials and the public, and perhaps even the courts, where fundamental constitutional rights may have been abridged, will act fairly.

"Many prison officials, on the spot and with the responsibility for the safety of inmates and staff, are reluctant to extend the unqualified right to call witnesses; and in our view, they must have the necessary discretion without be-ing subject to unduly crippling constitutional impediments. There is much play in the joints of the Due Process Clause, and we stop short of imposing a more demanding rule with respect to witnesses and documents . . . As the nature of the prison disciplinary process changes in future years, circumstances may then exist which will require further considerations and reflection of this Court. It is our view, however, that the procedures we have now required in prison discipli-nary proceedings represent a reasonable accommodation between the interests of the inmates and the needs of the institution.

"We think it entirely appropriate that the State require any such communi-cations [between an attorney and an inmate] be specially marked as originating from an attorney, with his name and address being given, if they are to receive special treatment. It would also certainly be permissible that prison authorities require that a lawyer desiring to correspond with a prisoner, first identify him-self and his client to the prison officials, to assure that the letters marked privi-leged are actually from members of the bar. As to the ability to open the mail in the presence of inmates, this could in no way constitute censorship, since the mail would not be read. Neither could it chill such communications, since the inmate's presence insures that prison officials will not read the mail . . . We think that petitioners, by acceding to a rule whereby the inmate is present when mail from attorneys is inspected, have done all, and perhaps even more, than the Constitution requires."

CASE SIGNIFICANCE: This is an important case, because, for the first time, the Court acknowledged that inmates are entitled to certain due process rights during prison disciplinary proceedings. These due process rights are not the same as those enjoyed by people in the free world, but they provide a measure of protection against arbitrariness. The Court said that a prisoner "is not wholly stripped of constitutional protections" and that disciplinary proceedings must "be governed by a mutual accommodation between institutional needs and gen-erally applicable constitutional requirements." The Court did not give the in-mates all the rights they sought. Specifically, the Court said that an inmate has no constitutional right to: (1) confrontation and cross-examination, although such is discretionary with the prison officials, and (2) retained or appointed counsel.

The rights given in this case do not apply to all disciplinary cases, but only to situations involving serious misconduct, meaning misconduct that can result in forfeiture of good-time credits or punitive segregation. They do not apply to minor offenses, although jail and prison administrators are likely to give the above rights in all disciplinary cases anyway, either because of agency rules or court mandate.

It is important to realize that the term "due process" does not have a fixed meaning in law. Although it basically means "fundamental fairness," what is fundamentally fair varies from one case to another even in a prison setting. The question asked is: What process is due in a particular proceeding? For example, due process in prison disciplinary proceedings, where prisoners have diminished constitutional rights, is different from due process in criminal trials in which the right to due process is at its fullest. Even in prison, the concept of due process varies. The kind of due process needed in prison disciplinary proceedings is different from that required to place an inmate in administrative segregation. Many of the prison due process cases decided after *Wolff* deal with the question of what rights should be given an inmate in a particular prison proceeding, be it an issue of transfer to other facilities, classification, or transfer from prison to a mental institution. Due process rights in these cases are not always the same as those given in *Wolff*.

Although the inmates raised two other issues in this case, *Wolff* is best known as a prison disciplinary proceeding case in which due process rights were given to inmates. The two other issues raised were whether the regulations governing inmates' mail and the inmate legal assistance programs were constitutional. The Court upheld the mail regulation, but remanded the legal assistance issue to the lower court.

Baxter v. Palmigiano
425 U.S. 308 (1976)

CAPSULE: Inmates are not entitled to counsel or cross-examination in prison disciplinary hearings. In addition, silence by the inmate in a disciplinary proceeding may be given adverse evidentiary significance.

FACTS: Palmigiano, an inmate serving a life sentence for murder at the Rhode Island Adult Correctional Institution, was charged by correctional officers with inciting a disturbance and disruption of prison operations, which may have resulted in a riot. Summoned before the prison disciplinary board, he was informed that there was a possibility that he would be prosecuted for a violation of state law but that no charges were pending. He was advised that he should consult his attorney, although the board had not permitted his attorney to be present at the hearing. He was also advised that he had a right to remain silent during the hearing, but that if he did so it would be held against him. Prison rules provided for a counsel-substitute; the prisoner availed himself of these services and remained silent during the hearing. The board decided that Palmigiano should be placed in punitive segregation for 30 days and that his classification status should be downgraded thereafter.

The prisoner filed an action under 42 U.S.C. §1983 for damages and injunctive relief, claiming that the disciplinary hearing violated the due process clause of the Fourteenth Amendment.

ISSUE: Did the prison disciplinary proceedings in the Rhode Island Adult Correctional Institution violate the equal protection or the due process clauses of the Fourteenth Amendment? NO.

DECISION: Prison inmates do not have the right to either retained or appointed counsel in disciplinary hearings that are not part of a criminal prosecution, nor are they entitled to confront and cross-examine witnesses at all times. Further, an inmate's decision to assert his Fifth Amendment rights and remain silent at a disciplinary proceeding can be given adverse evidentiary significance by the prison board.

REASON: "We see no reason to alter our conclusion so recently made in *Wolff* that inmates do not 'have a right to either retained or appointed counsel in disciplinary hearings.' 418 U.S., at 570. Plainly, therefore, state authorities were not in error in failing to advise Palmigiano to the contrary, i.e., that he was entitled to counsel at the hearing and that the State would furnish counsel if he did not have one of his own.

"No criminal proceedings are or were pending against Palmigiano. The State has not, contrary to *Griffin*, sought to make evidentiary use of his silence at the disciplinary hearing in any criminal proceeding. Rhode Island neither insisted nor asked that Palmigiano waive his Fifth Amendment privilege. He was notified that he was privileged to remain silent if he chose. He was also advised that his silence could be used against him, but a prison inmate in Rhode Island electing to remain silent during his disciplinary hearing, as respondent Palmigiano did here, is not in consequence of his silence automatically found guilty of the infraction with which he has been charged. Under Rhode Island law, disciplinary decisions 'must be based on substantial evidence manifested in the record of the disciplinary proceeding.' *Morris v. Travisono*, 310 F. Supp.

857, 873 (D.R.I. 1970). It is thus undisputed that an inmate's silence in and of itself is insufficient to support an adverse decision by the Disciplinary Board.

"In criminal cases, where the stakes are higher and the State's sole interest is to convict, *Griffin* prohibits the judge and prosecutor from suggesting to the jury that it may treat the defendant's silence as substantive evidence of guilt. Disciplinary proceedings in state prisons, however, involve the correctional process and important state interests other than conviction for crime. We decline to extend the *Griffin* rule to this context.

"We said in *Wolff v. McDonnell*: 'As the nature of the prison disciplinary process changes in future years, circumstances may then exist which will require further consideration and reflection of this Court. It is our view, however, that the procedures we have now required in prison disciplinary proceedings represent a reasonable accommodation between the interests of the inmates and the needs of the institution.' 418 U.S., at 572. We do not retreat from that view. However, the procedures required by the Courts of Appeals in Nos. 74-1187 and 74-1194 are either inconsistent with the 'reasonable accommodation reached in *Wolff*, or premature on the bases of the records before us."

CASE SIGNIFICANCE: The Court in this case refused to give inmates more due process rights than those already given to them in *Wolff v. McDonnell*. The significance of this case lays in the statement of the Court that "permitting an adverse inference to be drawn from an inmate's silence at his disciplinary proceedings is not, on its face, an invalid practice . . ." This is different from a criminal trial in which silence on the part of the accused cannot in any way be taken as an indication of guilt, nor can it be commented on by the prosecutor. The Court justified this decision by saying that there must be a "reasonable accommodation" between the interests of the inmates and the needs of the institution. This decision strengthens the hand of prison administrators in running prisons and reiterates the principle that prisoners have diminished constitutional rights.

Cleavinger v. Saxner
106 S. Ct. 496 (1985)

CAPSULE: Prison disciplinary board members are entitled to qualified immunity, not absolute immunity.

FACTS: David Saxner and Alfred Cain, Jr., inmates at the Federal Correctional Institution in Terre Haute, Indiana, were found guilty by a prison disciplinary committee of encouraging other inmates to engage in a work stoppage and of other charges. They were ordered to be placed in administrative detention and to forfeit some "good-time" days. On appeal, ultimately to the Regional Director of the Bureau of Prisons, the inmates were ordered released from administrative detention and all materials relevant to the incident in question were ordered expunged from their records. They were later paroled and released.

They brought suit in federal court, alleging violation of various constitutional rights. After a jury trial, the members of the prison disciplinary committee were held to have violated the due process rights of inmates Saxner and Cain; the inmates were awarded damages.

ISSUE: Are members of a federal prison's Institution Discipline Committee, who hear cases in which inmates are charged with rule infractions, entitled to absolute immunity from personal damages for actions that violate inmates' constitutional rights? NO.

DECISION: Members of prison disciplinary committees are entitled to qualified immunity, not absolute immunity, in the performance of their responsibilities.

REASON: "We conclude, nonetheless, that these concerns, to the extent they are well grounded, are overstated in the context of constitutional violations. We do not perceive the discipline committee's function as a 'classic' adjudicatory one, as petitioners would describe it. Surely, the members of the committee, unlike a federal or state judge, are not 'independent'; to say that they are is to ignore reality. They are not professional hearing officers, as are administrative law judges. They are, instead, prison officials, albeit no longer of the rank and file, temporarily diverted from their usual duties. They are employees of the Bureau of Prisons and they are the direct subordinates of the warden who reviews their decision. They work with the fellow employee who lodges the charge against the inmate upon whom they sit in judgment. The credibility determination they make often is one between a co-worker and an inmate. They thus are under obvious pressure to resolve a disciplinary dispute in favor of the institution and their fellow employee. See *Ponte v. Real*, 471 U.S. 491, ____ (1985) (dissenting opinion). It is the old situational problem of the relationship between the keeper and the kept, a relationship that hardly is conducive to a truly adjudicatory performance.

"Neither do we equate this discipline committee membership to service upon a traditional parole board. The board is a 'neutral and detached' hearing body. *Morrissey v. Brewer*, 408 U.S. 471, 489 (1972). The parole board member has been described as an impartial professional serving essentially 'as an arm of the sentencing judge.' *Sellars v. Procunier*, 641 F.2d, at 1302, n. 15, quoting *Bricker v. Michigan Parole Board*, 405 F. Supp. 1340, 1345 (E.D. Mich. 1975). And in the penalty context, the parole board is constitutionally required to provide greater due process protection than is the institution discipline committee. *Wolff v. McDonnell*, 418 U.S., at 561.

"We relate this committee membership, instead, to the school board service the Court had under consideration in *Wood v. Strickland*, 420 U.S. 308 (1975). The school board members were to function as 'adjudicators in the school disciplinary process,' and they were to 'judge whether there have been violations of school regulations and, if so, the appropriate sanctions for the violations.' Id., at 319. Despite the board's adjudicative function of that extent, the Court concluded that the board members were to be protected by only qualified immunity. After noting the suggestion of the presence of a deterrence-from-service factor, the Court concluded 'that absolute immunity would not be justified since it would not sufficiently increase the ability of school officials to exercise their discretion in a forthright manner to warrant the absence of a remedy for students subjected to intentional or otherwise inexcusable deprivations.' Id., at 320."

CASE SIGNIFICANCE: This case is significant because it tells us what type of immunity members of a prison disciplinary board are entitled to when deciding prison disciplinary cases. The committee in this case (composed of the associate warden, a correctional supervisor, and the chief of case management) claimed that, like judges, they enjoyed absolute immunity, meaning that they could not be held liable for anything they did in carrying out their duties. The Court conceded that members of a prison disciplinary board do, in a sense, perform "an adjudicatory function in that they hear testimony and receive documentary evidence; and in that they render a decision." Nonetheless, the Court concluded that they are not in the same category as judges and therefore should not be given absolute immunity. Said the Court:

> Surely the members of the committee, unlike a federal or state judge, are not 'independent'; to say that they are is to ignore reality. They are not professional hearing officers, as are administrative judges. They are, instead, prison officials, albeit no longer of the rank and file, temporarily diverted from their usual duties. They are employees of the Bureau of Prisons and they are the direct subordinates of the warden who reviews their decision.

The Court then decided that prison disciplinary board members enjoy only qualified immunity, which means that they are immune from civil liability only if they act in good faith. This is the same type of immunity given to prison correctional officers and most other officials in the criminal justice system. Although this case involved the federal prison system, the decision is equally applicable to state prison disciplinary boards.

Ponte v. Real
37 Cr. L. 3051 (1985)

CAPSULE: Reasons for refusing to call witnesses requested by an inmate in a disciplinary hearing need not be placed in writing or made part of the disciplinary record.

FACTS: Real, an inmate at the Massachusetts Correctional Institution at Walpole, was charged with violations of three prison regulations. He notified prison officials that he wished to call four witnesses during his disciplinary hearing. The witnesses were: the charging correctional officer, the officer who was involved in the fights, and two fellow inmates. At the hearing, the charging officer appeared and testified against Real. The other three witnesses were not called by the board. Real was not given any reason for the denial of his request for the appearance of the other three witnesses. The record of the disciplinary hearing also did not give the reason for the board not calling the witnesses. Real was found guilty as charged. On appeal, the penalties were reduced and Real received 25 days in isolation and the loss of 150 days of good-time credits. He challenged these sanctions in a habeas corpus case, alleging that he had been deprived of due process of law guaranteed by the Fourteenth Amendment, because no reasons were given by Ponte, the Superintendent of the M.C.I. at Walpole, in court as to why Real was not allowed to call the witnesses at the disciplinary hearing.

ISSUE: Does the due process clause of the Fourteenth Amendment require that prison officials' reasons for denying an inmate's witness request appear in the administrative record of the disciplinary hearing? NO.

DECISION: Prison officials' reasons for refusing to call witnesses requested by an inmate at a disciplinary hearing need not be placed in writing or made part of the administrative record, but, if not stated at the time of the hearing, the reasons for refusal must be presented by way of testimony if the officials' decision is subsequently challenged in a judicial action.

REASON: "Chief among the Due Process minima outlined in *Wolff* was the right of an inmate to call and present witnesses and documentary evidence in his defense before the disciplinary board . . . Notwithstanding our suggestion that the board give reasons for denying an inmate's witness request, nowhere in *Wolff* or *Baxter* did we require the disciplinary board to explain why it denied the prisoner's request, nor did we require that those reasons otherwise appear in the administrative record.

"The question is exactly that posed by the Supreme Judicial Court in its opinion: 'whether the Federal due process requirements impose a duty on the board to explain, in any fashion, at the hearing or later, why witnesses were not allowed to testify.' 390 Mass., at 405, 456 N.E.2d, at 1115. We think the answer to that question is that prison officials may be required to explain, in a limited manner, the reason why witnesses were not allowed to testify, but that they may do so either by making the explanation a part of the 'administrative record' in the disciplinary proceeding, or by presenting testimony in court if the deprivation of a 'liberty' interest is challenged because of that claimed defect in the hearing. In other words, the prison officials may choose to explain their decision at the hearing, or they may choose to explain it 'later.' Explaining the decision at the hearing will of course not immunize prison officials from a subsequent court challenge to their decision, but so long as the reasons are logically related to preventing undue hazards to 'institutional safety or correctional goals,' the explanation should meet the Due Process requirements as outlined in *Wolff*."

CASE SIGNIFICANCE: This case further clarifies the extent of inmates' rights in prison disciplinary proceedings. In *Wolff v. McDonnell*, 418 U.S. 539 (1974), the Court said that in prison disciplinary cases, an inmate should be allowed to call witnesses and present documentary evidence in his or her defense, providing there is no undue hazard to institutional safety or correctional goals. Thus, the disciplinary board may refuse an inmate's request to call witnesses in his or her behalf, if such presents an undue hazard to institutional safety or correctional goals as determined by the disciplinary board itself.

Such discretionary power may be abused by the board, hence the need for a safeguard. That safeguard is provided by the requirement that the reason or reasons for such refusal be given, but it may be given in two ways: (1) by placing it in writing as part of the administrative record, or (2) by giving those reasons in the form of testimony in a subsequent judicial action if the decision by the board is challenged in court. In this case, the inmate argued that not having those reasons stated in writing as part of the administrative record violated his due process rights. The Court disagreed, giving the board the option to do it that way or present those reasons later in a court of law. Said the Court: "But the primary business of prisons is the supervision of inmates, and it may well be that those charged with this responsibility feel that the additional administrative burdens that would be occasioned by such a requirement detract from the ability to perform the principal mission of the institution." The Court refused to limit the options available to prison administrators and upheld instead the authority given to prison officials as to when and how the reasons for refusing to call witnesses should be made public.

Superintendent, Walpole v. Hill
37 Cr. L. 3107 (1985)

CAPSULE: Disciplinary board findings that result in loss of good-time credits must be supported by a "modicum" of evidence to satisfy due process requirements.

FACTS: Gerald Hill and Joseph Crawford, inmates at the Massachusetts State Prison in Walpole, each received a prison disciplinary report charging them with assaulting another inmate. At separate hearings, a prison disciplinary board heard testimony and had a written report from a correctional officer stating that while working at the prison on the day in question the officer heard an inmate ask "What's going on?" twice. The officer opened the door to the walkway and found an inmate bleeding from the mouth and suffering from a swollen eye. There was also dirt scattered about the area, which the officer viewed as further evidence of a fight. He saw three inmates, including Hill and Crawford, leaving the walkway. The correctional officer observed that there were no other inmates in the area, which was enclosed by a chain-link fence. He concluded that one or more of the three inmates leaving had assaulted the fourth inmate. Testimony at the disciplinary hearing from the officer indicated that a prison medic also told him that the injured inmate had been beaten. Both Hill and Crawford declared their innocence before the prison disciplinary board. The injured inmate gave written statements that the three other inmates had not caused his injuries.

The prison disciplinary board found both Hill and Crawford guilty of violating prison regulations because of their involvement in the assault. The board decided that each inmate would lose 100 days of good-time credits and would be confined in isolation for 15 days. The inmates appealed the board's decision to the Superintendent of the prison, but this appeal was denied. Hill and Crawford then filed a complaint in the Massachusetts Superior Court, alleging that their constitutional rights had been violated because there was no evidence to confirm that the assault took place and there was no evidence to show that the inmates were involved in the assault if it did take place.

ISSUE: Must findings of a prison disciplinary board that result in the loss of good-time credits be supported by a certain amount of evidence in order to satisfy the due process clause of the Fourteenth Amendment? YES.

DECISION: According to Massachusetts law, good-time credits constitute a protected liberty interest and the revocation of such credits must be supported by a modicum of evidence to satisfy the minimum requirements of procedural due process. In this case, however, the evidence before the disciplinary board was sufficient to meet the requirements imposed by the due process clause of the Fourteenth Amendment.

REASON: "Where a prisoner has a liberty interest in good time credits, the loss of such credits threatens his prospective freedom from confinement by extending the length of imprisonment. Thus the inmate has a strong interest in assuring that the loss of good time credits is not imposed arbitrarily. This interest, however, must be accommodated in the distinctive setting of a prison, where disciplinary proceedings 'take place in a closed, tightly controlled environment peopled by those who have chosen to violate the criminal law and who have been lawfully incarcerated for doing so.' *Wolff v. McDonnell*, 418 U.S., at 561. Consequently, in identifying the safeguards required by due process, the Court has recognized the legitimate institutional needs of assuring the safety of inmates and prisoners, avoiding burdensome administrative requirements that might be susceptible to manipulation, and preserving the disciplinary process as a means of rehabilitation.

"Requiring a modicum of evidence to support a decision to revoke good time credits will help to prevent arbitrary deprivations without threatening institutional interests or imposing undue administrative burdens . . . Because the written statement mandated by *Wolff* requires a disciplinary board to explain the evidence relied upon, recognizing that due process requires some evidentiary basis for a decision to revoke good time credits will not impose significant new burdens on proceedings within the prison. Nor does it imply that a disciplinary board's factual findings or decisions with respect to appropriate punishment are subject to second-guessing upon review.

"We hold that the requirements of due process are satisfied if some evidence supports the decision by the prison disciplinary board to revoke good time credits. This standard is met if 'there was some evidence from which the conclusion of the administrative tribunal could be deduced . . .' *United States ex rel. Vajtauer v. Commissioner of Immigration*, 273 U.S., at 106. Ascertaining whether this standard is satisfied does not require examination of the entire record, independent assessment of the credibility of the witnesses, or weighing of the evidence. Instead, the relevant question is whether there is any evidence in the record that could support the conclusion reached by the disciplinary board. We decline to adopt a more stringent evidentiary standard as a constitutional requirement. Prison disciplinary proceedings take place in a highly charged atmosphere, and prison administrators must often act swiftly on the basis of evidence that might be insufficient in less exigent circumstances. See *Wolff*, 418 U.S., at 562-563, 567-569 . . . Revocation of good time credits is not comparable to a criminal conviction, id. at 556, and neither the amount of evidence necessary to support such a conviction, see *Jackson v. Virginia*, 443 U.S. 307

(1979), nor any other standard greater than some evidence applies in this context.

"Turning to the facts of this case, we conclude that the evidence before the disciplinary board was sufficient to meet the requirements imposed by the Due Process Clause. The disciplinary board received evidence in the form of testimony from the prison guard and copies of his written report . . . The Supreme Judicial Court found that this evidence was constitutionally insufficient because it did not support an inference that more than one person had struck the victim or that either of the respondents was the assailant or otherwise participated in the assault. This conclusion, however, misperceives the nature of evidence required by the Due Process Clause.

"Instead, due process in this context requires only that there be some evidence to support the findings made in the disciplinary hearing. Although the evidence in this case might be characterized as meager, and there was no direct evidence identifying any one of three inmates as the assailant, the record is not so devoid of evidence that the findings of the disciplinary board were without support or otherwise arbitrary."

CASE SIGNIFICANCE: An earlier case, *Wolff v. McDonnell* (1974), held that inmates are entitled to due process rights in prison disciplinary hearings. *Wolff* was followed by *Baxter v. Palmigiano* (1976), which examined the question of the right to an attorney at such a hearing, and the implications of a prisoner's silence at a disciplinary hearing. The Court in this case held that due process requires that some evidence is necessary for a decision that involves a liberty interest, but that the amount of evidence need not be as much as that required in a trial court. The Supreme Court describes the amount necessary as a "modicum," meaning *less* or *limited*. In this decision, the Court underscores the unique atmosphere that exists in a prison and the competing interests of the inmates and the prison administrators. The Court struck a balance, saying that a "modicum" of evidence is required in prison disciplinary hearings. "Modicum" has been defined as "a small portion," or a "limited quantity." This is less evidence than that required in criminal trials or other administrative proceedings, indeed more proof that the Court considers prisoners as having diminished constitutional rights.

H. Discrimination—Indigents

Smith v. Bennett
365 U.S. 708 (1961)

CAPSULE: A $4 filing fee violates the constitutional rights of indigent inmates.

FACTS: Neal Merle Smith was sentenced to 10 years in the Iowa State Penitentiary for breaking and entering. He was released on parole but his parole was later revoked for violations of conditions. He was arrested and returned to the state penitentiary. Smith then forwarded a petition for a writ of habeas corpus (seeking release from confinement) to the local District Clerk. Accompanying the petition was a motion to proceed *in forma pauperis* (which means "in the manner of a pauper") and an affidavit of poverty. The Clerk refused to docket the petition without a $4 filing fee. Smith then filed a motion in the Iowa Supreme Court for leave to appeal *in forma pauperis*, accompanied by a pauper's oath. That court denied the motion without opinion. The United States Supreme Court granted certiorari.

ISSUE: Does the Iowa law that requires the payment of statutory filing fees by an indigent prisoner before an application for a writ of habeas corpus or the allowance of an appeal violate the equal protection clause of the Fourteenth Amendment? YES.

DECISION: The State of Iowa violates the equal protection clause of the Fourteenth Amendment by failing to extend the privilege of the writ of habeas corpus to its indigent prisoners.

REASON: "It has long been available in the federal courts to indigent prisoners of both the State and Federal Governments to test the validity of their detention . . . When an equivalent right is granted by a State, financial hurdles must not be permitted to condition its exercise.

"Throughout the centuries the Great Writ has been the shield of personal freedom, insuring liberty to persons illegally detained. Respecting the State's grant of a right to test their detention, the Fourteenth Amendment weighs the interest of rich and poor criminals in equal scale, and its hand extends as far to each. In failing to extend the privilege of the Great Writ to its indigent prisoners, Iowa denies them equal protection of the laws."

CASE SIGNIFICANCE: This case is significant because the Court ruled that a prisoner cannot be denied access to court if he or she is too poor to pay a filing fee. The amount involved was small ($4), but that did not matter to the Court, because the prisoner involved was indigent and could not possibly have paid the fee.

In an earlier case, *Griffin v. Illinois*, 351 U.S. 12 (1956), the Court said that "there can be no equal justice where the kind of trial a man gets depends on the amount of money he has." This principle has since been applied to situations other than trials. For example, in *Douglas v. California*, 372 U.S. 353 (1963), the Court applied the "equal justice" principle to an indigent who sought the help of counsel on first direct appeal. In *Roberts v. LaVallee*, 389 U.S. 40 (1967), the Court held that an indigent person is entitled to a free transcript of his preliminary hearing for use at trial. And in *Williams v. Illinois*, 399 U.S. 235 (1970), the Court ruled that "a State cannot subject a certain class of convicted defendants to a period of imprisonment beyond the statutory maximum solely because they are too poor to pay the fine."

This case is also significant because it implies that the equal protection clause of the Fourteenth Amendment applies equally to prisoners in cases involving money. The fact that prisoners have been convicted and are serving time for crimes committed does not make them a different class for purposes of the equal protection clause. Indigents enjoy the protection of the Constitution whether they are in prison or are free.

I. Discrimination—Racial

Lee v. Washington
390 U.S. 333 (1968)

CAPSULE: Racial segregation in prisons is unconstitutional, except when a compelling state interest justifies it.

FACTS: Inmates in the Alabama prison system filed an action for declaratory and injunctive relief (an order from the court to force public officials to do something) concerning racial segregation in the Alabama state penal system and in county and local jails. The inmates contended that racial segregation was a violation of the Fourteenth Amendment. The Commissioner of Corrections of Alabama argued that racial segregation was necessary to maintain security and order.

ISSUE: Are the Alabama statutes requiring segregation of the races in prisons and jails unconstitutional in violation of the Fourteenth Amendment? YES.

DECISION: The Alabama statutes requiring racial segregation in prisons and jails are unconstitutional under the equal protection clause of the Fourteenth Amendment.

REASON: "This appeal challenges a decree of a three-judge District Court declaring that certain Alabama statutes violate the Fourteenth Amendment to the extent that they require segregation of the races in prisons and jails, and establishing a schedule for desegregation of these institutions. The State's contentions that Rule 23 of the Federal Rules of Civil Procedure, which relates to class actions, was violated in this case and that the challenged statutes are not unconstitutional, are without merit. The remaining contention of the State is that the specific orders directing desegregation of prisons and jails make no allowance for the necessities of prison security and discipline, but we do not so read the 'Order, Judgment, and Decree' of the District Court, which when read as a whole we find unexceptionable."

CASE SIGNIFICANCE: This case was the first case to address racial segregation in prisons. Earlier cases had addressed racial segregation in schools, restaurants, and retail stores. As expected, the U.S. Supreme Court ruled that racial segregation violates the Fourteenth Amendment. In a concurring opinion, Justice Black said that "prison authorities have the right, acting in good faith and in particularized circumstance, to take into account racial tensions in maintaining security, discipline, and good order in prisons and jails." Written in 1968, this statement allows prison authorities to take race into account when trying to ease tension, maintain security, discipline, and good order in prisons. This should be done, however, only with extreme caution and when a compelling state interest is involved, such as in an emergency situation when there is a prison riot. At present, any prison administrator who takes race into consideration when making decisions flirts with a civil rights lawsuit, except perhaps in extreme circumstances.

J. Due Process

Estelle v. Williams
425 U.S. 501 (1976)

CAPSULE: An accused cannot be compelled to stand trial before a jury while dressed in identifiable prison clothes.

FACTS: Williams was charged with assault with intent to commit murder after he severely wounded his landlord by stabbing him with a knife in the neck, chest, and abdomen. He was unable to post bail and subsequently was jailed until his trial. On the day of trial, he requested his civilian clothes from an officer at the jail. The request was denied and he appeared at trial with clothes that were distinctly marked as prison issue. During voir dire, his counsel expressly referred to his jail attire. At no time during the trial, however, did the defendant or his attorney raise an objection to this prison attire. Williams was convicted of the above offense, and the conviction was affirmed by the Texas Court of Criminal Appeals.

 While in prison, Williams filed a writ of habeas corpus, alleging that requiring a defendant to stand trial in his prison clothing was in violation of the due process and equal protection clauses of the Fourteenth Amendment.

ISSUE: Is an accused who is compelled to wear identifiable prison clothing at his trial by jury denied due process or equal protection of the laws under the Fourteenth Amendment? YES.

DECISION: The State cannot compel an accused to stand trial before a jury while dressed in identifiable prison clothes. In this case, however, the failure to object to the court about being tried in such clothes negates the presence of the compulsion necessary to establish a constitutional violation.

REASON: "Courts have therefore required an accused to object to being tried in jail garments, just as he must invoke or abandon other rights . . . The record is clear that no objection was made to the trial judge concerning the jail attire either before or at any time during the trial. This omission plainly did not result from any lack of appreciation of the issue, for respondent had raised the question with the jail attendant prior to trial. At trial, defense counsel expressly referred to respondent's attire during voir dire. The trial judge was thus informed that respondent's counsel was fully conscious of the situation.

 "Significantly, at the evidentiary hearing respondent's trial counsel did not intimate that he feared any adverse consequences attending an objection to the procedure. There is nothing to suggest that there would have been any prejudicial effect on defense counsel had he made objection, given the decisions on this point in that jurisdiction . . . Nothing in this record, therefore, warrants a conclusion that respondent was compelled to stand trial in jail garb or that there was sufficient reason to excuse the failure to raise the issue before trial. Nor can the trial judge be faulted for not asking the respondent or his counsel whether he was deliberately going to trial in jail clothes.

"Accordingly, although the State cannot, consistently with the Fourteenth Amendment, compel an accused to stand trial before a jury while dressed in identifiable prison clothes, the failure to make an objection to the court as being tried in such clothes, for whatever reason, is sufficient to negate the presence of compulsion necessary to establish a constitutional violation."

CASE SIGNIFICANCE: This case holds that the state cannot compel an accused to stand trial before a jury while dressed in identifiable prison clothes, because that would be fundamentally unfair and therefore a violation of the Fourteenth Amendment due process clause. The problem in this case, however, was the lack of evidence to support the inmate's allegation that he was compelled to stand trial in jail clothes, or that the failure to raise the issue before trial was excusable.

The significance of this case for defendants and lawyers is clear: proper objection must be made before or during trial if the defendant is compelled to wear jail clothes that would predispose the jury to associate the defendant's clothing with guilt. Failure to object means that there may be no sufficient proof later, on which to raise an appeal. Note, however, that in this case the defendant did ask to change to his civilian clothes, but the request was denied by the jailer. The defendant must have thought that the jailer spoke for the court when the denial was made. The principle the case establishes is quite simple: objections to violations of constitutional rights must be made before or during trial, regardless of how obvious that violation might be, or there may be no basis to raise them on appeal.

Hughes v. Rowe
449 U.S. 5 (1980)

CAPSULE: Placing a prisoner in segregation without a hearing is unconstitutional, unless justified by emergency conditions. The award of attorney's fees against the prisoner in this case was not proper.

FACTS: Hughes, a state prisoner in Illinois, was charged with violation of prison regulations and placed in segregation without a prior hearing. Two days later, Hughes was given a disciplinary hearing and at that time he admitted that he and two other inmates had consumed a homemade alcoholic beverage. Hughes was punished with segregation for 10 days, demotion to C-grade status, and loss of 30 days of statutory good time. He filed a §1983 case alleging that the decision to place him in a segregation cell (for the first two days) without a hearing was unconstitutional because it was not justified by any emergency conditions. He also alleged that the order of the District Court directing him to pay counsel fees of $400 for services rendered by the Attorney General of Illinois in representing the prison officials in the case was improper.

ISSUES:
1. Did the inmate's segregation in this case without a hearing violate his constitutional right to due process? YES.
2. Was the award of attorney's fees against the prisoner proper? NO.

DECISIONS:
1. Segregation without a prior hearing may violate due process if the hearing postponement is not justified by emergency conditions; such conditions must be related to concern for institutional security and safety.
2. The award of attorney's fees against the inmate was not proper because such award could be made only if the District Court had found "that the plaintiff's action was frivolous, unreasonable, or without foundation." No such finding supported the fee award in this case.

REASON: "Segregation of a prisoner without a prior hearing may violate due process if the postponement of procedural protections is not justified by apprehended emergency conditions. The amended complaint alleged that segregation was unnecessary in petitioner's case because his offense did not involve violence and he did not present a 'clear and present danger.' There is no suggestion in the record that immediate segregation was necessitated by emergency conditions. Defendants did make the unsworn assertion that petitioner was placed in segregation on 'temporary investigative status,' but the significance of this designation is unclear and it does not, without more, dispose of petitioner's procedural due process claim. The District Court, in dismissing the amended complaint, merely concluded that temporary segregation pending investigation was not actionable. The court cited an Illinois Department of Corrections Administrative Regulation which authorized segregation of prisoners pending investigation of disciplinary matters, where required 'in the interest of institutional security and safety.' In the absence of any showing that concern for institutional security and safety was the basis for immediate segregation of petitioner without a prior hearing, this regulation does not justify dismissal of petitioner's suit for failure to state a claim.

"In *Christianburg Garment Co. v. EEOC*, 434 U.S. 412 (1978), we held that the defendant in an action brought under Title VII of the Civil Rights Act of 1964 may recover attorney's fees from the plaintiff only if the District Court finds 'that the plaintiff's action was frivolous, unreasonable, or without foundation, even though not brought in subjective bad faith.' Although arguably a different standard might be applied in a civil rights action under 42 U.S.C. Section 1983, we can perceive no reason for applying a less stringent standard. The plaintiff's action must be meritless in the sense that it is groundless or without foundation. The fact that a plaintiff may ultimately lose his case is not in itself a sufficient justification for the assessment of fees. As we said in *Christianburg*:

> To take the further step of assessing attorney's fees against plaintiffs simply because they do not finally prevail would substantially add to the risks inhering in most litigation and would undercut the efforts of Congress to promote the vigorous enforcement of the provisions of Title VII. Hence, a plaintiff should not be assessed his opponent's attorney's fees unless a court finds that his claim was frivolous, unreasonable, or groundless, or that the plaintiff continued to litigate after it clearly became so.

CASE SIGNIFICANCE: In an earlier case (*Wolff v. McDonnell*, 418 U.S. 539, [1974]), the Court said that a hearing is required before an inmate can be placed in punitive segregation. This case presents a slightly different issue. May an inmate ever be placed in solitary confinement without being given a hearing? The Court replied yes, but only if immediate segregation is necessitated by emergency conditions that would make a hearing impractical. The Court then said, however, that "here, the record did not show that petitioner's immediate segregation was necessitated by emergency conditions, and an administrative regulation authorizing segregation pending investigation of disciplinary matters, where required 'in the interest of institutional security and safety,' did not justify dismissal of the suit in the absence of any showing that concern for institutional security and safety was the basis for petitioner's immediate segregation without a prior hearing." In short, the Court said that inmates may be placed in punitive segregation without a hearing, but only if necessitated by emergency conditions, such emergency conditions being interpreted to mean "concern for institutional security and safety." The placement of inmates in segregation without a hearing has therefore been strictly limited by the Court.

This case is also significant for what it says about when an inmate may be made to pay attorney's fees. The Attorney's Fees Act of 1976 provides that the trial judge may require a party in a §1983 lawsuit to pay attorney's fees "if the opposing party [the inmate] prevails in at least one of the allegations." In this case, the District Court judge imposed a $400 counsel fee not for, but against the inmate for services rendered by the Attorney General of Illinois in representing state prison officials in this action. The Court rejected the fee as improper, saying that such fee is proper only if the district court finds the plaintiff's action to be "frivolous, unreasonable, or without foundation." The Court concluded that there was no such finding in this case, hence the fee could not be awarded. Clearly, this sets two different standards for recovery of attorney's fees. The Attorney's Fees Act of 1976 makes it easier for inmates to file cases because if they prevail in at least one allegation the judge can then order prison officials and the state to pay inmates' lawyer's fees. This case reaffirms the Court's ruling in the *Christianburg* case, mentioned above, and refuses to open the door wider for prison officials to recover attorney's fees from inmates.

Parratt v. Taylor
451 U.S. 527 (1981)

CAPSULE: **Loss of inmate hobby materials because a correctional officer failed to follow prison regulations does not amount to a violation of an inmate's due process rights under the Constitution.**

FACTS: Taylor, an inmate at the Nebraska Penal and Correctional Complex, ordered hobby materials through the mail at an estimated cost of $23.50. When these materials arrived at the prison hobby center, two employees signed for them. At the time, Taylor was in segregation and was not permitted to have these materials. Prison procedure for the handling of packages provided that the package be delivered to the inmate and a receipt signed or that the prisoner be notified to pick up a package and a receipt be signed. Prison policy allowed only the inmate to whom the package was addressed to sign a receipt for it.

When Taylor was released from segregation he contacted several prison officials to locate his package. These officials could not find his package nor could they determine what caused the package to disappear. Taylor brought action in Federal District Court under 42 U.S.C. §1983 against prison officials, to recover the value of his hobby materials. He claimed that officials were negligent in losing the materials by not following prison regulations and thereby deprived him of property without due process of law in violation of the Fourteenth Amendment.

ISSUE: Did inmate Taylor suffer deprivation of property without due process of law in violation of the Fourteenth Amendment? NO.

DECISION: To succeed in a §1983 case, the plaintiff must prove the following: (1) that the conduct complained of was committed by a person acting under color of state law; and (2) that the conduct deprived a person of rights, privileges, or immunities secured by the Constitution or laws of the United States. In this case, the plaintiff established that the prison authorities acted under color of state law, but could not prove that the loss of hobby materials, due to prison officials not strictly following prison procedure, constituted a violation of the prisoner's right to due process.

REASON: "Unquestionably, respondent's claim satisfies three prerequisites of a valid due process claim: the petitioners acted under color of state law; the hobby kit falls within the definition of property; and the alleged loss, even though negligently caused, amounted to a deprivation. Standing alone, however, these three elements do not establish a violation of the Fourteenth Amendment. Nothing in that Amendment protects against all deprivations of life, liberty, or property by the State. The Fourteenth Amendment protects only against deprivations 'without due process of law.' *Baker v. McCollan*, 443 U.S., at 145. Our inquiry therefore must focus on whether the respondent has suffered a deprivation of property without due process of law. In particular, we must decide whether the tort remedies which the State of Nebraska provides as a means of redress for property deprivations satisfy the requirements of procedural due process.

"The justifications which we found sufficient to uphold takings of property without any predeprivation process are applicable to a situation such as the present one, involving a tortious loss of a prisoner's property as a result of a random and unauthorized act by a state employee. In such a case, the loss is not a result of some established state procedure and the State cannot predict precisely when the loss will occur. It is difficult to conceive of how the State could provide a meaningful hearing before the deprivation takes place. The loss of property, although attributable to the State as action under 'color of law,' is in almost all cases beyond the control of the State. Indeed, in most cases it is not only impracticable, but impossible, to provide a meaningful hearing before the deprivation.

"Our decision today is fully consistent with our prior cases. To accept respondent's argument that the conduct of the state officials in this case constituted a violation of the Fourteenth Amendment would almost necessarily result in turning every alleged injury which may have been inflicted by a state official acting under 'color of law' into a violation of the Fourteenth Amendment cognizable under Section 1983. It is hard to perceive any logical stopping place to such a line of reasoning . . . Such reasoning 'would make of the Fourteenth Amendment a font of tort law to be superimposed upon whatever systems may already be administered by the States.' *Paul v. Davis*, 424 U.S. 693, 701 (1976). We do not think that the drafters of the Fourteenth Amendment intended the Amendment to play such a role in our society."

CASE SIGNIFICANCE: The Court in this case said that the loss suffered by the inmate as a result of the negligence of prison officials in not following proper procedures did not constitute a violation of a constitutional right. This case says in effect that not every misconduct or negligence of a prison official constitutes a violation of a prisoner's constitutional right. To prove a violation of the constitutional right to due process the inmate must establish something more than the type of negligence involved in this case. Moreover, the inmate had a remedy available to him under Nebraska tort law, which he did not use. Such procedure could have fully compensated the inmate for the loss of property. In a subsequent case, however (*Daniels v. Williams*, 474 U.S. 327 [1986]), the Court held that federal law (42 U.S.C. §1983) would not be available to an inmate in these types of cases even if the inmate had no effective remedy under state tort law, therefore overturning this part of the *Taylor* decision.

Daniels v. Williams
474 U.S. 327 (1986)

CAPSULE: A negligent act of a prison official (such as leaving a pillow on the stairs) does not violate the due process rights of inmates.

FACTS: Daniels, an inmate at the city jail in Richmond, Virginia, slipped on a pillow left on a stairway. He sustained back and ankle injuries as a result of his fall. Daniels brought suit under 42 U.S.C. §1983, against Williams, a correctional deputy stationed at the jail, who had left the pillow on the stairs. Daniels claimed that Williams' negligence deprived him of his "liberty" interest "without due process of law" within the meaning of the due process clause of the Fourteenth Amendment. Daniels also claimed that he was without an "adequate" state remedy because Williams maintained that he was entitled to sovereign immunity.

ISSUE: Is the due process clause of the Fourteenth Amendment violated by a state official's negligent act that causes unintended loss of, or injury to, an inmate's life, liberty, or property? NO.

DECISION: The due process clause is not violated by a state official's negligent act that causes unintended loss of, or injury to, life, liberty, or property. To hold that injury caused by such conduct is a deprivation within the meaning of the due process clause would trivialize the centuries-old principle of due process of law.

REASON: "No decision of this Court before *Parratt* supported the view that negligent conduct by a state official, even though causing injury, constitutes a deprivation under the Due Process Clause. This history reflects the traditional and common-sense notion that the Due Process Clause, like its forebear in the Magna Carta, . . . was 'intended to secure the individual from the arbitrary exercise of the powers of government,' *Hurtado v. California*, 110 U.S. 516, 527 (1884).

"Far from an abuse of power, lack of due care suggests no more than a failure to measure up to the conduct of a reasonable person. To hold that injury caused by such conduct is a deprivation within the meaning of the Fourteenth Amendment would trivialize the centuries-old principle of due process of law.

"The only tie between the facts of this case and anything governmental in nature is the fact that respondent was a sheriff's deputy at the Richmond city jail and petitioner was an inmate confined in that jail. But while the Due Process Clause of the Fourteenth Amendment obviously speaks to some facets of this relationship, *see, e.g., Wolff v. McDonnell, supra*, we do not believe its protections are triggered by lack of due care by prison officials.

"Jailers may owe a special duty of care to those in their custody under state tort law, *see Restatement (Second) of Torts* §314A(4) (1965), but for the reasons previously stated we reject the contention that the Due Process Clause of the Fourteenth Amendment embraces such a tort law concept. Petitioner alleges that he was injured by the negligence of respondent, a custodial official at the city jail. Whatever other provisions of state law or general jurisprudence he may rightly invoke, the Fourteenth Amendment to the United States Constitution does not afford him a remedy."

CASE SIGNIFICANCE: By ruling that a negligent act of a prison officer of the kind involved here (leaving a pillow on the stairs, which caused the inmate to slip) does not fall under the due process clause, the Court severely restricted the scope of the Fourteenth Amendment prisoners' claims in negligence cases. Note, however, that this case dealt with "mere" negligence. What if the act by a prison official constitutes "gross" negligence? Some lower courts have decided that §1983 can be used as remedy for prisoners in cases of gross negligence, but other lower courts disagree. Scholars also disagree on this issue, which the Court will have to resolve in the future. This case says, however, that "mere" negligence is not a violation of constitutional rights under the Fourteenth Amendment.

The Court in this case also said that even if state tort law does not provide an effective remedy for these types of negligence, it is not actionable anyway under federal law. This overturns a section of the decision in *Parratt v. Taylor*

(451 U.S. 527 [1981]), discussed above, which implied that the Court might allow federal courts to be used if state law did not afford the inmate an effective remedy.

K. Use of Force

Whitley v. Albers
475 U.S. 312 (1986)

CAPSULE: The shooting of a prisoner, without prior verbal warning, to suppress a prison riot did not violate the prisoner's right against cruel and unusual punishment. Liability arises only if such deadly force was used with "obduracy and wantonness."

FACTS: A corrections officer was taken hostage and held in a cell on the upper tier of a cellblock during a riot in an Oregon penitentiary. The prison security manager consulted with two other prison officials and it was agreed that forceful intervention was necessary to protect both the hostage and the non-participating inmates. A squad of officers armed with shotguns entered the cellblock in order to rescue the hostage. One officer was ordered to fire a warning shot and to shoot low at any prisoner climbing the stairs toward the hostage cell. After the rescue squad began moving up the stairs, a warning shot was fired, followed by another shot. A third shot hit the respondent in the left knee as he was climbing up the stairs. As a result, the inmate sustained severe damage to his left leg as well as mental and emotional distress. He brought suit under 42 U.S.C. §1983 against the prison officials, alleging violation of his Eighth and Fourteenth Amendment rights.

ISSUE: Is the infliction of pain in the course of prison security measures a violation of the right to be free from cruel and unusual punishment under the Eighth Amendment? NO.

DECISION: The infliction of pain in the course of prison security measures is a violation of the Eighth Amendment only if inflicted unnecessarily and wantonly. The shooting of a prisoner without prior verbal warning, in an effort to suppress a prison riot, did not violate his right to be free from cruel and unusual punishment. There is liability in these cases only if the use of deadly force was with obduracy and wantonness.

REASON: "It is obduracy and wantonness, not inadvertence or error in good faith, that characterize the conduct prohibited by the Cruel and Unusual Punishment Clause, whether that conduct occurs in connection with establishing conditions of confinement, supplying medical needs, or restoring control over a tumultuous cell block. The infliction of pain in the course of a prison security measure, therefore, does not amount to cruel and unusual punishment simply because it may appear in retrospect that the degree of force authorized or applied for security purposes was unreasonable, and hence unnecessary in the strict sense.

"Viewing the evidence in the light most favorable to respondent, as must be done in reviewing the decision reversing the trial court's directed verdict for petitioners, it does not appear that the evidence supports a reliable inference of wantonness in the infliction of pain under the above standard. Evidence arguably showing that the prison officials erred in judgment when they decided on a plan that employed potentially deadly force, falls far short of a showing that there was no plausible basis for their belief that this degree of force was necessary."

CASE SIGNIFICANCE: This case is consistent with the trend that gives prison administrators and personnel more discretion in dealing with inmates, particularly in an emergency situation. The Court said that there is liability in these cases, but only if the use of deadly force was obdurate and wanton. One dictionary defines "obdurate" as "hardened in feelings"; it defines "wanton" as "merciless, inhumane, and malicious." What the officers did in this case did not amount to obduracy or wantonness.

Does the standard apply to all use-of-force cases or only cases involving use of deadly force? The decision itself is unclear on that issue. The Court said: "It is obduracy and wantonness, not inadvertence or error in good faith, that characterize the conduct prohibited by the Eighth Amendment, whether that conduct occurs in connection with establishing conditions of confinement, supplying medical needs, or restoring control over a tumultuous cell block." (emphasis added). In another part of the decision, however, the Court says: "Where a prison security measure is undertaken to resolve a disturbance that poses significant risks to safety of inmates and prison staff, the question whether the measure taken inflicted wanton pain in violation of the Eighth Amendment ultimately turns on whether the force applied was applied in a good faith effort to maintain or restore discipline or maliciously and sadistically for the purpose of causing harm . . ." A subsequent case (*Hudson v. McMillian*, 60 L.W. 4151 [1992]), however, implies that the standard set in *Whitley v. Albers* is limited only to use of deadly force cases. The Court set a different standard for liability in non-deadly force cases, as the next case indicates.

Hudson v. McMillian
60 L.W. 4151 (1992)

CAPSULE: Use of excessive physical force against a prisoner may constitute cruel and unusual punishment, even though no serious injury results, if that force was used "maliciously and sadistically" to cause harm.

FACTS: Keith Hudson, a prison inmate in Louisiana, brought a 42 U.S.C. §1983 lawsuit against correctional officers McMillian and Woods, as a result of the beating Hudson received from the two officers when they took Hudson out of his cell one morning and walked him toward the prison's administrative lockdown area. Hudson testified that McMillian punched him in the mouth, eyes, chest, and stomach, while Woods held him in place and kicked and punched him from behind. The prisoner also alleged that Mezo, the supervisor on duty, watched the beating but merely told the officers "not to have too much fun." As a result of the beating, the prisoner suffered minor bruises and swelling of the face, mouth, and lip. The beating also loosened Hudson's teeth and cracked his partial dental plate, making it unusable for months. The Federal Magistrate found excessive use of force by the officers and condonation of their actions by the supervisor. The prisoner was awarded $800 in damages. The Fifth Circuit Court of Appeals reversed, holding that there was no violation of the Eighth Amendment prohibition against cruel and unusual punishment because there was no "significant injury," and that whatever injuries were inflicted were "minor," and required no medical treatment.

ISSUE: Is the use of excessive force against a prisoner cruel and unusual punishment and therefore unconstitutional even if the inmate does not suffer serious injury? YES.

DECISION: The use of excessive physical force by prison officials against a prisoner may constitute cruel and unusual punishment, and is therefore unconstitutional, even if the inmate does not suffer serious injury if such force was used "maliciously and sadistically" to cause harm.

REASON: "In *Whitley v. Albers*, 475 U.S. 312 (1986), the principal question before us was what legal standard should govern the Eighth Amendment claim of an inmate shot by a guard during a prison riot. We based our answer on the settled rule that 'the unnecessary and wanton infliction of pain . . . constitutes cruel and unusual punishment forbidden by the Eighth Amendment.'

"What is necessary to establish an 'unnecessary and wanton infliction of pain,' we said, varies according to the nature of the alleged constitutional violation. 475 U.S., at 320. For example, the appropriate inquiry when an inmate alleges that prison officials failed to attend to serious medical needs is whether the officials exhibited 'deliberate indifference.' See *Estelle v. Gamble*, 429 U.S. 97, 104 (1976). This standard is appropriate because the State's responsibility to provide inmates with medical care ordinarily does not conflict with competing administrative concerns. *Whitley, supra*, at 320.

"By contrast, officials confronted with a prison disturbance must balance the threat unrest poses to inmates, prison workers, administrators, and visitors against the harm inmates may suffer if guards use force. Despite the weight of these competing concerns, corrections officials must make their decisions 'in haste, under pressure, and frequently without the luxury of a second chance.' 475 U.S., at 320. We accordingly concluded in *Whitley* that application of the deliberate indifference standard is inappropriate when authorities use force to put down a prison disturbance. Instead, 'the question whether the measure taken inflicted unnecessary and wanton pain and suffering ultimately turns on 'whether force was applied in a good faith effort to maintain or restore discipline or maliciously and sadistically for the very purpose of causing harm.' "

"Many of the concerns underlying our holding in *Whitley* arise whenever guards use force to keep order. Whether the prison disturbance is a riot or a lesser disruption, corrections officers must balance the need 'to maintain or restore discipline' through force against the risk of injury to inmates. Both situations may require prison officials to act quickly and decisively. Likewise, both implicate the principle that '[p]rison administrators . . . should be accorded wide-ranging deference in the adoption and execution of policies and practices that in their judgment are needed to preserve internal order and discipline and to maintain institutional security.' In recognition of these similarities, we hold that whenever prison officials stand accused of using excessive physical force in violation of the Cruel and Unusual Punishments Clause, the core judicial inquiry is that set out in *Whitley*: whether force was applied in a good-faith effort to maintain or restore discipline, or maliciously and sadistically to cause harm."

CASE SIGNIFICANCE: This case is significant because it defines when the use of non-deadly force by correctional officers becomes a violation of the constitutional rights of inmates. The Court said that the injury to the prisoner does not have to be "serious" or "significant" for it to become a constitutional violation. Instead, the Court used this standard: whether the force was applied in a good faith effort to maintain or restore discipline, or maliciously and sadistically to cause harm. In this case, the majority of the Court concluded that Hudson's constitutional right against cruel and unusual punishment was violated because the correctional officers used force "maliciously and sadistically to cause harm."

The standard used by the court to impose damages in this case is easier for the prisoner to meet than the standard used in previous cases. The cruel and unusual punishment clause of the Eighth Amendment has been the subject of several Court decisions. In one of the earliest cases (*Estelle v. Gamble*, 429 U.S. 97 [1976]), the Court held that "deliberate indifference" to an inmate's medical needs constitutes a violation of the Eighth Amendment. In a subsequent case (*Whitley v. Albers*, 475 U.S. 312 [1986]), the Court applied a different standard in the use of deadly force by prison officials to put down a prison riot. In the present case, the majority of the Court concluded that Hudson's constitutional right against cruel and unusual punishment was violated because the correctional officers used force maliciously and sadistically to cause harm.

This decision does not imply that any injury caused by correctional officers in the performance of responsibilities is *per se* a violation of the Eighth Amendment and therefore leads to civil liability. The Court specifically rejected such view, holding instead that this decision does not "say that every malevolent touch by a prison guard gives rise to a federal cause of action." The Court quoted, with approval, a decision by the Second Circuit Court of Appeals (*Johnson v. Glick*, 481 F.2d, at 1033) which says that "not every push or shove, even if it may later seem unnecessary in the peace of a judge's chambers, violates a prisoner's constitutional rights." The question to be asked in each case is: "Was the use of force by the prison guard repugnant to the conscience of mankind?" using contemporary standards. The Court found that what the officers did to Hudson violated this standard, and thus held them civilly liable for the injuries inflicted, even though the injuries were considered "minor" by the lower court.

This case was decided by a 7-2 vote, the two dissenters being Justices Thomas and Scalia. In his dissent, Justice Thomas wrote: "In my view, a show of force that causes only insignificant harm to a prisoner may be immoral, it may be tortious, it may be criminal, and it may even be remediable under other provisions of the Federal Constitution, but it is not 'cruel and unusual punishment.' " Thomas and Scalia felt that because the lower court found the injuries to the prisoner to be "minor," no damages ought to have been imposed. The dissent also charged that the majority opinion expanded the interpretation of the cruel and unusual punishment clause "beyond all bounds of history and precedent." It must be pointed out, however, that the dissent did not approve of or condone what the officers in this case did to the prisoner. Said the dissent: "Abusive behavior by prison guards is deplorable conduct that properly evokes outrage and contempt. But that does not mean that it is invariably unconstitutional. The Eighth Amendment is not, and should not be turned into a National Code of Prison Regulation." They differed with the majority in that they believed this type of injury does not constitute cruel and unusual punishment in violation of the Eighth Amendment.

L. Good Faith Defense

Harlow v. Fitzgerald
457 U.S. 800 (1982)

CAPSULE: Government officials performing discretionary functions are civilly liable only if their conduct violates a clearly established statutory or constitutional right of which a reasonable person would have known.

FACTS: Harlow and Butterfield, senior aides of President Nixon, were accused of violating Fitzgerald's constitutional rights by conspiring to have Fitzgerald dismissed as an Air Force official. Fitzgerald's allegations against Harlow stemmed from several conversations in which Harlow discussed Fitzgerald's dismissal with the Air Force Secretary. Allegations against Butterfield were based on a memorandum circulated by Butterfield in which he claimed that Fitzgerald planned to "blow the whistle" on Air Force purchasing practices. Fitzgerald alleged that his dismissal was in retaliation for these actions. Fitzgerald filed a lawsuit for unlawful discharge.

ISSUE: Do government officials have absolute immunity when performing discretionary official functions, such as dismissing a subordinate? NO.

DECISION: Government officials performing discretionary functions are civilly liable only if their conduct violates clearly established statutory or constitutional rights of which a reasonable person would have known.

REASON: "Reliance on the objective reasonableness of an official's conduct, as measured by reference to clearly established law, should avoid excessive disruption of government . . . On summary judgment, the judge appropriately may determine, not only the applicable law, but whether that law was clearly established at the time an action occurred. If the law at that time was not clearly established, an official could not reasonably be expected to anticipate subsequent legal developments, nor could he fairly be said to 'know' that the law forbade conduct not previously identified as unlawful . . . If the law was clearly established, the immunity defense ordinarily should fail, since a reasonably competent public official should know the law governing his conduct. Nevertheless, if the official pleading the defense claims extraordinary circumstances and can prove that he neither knew nor should have known the relevant legal standard, the defense should be sustained . . ."

CASE SIGNIFICANCE: This case involved officials in the office of the United States President, not prison officials. The principle of the case, however, applies to all public officials. The *Fitzgerald* case is important because it set a new test for the "good faith" defense available to public officials, including prison officers. The old test (enunciated by the Court in *Wood v. Strickland*, 420 U.S. 308 [1975]) was that a government official asserting the defense "took action with malicious intention to cause deprivation of constitutional rights or other injury." The new test, under *Fitzgerald*, is that public officials are not civilly liable "if their conduct does not violate clearly established statutory or constitutional rights of which a reasonable person would have known." This new test has "good news and bad news" sides to it. The "good news" is that not every violation of a constitutional right by a prison official leads to civil liability. There is civil liability only if the official violated a "clearly established statutory or constitutional right of which a reasonable person would have known." This means that the "good faith" defense requires that for an official to be held liable, the following must be established by the plaintiff: (1) there must be a violation of a clearly established constitutional right, (2) of which a reasonable person would have known. The "bad news" is that prison officials have an obligation to know the clearly established rights of prisoners and detainees. After a period of time, they cannot plead ignorance of a new court decision giving rights to inmates.

M. Good-Time Reduction

Weaver v. Graham
450 U.S. 24 (1981)

CAPSULE: A state statute that repeals an earlier statute and reduces the amount of good time deducted from a convicted inmate's sentence is unconstitutional if applied to an inmate whose offenses were committed before the law took effect.

FACTS: Weaver was convicted of second-degree murder and was sentenced to 15 years in prison. At the time of his conviction and sentencing, Florida statute provided a formula for deducting gain-time credits from sentences of all of its prisoners. Three years later, the legislature repealed this statute and enacted another, which lessened the amount of gain-time credits that could be earned. The state applied this new law to all its prisoners, including those whose offenses were committed before the law took effect.

Weaver sought a writ from the Supreme Court of Florida on the ground that the new statute as applied to him was *ex post facto,* prohibited by both the United States and Florida Constitutions. The State Supreme Court denied the petition.

ISSUE: Does the *ex post facto* prohibition of the U.S. Constitution apply to a Florida statute that repeals an earlier statute and reduces the amount of good time deducted from a convicted inmate's sentence? YES.

DECISION:

1. For a criminal or penal law to be *ex post facto,* it must satisfy two requirements: (1) it must be retrospective (i.e., apply to events occurring before its enactment), and (2) it must disadvantage the offender affected by it.

2. This new statute limits the inmate's opportunity to earn early release and thereby makes more onerous the punishment for crimes committed before its enactment. This violates the *ex post facto* prohibition of the U.S. Constitution.

REASON: "The *ex post facto* prohibition forbids the Congress and the States to enact any law 'which imposes a punishment for an act which was not punishable at the time it was committed; or imposes additional punishment to that then prescribed.' . . . In accord with these purposes, our decisions prescribe that two critical elements must be present for a criminal or penal law to be *ex post facto*: It must be retrospective, that is, it must apply to events occurring before its enactment, and it must disadvantage the offender affected by it. *Lindsey v. Washington, supra,* at 401 . . .

"Under this inquiry, we conclude Section 944.275(1) [the Florida statute in question] is disadvantageous to petitioner and other similarly situated prisoners. On its face, the statute reduces the number of monthly gain-time credits available to an inmate who abides by prison rules and adequately performs his assigned tasks. By definition, this reduction in gain-time accumulation lengthens the period that someone in petitioner's position must spend in prison.

"The fact remains that an inmate who performs satisfactory work and avoids disciplinary violations could obtain more gain time per month under the repealed provision, . . . than he could for the same conduct under the new provisions . . . To make up the difference, the inmate has to satisfy the extra conditions specified by the discretionary gain-time provisions. Even then, the award of the extra gain time is purely discretionary, contingent on both the wishes of the correctional authorities and special behavior by the inmate, such as saving a life or diligent performance in an academic program . . . In contrast, under both the new and old statutes, an inmate is automatically entitled to the monthly gain time simply for avoiding disciplinary infractions and performing his assigned tasks . . . Thus, the new provision constricts the inmate's opportunity to earn early release, and thereby makes more onerous the punishment for crimes committed before it enactment. This result runs afoul of the prohibition against *ex post facto* laws."

CASE SIGNIFICANCE: An *ex post facto* (after the fact) law provides for punishment after an act has taken place. Such laws are prohibited by the Constitution because they are patently unfair to the person who committed the act.

This case presents a variation of that problem in that it determines whether a law that reduces the amount of good time from an inmate's sentence is constitutional when applied to an inmate whose offenses were committed before the law took effect. The Court found the law unconstitutional, saying that it makes more onerous the punishment for crimes committed before its enactment.

This case is significant for parole because it prohibits the application of new parole laws, if those laws are unfavorable to inmates, to offenders who committed offenses before the new parole laws were passed. This does not mean that parole laws cannot be changed. What it means is that if parole laws are changed, those changes cannot be applied to inmates who have committed prior offenses if those changes are unfavorable to the inmate. The changes apply only to future offenders. It must be noted, however, that changes favorable to inmates may take effect immediately if that is the intent of the law.

N. Habeas Corpus

Ex parte Hull
61 S. Ct. 640 (1941)

CAPSULE: A state and its officers cannot abridge or impair a prisoner's right, given by federal law, to apply for a federal writ of habeas corpus.

FACTS: Hull was convicted of a sex offense and incarcerated in the Michigan State Prison in Jackson, Michigan. He was later paroled, but then returned to prison because he was convicted of a new sex offense. He prepared a petition for a writ of habeas corpus and exhibits to file before the U.S. Supreme Court. He took the papers to a prison official and asked him to notarize them. Instead, the official advised the inmate that the papers and a registered letter to the clerk of the court would not be accepted for mailing. Hull attempted to mail them by giving them to his father, but the guards confiscated them. Several days later Hull again attempted to mail a letter concerning his case to the clerk of the U.S.

Supreme Court but the letter was intercepted and sent to the investigator for the state parole board.

Hull prepared another document which his father filed with the clerk of the U.S. Supreme Court. The document detailed his efforts to file the confiscated papers and he contended that he was unlawfully restrained, requesting release from the prison. Prison officials cited a regulation which stated that all legal documents had to be submitted to the institutional welfare office and then to a legal investigator for the parole board before they could be forwarded to the court.

ISSUE: Is a prison regulation requiring a petition for a writ of habeas corpus to be submitted to the institutional welfare office and then to a legal investigator for the parole board valid? NO.

DECISION:
1. A state and its officers may not abridge or impair a prisoner's right, given by federal law, to apply for a writ of habeas corpus.

2. The invalidity of a prison regulation requiring a petition for a writ of habeas corpus to be submitted to the institutional welfare office and then to a legal investigator for the parole board does not imply that the prisoner should be released.

REASON: "The regulation is invalid. The considerations that prompted its formulations are not without merit, but the state and its officers may not abridge or impair petitioner's right to apply to a federal court for a writ of habeas corpus. Whether a petition for writ of habeas corpus addressed to a federal court is properly drawn and what allegations it must contain are questions for that court alone to determine.

"However, the invalidity of the prison regulation does not compel petitioner's release. For that reason it is necessary to examine the petition annexed to the response . . . the next question, therefore, is whether the petition is premature. The petition is not premature . . . There is no reason to suppose that he can compel the parole board to review the record of the second conviction, or to make a declaratory ruling that if that conviction is void his parole will be reinstated."

CASE SIGNIFICANCE: A writ of habeas corpus is a post-conviction proceeding that enables an offender access to court even after the appeal process has been exhausted and the offender has started serving his or her sentence. It is an avenue whereby prisoners retain access to court despite a final conviction. The purpose of a habeas corpus petition is to secure release on the ground that the prisoner has been deprived of freedom unconstitutionally. It is a basic constitutional right that courts guard zealously and is always available to inmates regardless of the type of sentence and the length of time served. It seldom succeeds, but the right to file a habeas petition is always available.

In this case, the State of Michigan imposed a limitation on a prisoner's habeas corpus access by providing that all legal documents had to be submitted to the institutional welfare office and then to a legal investigator for the parole board before they could be forwarded to the court. This regulation was declared unconstitutional because it impaired a prisoner's access to courts through the use of this remedy. However, the invalidity of this regulation did not mean that the prisoner could be released.

Rose v. Lundy
455 U.S. 509 (1982)

CAPSULE: Under federal law, state prisoners must exhaust state court remedies before filing for a writ of habeas corpus in federal court.

FACTS: Noah Lundy was convicted in Tennessee of rape and crime against nature and was sent to state prison. The Tennessee Court of Criminal Appeals affirmed his convictions and the Tennessee Supreme Court denied review. Lundy filed a petition for post-conviction relief in state court, which was denied. He then filed a petition for a writ of habeas corpus in federal district court under 28 U.S.C. §2254, alleging the following: "(1) that he had been denied the right to confrontation because the trial court limited the defense counsel's questioning of the victim; (2) that he had been denied the right to a fair trial because the prosecuting attorney stated that the respondent had a violent character; (3) that he had been denied the right to a fair trial because the prosecutor improperly remarked in his closing argument that the State's evidence was uncontradicted; and (4) that the trial judge improperly instructed the jury that every witness is presumed to swear the truth." The Federal District Court granted the writ of habeas corpus despite claims (3) and (4) not having been litigated in state court. The Court of Appeals affirmed the decision of the Federal District Court; the government appealed.

ISSUE: Does federal law (28 U.S.C. §2254 [b] and [c]) require a federal district court to dismiss a state prisoner's petition for a writ of habeas corpus that contains claims that have not been exhausted in the state court? YES.

DECISION: A district court must dismiss "mixed petitions" (meaning petitions that contain claims that have been exhausted and others that have not been exhausted in state court) because such dismissal furthers the purposes underlying the federal habeas corpus statute.

REASON: "The exhaustion doctrine is principally designed to protect the state courts' role in the enforcement of federal law and prevent disruption of state judicial proceedings. Under our federal system, the federal and state 'courts [are] equally bound to guard and protect rights secured by the Constitution.' Because 'it would be unseemly in our dual system of government for a federal district court to upset a state court conviction without an opportunity for the state courts to correct a constitutional violation,' federal courts apply the doctrine of comity, which 'teaches that one court should defer action on causes properly within its jurisdiction until the courts of another sovereignty with concurrent powers, and already cognizant of the litigation, have had an opportunity to pass upon the matter.'

"A rigorously enforced total exhaustion rule will encourage state prisoners to seek full relief first from the state courts, thus giving those courts the first opportunity to review all claims of constitutional error. As the number of prisoners who exhaust all of their federal claims increases, state courts may become increasingly familiar with and hospitable toward federal constitutional issues. Equally as important, federal claims that have been fully exhausted in state courts will more often be accompanied by a complete factual record to aid the federal courts in their review.

"The facts of the present case underscore the need for a rule encouraging exhaustion of all federal claims. In his opinion, the District Court Judge wrote that 'there is such mixture of violations that one cannot be separated from and considered independently of the others.' Because the two unexhausted claims for relief were intertwined with the exhausted one, the judge apparently considered all of the claims in ruling on the petition. Requiring dismissal of petitions containing both exhausted and unexhausted claims will relieve the district courts of the difficult if not impossible task of deciding when claims are related, and will reduce the temptation to consider unexhausted claims."

CASE SIGNIFICANCE: Despite the absence of a constitutional issue, this case is significant because it makes clear when state prisoners can file habeas corpus petitions in federal courts. Habeas corpus petitions are filed by inmates to gain freedom, alleging that something was wrong with their conviction and therefore they are in prison unconstitutionally. This is the prisoner's last hope of freedom after conviction has been affirmed by the courts. Although habeas corpus cases seldom succeed, they give prisoners another judicial avenue to pursue when they feel they have been wrongly convicted.

The "exhaustion of state remedies" doctrine provides that remedies in state courts must be exhausted before a case can be heard in federal court. As this case states, "the exhaustion doctrine existed long before its codification by Congress in 1948." Although now codified, the "mixed petition" issue was not addressed in the codification, hence the need to clarify it in this case. The purpose of the exhaustion doctrine is to avoid piecemeal litigation. Its benefits are obvious. In the words of the Court: "To the extent that the exhaustion requirement reduces piecemeal litigation, both the courts and the prisoners should benefit, for as a result the district court will be more likely to review all of the prisoner's claims in a single proceeding, thus providing for a more focused and thorough review."

There are two kinds of habeas corpus proceedings: state habeas corpus and federal habeas corpus (under 28 U.S.C. §2254 [b] and [c]). Both are available to prisoners, but this case states that issues brought to federal courts on habeas corpus grounds must first be litigated in state courts. In this case, the prisoner alleged four grounds for relief; two grounds were litigated in state court, whereas the other two grounds were not litigated. The issue was whether such a "mixed petition" ought to be entertained by the federal court. The Court decided that 28 U.S.C. §2254 "requires a federal district court to dismiss a petition for a writ of habeas corpus containing any claims that have not been exhausted in the state courts." This is significant because it lengthens the time of potential relief for state prisoners in habeas corpus proceedings. It usually takes a number of years for prisoner habeas corpus cases to be decided in state court. Only after that will the federal forum be available to a state prisoner. This therefore further delays the availability of the federal habeas corpus remedy because state prisoners must first go through state process before taking their case to a federal court, even when some of the allegations have been litigated in state court. It is to be noted, however, that federal prisoners do not have to exhaust state proceedings because they have been convicted under federal law and were tried in federal court.

McCleskey v. Zant
59 L.W. 4288 (1991)

CAPSULE: Failure to claim violation of a constitutional right in a first federal habeas corpus petition constitutes an abuse of the writ and precludes a claim in a second habeas corpus petition.

FACTS: McCleskey was charged with murder and armed robbery. At his 1978 trial, the State of Georgia called Offie Evans, the occupant of the jail cell next to McCleskey, to rebut the petitioner's alibi defense. Evans testified that McCleskey had admitted to and boasted about the killing. Due to this testimony and other supporting evidence, the jury convicted McCleskey and sentenced him to death. After the Georgia Supreme Court affirmed the trial decision,

McCleskey initiated post-conviction proceedings by filing a state habeas corpus petition. McCleskey alleged that his statements to Evans were acquired by the state creating a situation that induced him to make incriminating statements without the assistance of counsel, in violation of the Sixth Amendment. He was denied relief and filed his first federal habeas corpus and second state habeas corpus petitions, which did not contain the Sixth Amendment claim. Both petitions were also denied. He filed a second federal habeas petition in 1987, challenging on Sixth Amendment grounds a 21-page statement that Evans had made to the police. The statement was made available to McCleskey just weeks before he filed his second federal petition. The document not only contained conversations that were consistent with Evans' trial testimony, but also recounted the tactics used by Evans to engage McCleskey in conversation. At the petition hearing, a jailer who was present during McCleskey's pretrial incarceration gave testimony that indicated that Evans' cell assignment had been made at the state's behest.

ISSUE: Does the failure to include a claim of a violation of the Sixth Amendment in his first petition for a federal writ of habeas corpus constitute abuse of the writ? YES.

DECISION: The failure to include a claim of a violation of a constitutional right in the first federal habeas corpus petition constitutes an abuse of the writ, which precludes a similar claim in a second federal habeas petition.

REASON: "Much confusion exists as to the proper standard for applying the abuse of the writ doctrine, which refers to a complex and evolving body of equitable principles informed and controlled by historical usage, statutory developments, and judicial decisions. This Court has heretofore defined such abuse in an oblique way, through dicta and denials of certiorari petitions or stay applications and, because of historical changes and the complexity of the subject, has not always followed an unwavering line in its conclusions as to the writ's availability.

"Although this Court's federal habeas decisions do not admit of ready synthesis, a review of these precedents demonstrates that a claim need not have been deliberately abandoned in an earlier petition in order to establish that its inclusion in a subsequent petition constitutes abuse of the writ, *see, e.g., Sanders v. United States*, 373 U.S. 1, 18: that such inclusion constitutes abuse if the claim could have been raised in the first petition, but was omitted through inexcusable neglect, *see, e.g., Delo v. Stokes*, 495 U.S. ___, ___, and that, because the doctrines of procedural default and abuse of the writ implicate nearly identical concerns, the determination of inexcusable neglect in the abuse context should be governed by the same standard used to determine whether to excuse a habeas petitioner's state procedural defaults, *see, e.g., Wainright v. Sykes*, 433 U.S. 72. Thus, when a prisoner files a second or subsequent habeas petition, the government bears the burden of pleading abuse of the writ. This burden is satisfied if the government, with clarity and particularity, notes petitioner's prior writ history, identifies the claims that appear for the first time, and alleges that petitioner has abused the writ. The burden to disprove abuse then shifts to petitioner. To excuse his failure to raise the claim earlier, he must show cause—e.g., that he was impeded by some objective factor external to the defense, such as governmental interference or the reasonable unavailability of the factual basis for the claim—as well as actual prejudice resulting from the errors of which he complains. He will not be entitled to an evidentiary hearing if the district court determines as a matter of law that he cannot satisfy the cause and prejudice standard. However, if one cannot show cause, the failure to earlier raise the claim may nonetheless be excused if he can show that a fundamental miscarriage of justice—the conviction of an innocent person—would result from a failure to entertain the claim."

CASE SIGNIFICANCE: This case was decided on procedural grounds, but its implication is potentially far-reaching. Habeas corpus petitions by state prisoners seek release on the ground of unconstitutional confinement. Such petitions are first heard in state courts and, if denied, may be filed again in a federal court under the Federal Habeas Corpus Act. The prisoner in this case went twice to his state court and then filed a federal habeas corpus proceeding. In his first federal habeas corpus case, however, he failed to allege a violation of his Sixth Amendment rights. Having been turned down, he filed a second federal habeas corpus case but this time he raised a violation of his Sixth Amendment rights as the basis of his release. The Court considered this an abuse of the writ and prohibited him from raising it in the second federal habeas corpus case. The Court said that "such inclusion constitutes abuse if the claim could have been raised in the first petition, but was omitted through inexcusable neglect." The Court added that "to excuse his failure to raise the claim earlier, he must show cause— e.g., that he was impeded by some objective factor external to the defense, such as government interference or the reasonable availability of the factual basis for the claim—as well as actual prejudice resulting from the errors of which he complains." The prisoner failed to establish this in his second petition, hence the issue could no longer be raised.

The effect of this decision is to minimize successive filings of habeas corpus cases in federal court by state prisoners. In effect, the Court is saying that petitioners must include all constitutional claims in their first petition and not "serialize" them. Any claim not raised in the first petition cannot be raised in a subsequent petition unless there are justifiable reasons for failure to raise that claim in the first petition.

O. Mail

Turner v. Safley
482 U.S. 78 (1987)

CAPSULE: A prison regulation that impinges on inmates' constitutional rights (in this case the freedom to send and receive mail) is valid if it is reasonably related to legitimate penological interests.

FACTS: State prison inmates brought a class action challenging regulations of the Missouri Division of Corrections that permit correspondence between immediate family members who are inmates at different institutions and between inmates concerning legal matters, but allows other inmate correspondence only if each inmate's classification/treatment deems it in the best interest of the parties. This had the effect of prohibiting inmate-to-inmate correspondence, except among a few individuals.

ISSUE: Does a regulation that permits correspondence between immediate family members who are inmates at different institutions and between inmates concerning legal matters, but allows other correspondence only if it is in the best interests of the parties, violate the constitutional rights of inmates? NO.

DECISION: A prison regulation that impinges on inmates' constitutional rights is valid if it is reasonably related to legitimate penological interests. The factors to be considered in making the reasonableness determination include:
1. whether there is a valid, rational connection between the regulation and the legitimate government interest put forward to justify it;
2. whether there are alternative means of exercising the right that remains open to prisoners;
3. the impact that accommodation of the asserted right will have on guards and other inmates and on the allocation of prison resources generally; and
4. the existence of ready alternatives to the regulation.

Missouri's inmate-to-inmate correspondence rule is reasonably related to legitimate security concerns of prison officials and is therefore constitutional.

REASON: "The prohibition on correspondence between institutions is logically connected to these legitimate security concerns . . . The rule is content neutral, it logically advances the goals of institutional security and safety identified by Missouri prison officials, and it is not an exaggerated response to these objectives. On that basis, we conclude that the regulation does not unconstitutionally abridge the First Amendment rights of prison inmates.

CASE SIGNIFICANCE: This case is discussed more extensively at the beginning of this book (see page 3) as the case that sets the standard for courts to determine whether prison regulations that allegedly impinge on prisoners' constitutional rights are valid. The rights involved in the challenge were the First Amendment right to communication and the right to marry. On the issue of whether the prison regulation on sending and receiving mail by inmates was valid, the Court said that this prison regulation was reasonably related to legitimate penological interests in that "mail between prisons could be used to communicate escape plans, to arrange violent acts, and to foster prison gang activity." It added that "the prison regulation does not deprive prisoners of all means of expression, but simply bars communication with a limited class of people—other inmates—with whom authorities have particular cause to be concerned." Given these, the Court concluded that the four tests to determine whether a prison regulation was "reasonably related to legitimate penological interests" were complied with, hence the regulation was constitutional.

This case is significant because it sets the current standard for determining the validity of prison regulations on mail inspection. Prison mail regulation has been the subject of numerous court battles between prisoners and prisons. The current standard holds that prison mail regulations are valid as long as they are "reasonably related to a legitimate penological interest." What that means is ultimately decided by the courts on a case-by-case basis.

Thornburgh v. Abbott
109 S. Ct. 1874 (1989)

CAPSULE: Prison regulations regarding receipt of publications by inmates are valid if reasonably related to a legitimate penological interest.

FACTS: Inmates and certain publishers filed suit in District Court against the Federal Bureau of Prisons, claiming that the regulations allowing prisoners to receive publications from the outside world, but restricting these publications on the basis of their detriment to the "security, good order, or discipline of the institution" or on the basis of their facilitating criminal activity, violated their First Amendment rights according to the standards set forth in *Procunier v. Martinez*,

416 U.S. 396. These regulations provide procedural safeguards for the prisoner and for the publisher or sender. The warden is the sole authority for rejecting a publication although he may designate a staff member to screen and, where appropriate, to approve incoming publications. If the publication is rejected, the warden must advise the inmate promptly in writing of the reasons for rejection and provide the publisher or sender with a copy of the rejection letter. This notice must refer to "the specific articles(s) or material(s) considered objectionable," Section 540.71(d), with the option that the publisher or sender may request an independent review of the decision to reject by a timely writing to the Regional Director of the Bureau. Additionally, an inmate may appeal through the Bureau's Administrative Remedy Procedure. The warden must permit the prisoner to review the rejected material for the purpose of filing an appeal. However, the regulations allow the warden to deny review of the material if this review "may provide the inmate with information of a nature which is deemed to pose a threat or detriment to the security, good order or discipline of the institution or to encourage or instruct criminal activity." Section 540.71(d).

ISSUE: Are restrictions on receipt of publications from the outside world that are based on the publication's detriment to the security, good order, or discipline of the institution, or on the basis of the publication's facilitation of criminal activity, such determination to be made by the warden, unconstitutional? NO.

DECISION: Using the test prescribed in *Turner v. Safley*, the Federal Bureau of Prisons regulations are valid because they are reasonably related to a legitimate penological interest.

REASON: "In this case, there is no question that publishers who wish to communicate with those who, through subscription, willingly seek their point of view have a legitimate First Amendment interest in access to prisoners. The question here, as it has been in our previous First Amendment cases in this area, is what standard of review this Court should apply to prison regulations limiting that access.

"The Court set forth in *Turner* the development of this reasonableness standard in the respective decisions in *Pell* and *Jones* and in *Block v. Rutherford*, 468 U.S. 576 (1984), and we need not repeat that discussion here.

"The Court's decision to apply a reasonableness standard in these cases rather than Martinez' less deferential approach stemmed from its concern that language in Martinez might be too readily understood as establishing a standard of 'strict' or 'heightened' scrutiny, and that such a strict standard simply was not appropriate for consideration of regulations that are centrally concerned with the maintenance of order and security within prisons. See *Turner v. Safley*, 482 U.S., at 81, 87, 89. Specifically, the Court declined to apply the *Martinez* standard in 'prisoners' rights' cases because, as we noted in *Turner*, *Martinez* could be (and had been) read to require a strict 'least restrictive alternative' analysis, without sufficient sensitivity to the need for discretion in meeting legitimate prison needs. 482 U.S., at 89-90. The Court expressed concern that 'every administrative judgment would be subject to the possibility that some court somewhere would conclude that it had a less restrictive way of solving the problem at hand,' id., at 9, and rejected the costs of a 'least restrictive alternative' rule as too high. See also *O'Lone v. Estate of Shabazz*, 482 U.S. 342, 350 (1987) (refusing to apply a least restrictive alternative standard for regulation of prisoner work rules having an impact on religious observance).

"Furthermore, we acknowledge today that the logic of our analyses in *Martinez* and *Turner* requires that *Martinez* be limited to regulations concerning outgoing correspondence . . . Any attempt to justify a similar categorical distinction between incoming correspondence from prisoners (to which we applied a reasonableness standard in *Turner*) and incoming correspondence from nonprisoners would likely prove futile, and we do not invite it. To the extent that *Martinez* itself suggests such a distinction, we today overrule that case; the Court accomplished much of this step when it decided *Turner*.

"In doing so, we recognize that it might have been possible to apply a reasonableness standard to all incoming materials without overruling *Martinez*; we instead could have made clear that *Martinez* does not uniformly require the application of a 'least restrictive alternative' analysis. We choose not to go that route, however, for we prefer the express flexibility of the *Turner* reasonableness standard. We adopt the *Turner* standard in this case with confidence that, as petitioners here have asserted, 'a reasonableness standard is not toothless.' Pet. for Cert. 17, n. 10.

"The legitimacy of the Government's purpose in promulgating these regulations is beyond question. The regulations are expressly aimed at protecting prison security, a purpose this Court has said is 'central to all other corrections goals.' *Pell v. Procunier*, 417 U.S., at 823.

"Where the regulations at issue concern the entry of materials into the prison, we agree with the District Court that a regulation which gives prison authorities broad discretion is appropriate . . . A second factor the Court in *Turner* held to be 'relevant in determining the reasonableness of a prison restriction . . . is whether there are alternatives of exercising the right that remain open to prison inmates.' 482 U.S., at 90 . . . As the regulations at issue in the present case permit a broad range of publications to be sent, received, and read, this factor is clearly satisfied.

"In our view, when prison officials are able to demonstrate that they have rejected a less restrictive alternative because of reasonably founded fears that it will lead to greater harm, they succeed in demonstrating that the alternative they in fact selected was not an 'exaggerated response' under *Turner*."

CASE SIGNIFICANCE: This decision applies the standard set by the Court two years earlier in *Turner v. Safley*, 482 U.S. 78 (1987) to prison "receipt of publications" cases. In the *Turner* case, the Court held that prison regulations that impinge on inmates' constitutional rights are valid if they are "reasonably related to legitimate penological interests." The Court then enumerated four factors to be considered when making the reasonableness determination: (1) whether there is a valid, rational connection between the regulation and the legitimate government interest put forward to justify it; (2) whether there are alternative means of exercising the rights that remain open to prisoners; (3) the impact that accommodation of the asserted right will have on correctional officers and other inmates and on the allocation of prison resources generally; and (4) the existence of ready alternatives to the regulation. The Court applied these four tests to the federal prison regulation involved in this case and concluded that the regulation was constitutional. This case is significant in that it extends the *Turner* test to "receipt of publication" cases and also illustrates how those tests are applied to actual prison regulations. The *Turner* test makes it difficult for prisoners to overturn prison regulations even if they infringe on First Amendment rights, such as the regulations in question here did. The Court has certainly taken the side of prison administration in the balancing of interests between prison authorities and inmates, even when the constitutional right involved is as important as the First Amendment. This case involved the Federal Bureau of Prisons, but should apply to state prisons as well.

P. Medical Care

Estelle v. Gamble
429 U.S. 97 (1976)

CAPSULE: "Deliberate indifference" to inmate medical needs constitutes cruel and unusual punishment.

FACTS: J.W. Gamble, an inmate of the Texas Department of Corrections, was injured while performing a work assignment. He was granted a pass to the hospital where he was diagnosed with back strain, treated with medicine, and relieved of prison duty. The pain continued and the inmate was placed on a cell pass for three weeks. After three weeks, he was ordered back to work with continued medication. Gamble refused to work, claiming that he was in too much pain. He was placed in administrative segregation and directed to be seen by another doctor. The medical director treated him with medication for back pain and high blood pressure. However, the prescription took four days to fill because it was temporarily misplaced. Medication was continued for one month while he remained in administrative segregation.

At his next discipline committee hearing, testimony was given that Gamble was in "first-class" medical condition. He was ordered to work; he refused again, and was placed in solitary confinement. Gamble requested medical attention four days later for black-outs and chest pains. He was examined, treated, and placed in administrative segregation. A few days later, he again asked to see a doctor and was denied access for two days. Shortly thereafter, he brought a civil rights action under 42 U.S.C. §1983 against W.J. Estelle, Jr., Director of the Department of Corrections; H.H. Husbands, warden of the prison; and Dr. Ralph Gray, medical director. Gamble claimed that he was subjected to cruel and unusual punishment in violation of the Eighth Amendment because he received inadequate treatment for a back injury sustained while working in the prison. The District Court dismissed the complaint based on failure to state a claim upon which relief could be granted. The Court of Appeals ordered reinstatement of the complaint, holding that the alleged insufficiency of the medical treatment required it.

ISSUE: Did the action of the state constitute deliberate indifference to the prisoner's injury, thus violating the cruel and unusual punishment clause of the Eighth Amendment? NO.

DECISION: Deliberate indifference by prison personnel to a prisoner's serious illness or injury constitutes cruel and unusual punishment, in violation of the Eighth Amendment. In this case, however, the claims by the inmate do not constitute deliberate indifference. The facts show that the medical director and other prison medical personnel saw the inmate on 17 occasions during a three-month period and treated his injury and other problems. The failure to perform an X-ray or to use additional diagnostic techniques does not constitute cruel and unusual punishment, but is at most medical malpractice that can be redressed in state courts.

REASON: "We therefore conclude that deliberate indifference to serious medical needs of prisoners constitutes the 'unnecessary and wanton infliction of pain,' *Gregg v. Georgia, supra,* at 173 (joint opinion), proscribed by the Eighth Amendment . . . This conclusion does not mean, however, that every claim by a prisoner that he has not received adequate medical treatment states a violation of the Eighth Amendment . . . Medical malpractice does not become a constitutional violation merely because the victim is a prisoner. In order to state a cognizable claim, a prisoner must allege acts or omissions sufficiently harmful to evidence deliberate indifference to serious medical needs. It is only such indifference that can offend 'evolving standards of decency' in violation of the Eighth Amendment . . . Even applying these liberal standards, however, Gamble's claims against Dr. Gray, both in his capacity as treating physician and as medical director of the Corrections Department, are not cognizable under Section 1983 . . . A medical decision not to order an X-ray, or like measures, does not represent cruel and unusual punishment. At most, it is medical malpractice, and as such the proper forum is the state court under the Texas Tort Claims Act."

CASE SIGNIFICANCE: This case, decided in 1976, was the first major prison medical treatment case decided by the Supreme Court. It is important because it sets the standard by which violations of an inmate's constitutional rights in medical treatment cases are determined. The Court said that "deliberate indifference by prison personnel to a prisoner's serious illness or injury" constitutes cruel and unusual punishment. Having said that, the Court concluded that there was no violation in this case because the medical personnel saw the inmate on 17 occasions during a three-month span, adding that the failure to perform an X-ray or to use additional diagnostic techniques does not constitute cruel and unusual punishment. The remedy for malpractice in prisons lies in state courts, not in a civil rights (§1983) case.

What is "deliberate indifference" by which prison systems are judged in medical treatment cases? Quoting an earlier case, the Court said that "deliberate indifference to serious medical needs of prisoners constitutes the 'unnecessary and wanton infliction of pain . . .'" The Court then added: "This is true whether the indifference is manifested by prison doctors in their response to the prisoner's needs or by prison guards in intentionally denying or delaying access to medical care or intentionally interfering with the treatment once prescribed." In a footnote, the Court gave examples of deliberate indifference by prison doctors: (1) "doctors choosing the 'easier and less efficacious treatment' of throwing away the prisoner's ear and stitching the stump;" (2) "injection of penicillin with knowledge that the prisoner was allergic, and refusal of the doctor to treat the allergic reaction;" and (3) "prison physician refusing to administer the prescribed painkiller and renders leg surgery unsuccessful by requiring the prisoner to stand despite contrary instructions of the surgeon." These examples, taken by the Supreme Court from lower court cases, are much more severe than what the Texas Department of Corrections did to inmate Gamble, hence there was no violation of Gamble's constitutional right against cruel and unusual punishment.

The phrase "deliberate indifference," popularized by this case, has since been applied to other cases not involving medical care. However, despite the Court's attempt to provide a definition for deliberate indifference in medical cases (that definition being the "unnecessary and wanton infliction of pain"), its meaning in other prison cases remains elusive and difficult to apply. Nonetheless, it is a convenient tool by which cruel and unusual punishment is determined in prison cases.

West v. Atkins
108 S. Ct. 2250 (1988)

CAPSULE: Private physicians under contract with the state are "acting under color of state law" when treating prisoners.

FACTS: Inmate West tore his left Achilles tendon while playing volleyball at a state prison in North Carolina. A physician at the prison transferred West to the Central Prison Hospital in Raleigh for orthopedic consultation. Samuel Atkins, M.D., a private physician, provided orthopedic services at the prison hospital through a contract for professional services. He treated West's injury by placing his leg in a series of casts over several months.

West brought an action against Atkins under 42 U.S.C. §1983, alleging that his Eighth Amendment right to be free from cruel and unusual punishment had been violated. West claimed the Atkins knew that he needed surgery but refused to schedule it and eventually discharged him when his ankle was still swollen and painful. West alleged that Atkins was deliberately indifferent to his serious medical needs by failing to provide adequate treatment.

ISSUE: Is a physician who is under contract with the state to provide medical services to inmates at a state prison hospital on a part-time basis acting "under color of state law" within the meaning of 42 U.S.C. §1983 when treating an inmate? YES.

DECISION: A physician who is under contract with the state to provide medical services to inmates in a state prison hospital on a part-time basis acts "under color of state law" when treating an inmate. Therefore, although a private person, the physician can be sued under §1983.

REASON: "The traditional definition of acting under color of state law requires that the defendant in a Section 1983 action have exercised power 'possessed by virtue of state law and made possible only because the wrongdoer is clothed with the authority of state law.'

"We now make explicit what was implicit in our holding in *Estelle*: Respondent, as a physician employed by North Carolina to provide medical services to state prison inmates, acted under color of state law for purposes of Section 1983 when undertaking his duties in treating petitioner's injury. Such conduct is fairly attributable to the State.

"Under state law, the only medical care West could receive for his injury was that provided by the State. If Doctor Atkins misused his power by demonstrating deliberate indifference to West's serious medical needs, the resultant deprivation was caused, in the sense relevant for state-action inquiry, by the State's exercise of its right to punish West by incarceration and to deny him a venue independent of the State to obtain medical care.

"The State bore an affirmative obligation to provide adequate medical care to West; the State delegated that function to respondent Atkins; and respondent voluntarily assumed that obligation by contract . . . In the State's employ, respondent worked as a physician at the prison hospital fully vested with state authority to fulfill essential aspects of the duty, placed on the State by the Eighth Amendment and state law, to provide essential medical care to those the State had incarcerated. Doctor Atkins must be considered to be a state actor."

CASE SIGNIFICANCE: This case addresses the question whether private persons under contract with the state can be sued under §1983, or whether only public employees can be sued under this federal law. By deciding that private persons can be held liable and are acting under "color of law" when performing services, the Court expanded the number and categories of individuals who may be sued under §1983. This decision allows prisoners to bring actions under federal statutes against people working in prisons who may not be public employees, but who are under contract with the state to provide services to prisoners. The reason for this is that the state, by contracting with a private provider to perform an essential service, in fact delegated its power to that private person— hence, he or she acts under color of state law.

Washington v. Harper
58 L.W. 4249 (1990)

CAPSULE: A prisoner with a serious mental illness may be treated with antipsychotic drugs against his will. There must be a hearing prior to such treatment, but the hearing does not have to be before a judge; a hearing before a special committee (in this case composed of a psychiatrist, a psychologist, and a correctional official) is sufficient.

FACTS: Inmate Harper was sentenced to prison in 1976 for robbery. From 1976 to 1980, he was incarcerated at the Washington State Penitentiary, primarily in the mental health unit. Harper was paroled in 1980, one of the conditions being that he participate in psychiatric treatment. In December 1981, his parole was revoked after he assaulted two nurses at a hospital in Seattle.

Upon being returned to prison, Harper was sent to the Special Offender Center (SOC or the Center). The initial diagnosis of Harper indicated that he was suffering from a manic-depressive disorder. He gave voluntary consent to treatment, including the administration of antipsychotic drugs, until November 1982 when he refused to continue taking his prescribed medication. His physician sought to continue his medication despite his objections, pursuant to SOC Policy 600.30.

Policy 600.30 states that if a psychiatrist orders antipsychotic medication, an inmate may be involuntarily treated only if he (1) suffers from a "mental disorder" and (2) is "gravely disabled" or poses a "likelihood of serious harm" to himself or others. After a hearing in which the above conditions are judged to have been met, a special committee consisting of a psychiatrist, a psychologist, and a Center official, none of whom may be currently involved in the inmate's diagnosis or treatment, can order involuntary medication if the psychiatrist is in the majority. The inmate has a right to notice of the hearing, the right to attend, present evidence, and cross-examine witnesses. He or she has a right to a disinterested lay advisor versed in psychological issues, the right to appeal to the Center's Superintendent, and the right to periodic review of any involuntary medication ordered. The inmate also has a right to judicial review of a committee decision in state court by means of a personal restraint petition or extraordinary writ.

Harper was found to be a danger to others as a result of a mental disease or disorder and consequently the committee approved the involuntary administration of antipsychotic drugs. This decision was appealed to and upheld by the Superintendent. Harper was involuntarily medicated for one year, during which periodic reviews were conducted.

Following this year, Harper was transferred to another facility for one month. During this time, he was not taking medication. He was then transferred back to the Center where another committee meeting was held in accordance with policy. The committee approved involuntary medication and Harper was given antipsychotic drugs. He filed suit in state court under 42 U.S.C. §1983, claiming that failure to provide a judicial hearing before the involuntary administration of antipsychotic drugs violated the due process, equal protection, and free speech clauses of both the federal and state constitutions, as well as state tort law.

ISSUE: Does the treatment of a mentally ill prisoner with antipsychotic drugs against his will and without a judicial hearing violate the due process clause of the Fourteenth Amendment? NO.

DECISION:

1. The due process clause permits the state to treat a prisoner who has a serious mental illness with antipsychotic drugs against his will if he is a danger to himself or others and the treatment is in his medical interest. The state has a legitimate interest in medically treating a prisoner, where appropriate, for the purpose of reducing the danger the prisoner poses.

2. The Special Offender Center's Policy 600.30 concerning administrative hearing procedures comports with procedural due process. A judicial hearing is not required under the due process clause and the Policy's procedures satisfy due process requirements in other respects.

REASON: "In *Turner*, we considered various factors to determine the reasonableness of a challenged prison regulation. Three are relevant here. 'First, there must be a "valid, rational connection" between the prison regulation and the legitimate governmental interest put forward to justify it.' 482 U.S. at 89 (quoting *Block v. Rutherford*, 468 U.S. 576, 586 [1984]). Second, a court must consider 'the impact accommodation of the asserted constitutional right will have on guards and other inmates, and on the allocation of prison resources generally.' 482 U.S., at 90. Third, 'the absence of ready alternatives is evidence of the reasonableness of a prison regulation,' but this does not mean that prison officials 'have set up and then shot down every conceivable alternative method of accommodating the claimant's constitutional complaint.' Id., at 90-91; *see also Estate of Shabazz, supra*, at 350.

"Applying these factors to the regulation before us, we conclude that the Policy comports with constitutional requirements. There can be little doubt as to both the legitimacy and the importance of the governmental interest presented here . . . Special Offender Center Policy 600.30 is a rational means of furthering the State's legitimate objectives . . . There is considerable debate over the potential side effects of antipsychotic medications, but there is little dispute in the psychiatric profession that proper use of the drugs is one of the most effective means of treating and controlling a mental illness likely to cause violent behavior.

"We hold that, given the requirements of the prison environment, the Due Process Clause permits the State to treat a prison inmate who has a serious mental illness with antipsychotic drugs against his will, if the inmate is dangerous to himself or others and the treatment is in the inmate's medical interest. Policy 600.30 comports with these requirements; we therefore reject respondent's contention that its substantive standards are deficient under the Constitution.

"We address next what procedural protections are necessary to ensure that the decision to medicate an inmate against his will is neither arbitrary nor erroneous under the standards we have discussed above . . . We hold that the administrative hearing procedures set by the SOC Policy do comport with procedural due process, and conclude that the Washington Supreme Court erred in requiring a judicial hearing as a prerequisite for the involuntary treatment of prison inmates . . . The Policy provides for notice, the right to be present at an adversary hearing, and the right to present and cross-examine witnesses. *See Vitek, supra,* at 494-496. The procedural protections are not vitiated by meetings between the committee members and staff before the hearing. Absent evidence of resulting bias, or evidence that the actual decision is made before the hearing, allowing respondents to contest the staff's position at the hearing satisfies the requirement that the opportunity to be heard 'must be granted at a meaningful time and in a meaningful manner.' *Armstrong v. Manzo,* 380 U.S. 545, 552 (1965). We reject also respondent's contention that the hearing must be conducted in accordance with the rules of evidence or that a 'clear, cogent, and convincing' standard of proof is necessary. This standard is neither required nor helpful when medical personnel are making the judgment required by the regulations here. *See Vitek, supra,* at 494-495.

"In sum, we hold that the regulation before us is permissible under the Constitution. It is an accommodation between an inmate's liberty interest in avoiding the forced administration of antipsychotic drugs and the State's interests in providing appropriate medical treatment to reduce the danger that an inmate suffering from a serious mental disorder represents to himself or others. The Due Process Clause does require certain essential procedural protections, all of which are provided by the regulation before us."

CASE SIGNIFICANCE: This case answers the question of whether a state may treat a prisoner with antipsychotic drugs against his or her will and without a judicial hearing. The Court said yes, holding that the state has a legitimate interest in such treatment, where appropriate, for the purpose of reducing the danger the prisoner poses. The prisoner in this case argued that because of the liberty interest involved (being treated against his will), a hearing before a judge was necessary—in essence saying that the procedure followed by the State of Washington was unconstitutional because the decision was made not by a judge but by a special committee consisting of a psychiatrist, a psychologist, and a Center official. The Court disagreed, saying that the liberty interest of the inmate in this case was adequately protected by such procedure and "perhaps better served, by allowing the decision to medicate to be made by the medical professionals rather than a judge."

The Court's decision did not say that forced treatment of a prisoner who has a serious mental illness by prison authorities could be made arbitrarily. On the contrary, the Court said that due process was required prior to such treatment. In this case, however, the procedure provided by the State of Washington (which included a hearing before a committee, the right to notice, attend the hearing, present evidence, cross-examine witnesses, and the right to appeal to administrators as well as the right to a judicial review of a committee decision in a state court) satisfied the due process requirement of the Constitution. While the Court did not enumerate the due process rights an inmate is entitled to in forced treatment situations, the Court made clear that there was nothing wrong with the procedure used by the State of Washington. In sum, inmates are entitled to some due process rights prior to forced treatment, but these rights do not include a judicial hearing, nor do they include all the rights to which an inmate is entitled in a judicial hearing. The procedure used by the State of Washington complied with due process requirements.

Q. Freedom of the Press

Pell v. Procunier
417 U.S. 817 (1974)

CAPSULE: A state prison regulation prohibiting media interviews with specific inmates does not violate the constitutional rights of the media or the inmates as long as alternative means of communication are available.

FACTS: Three professional journalists and four California prison inmates brought suit against California prison authorities under 42 U.S.C. §1983, challenging the constitutionality of a regulation in the California Department of Corrections Manual stating that the press and other media interviews with "specific individual inmates will not be permitted." The policy was implemented following a violent prison disturbance that was partially attributed to a former rule allowing face-to-face, prisoner-press interviews. Correctional authorities saw these interviews as a way for a relatively small number of inmates to gain disproportionate notoriety and influence among their fellow inmates.

The new regulation was challenged as an infringement on the inmates' and journalists' First Amendment rights to freedom of speech and the journalists' right to a free press.

ISSUE: Does a prison regulation prohibiting media interviews with specific inmates violate the constitutional rights of the media and the inmates? NO.

DECISION:
1. Because alternative channels of communication are open to the inmates, the interview regulation does not violate freedom of speech. This right

must be balanced against the state's legitimate interest in confining prisoners, deterring crime, and protecting society.

2.   Because the press is not denied access to information available to the general public, the rights of the media are not infringed by the interview regulation. Reporters are free to visit both maximum- and minimum-security sections of California penal institutions and to speak with inmates whom they may encounter; they are also free to select inmates at random.

REASON: "Challenges to prison restrictions that are asserted to inhibit First Amendment interests must be analyzed in terms of the legitimate policies and goals of the corrections system, to whose custody and care the prisoner has been committed in accordance with due process of law. In order to evaluate the constitutionality of Section 415.071 [the prison regulation] we think that the regulation cannot be considered in isolation but must be viewed in the light of the alternative means of communication permitted under the regulations with persons outside the prison . . . One such alternative available to California prison inmates is communication by mail . . . Thus, it is clear that the medium of written correspondence affords inmates an open and substantially unimpeded channel for communication with persons outside the prison, including representatives of the news media.

"Moreover, the visitation policy of the California Corrections Department does not seal the inmate off from personal contact with those outside the prison. Inmates are permitted to receive limited visits from members of their families, the clergy, their attorneys, and friends of prior acquaintance. This is not a case in which the selection is based on the anticipated content of the communication between the inmate and the prospective visitor. If a member of the press fell within any of these categories, there is no suggestion that he would not be permitted to visit with the inmate. More importantly, however, inmates have an unrestricted opportunity to communicate with the press or any other member of the public through their families, friends, clergy, or attorneys who are permitted to visit them at the prison. Thus, this provides another alternative avenue of communication between prison inmates and persons outside the prison.

"The First and Fourteenth Amendments bar government from interfering in any way with a free press. The Constitution does not, however, require government to accord the press special access to information not shared by members of the public generally. It is one thing to say that a journalist is free to seek out sources of information not available to members of the general public, that he is entitled to some constitutional protection of the confidentiality of sources, cf. *Branzburg v. Hayes, supra,* and that government cannot restrain the publication of news emanating from such sources. Cf. *New York Times Co. v. United States, supra.* It is quite another thing to suggest that the Constitution imposes upon government the affirmative duty to make available to journalists sources of information not available to members of the public generally . . . Accordingly, since Section 415.071 does not deny the press access to sources of information available to members of the general public, we hold that it does not abridge the protections that the First and Fourteenth Amendments guarantee."

CASE SIGNIFICANCE: This case is significant because it was the first case decided by the Court on the issue of prisoner access to the media and vice versa. In this case, the media sought to declare as unconstitutional a rule prohibiting media interviews with specific inmates, a rule promulgated by prison authorities following a violent prison disturbance that authorities attributed, in part, to their former policy of free face-to-face, prisoner-press interviews. The Court said that the First Amendment rights of inmates were not violated because there were alternative means of communication available to them, such as correspondence by mail with persons on the outside, including media representatives. They also had visitation rights with family, the clergy, attorneys, and friends, and had un-restricted opportunity to communicate with the press or public through their prison visitors. As for the freedom of the press, the court reiterated an earlier statement in *Branzburg v. Hayes*, 408 U.S. 665, in which the Court said "the First Amendment does not guarantee the press a constitutional right of special access to information not available to the public generally." This decision cur-tails the First Amendment rights of inmates and press; such curtailment is con-stitutional as long as other avenues are open. What prison authorities cannot do is completely cut off communication between inmates and the press, and vice versa.

The holding in this was later extended to federal prisons in the case of *Saxbe v. Washington Post Company*, 417 U.S. 843 (1974).

Houchins v. KQED, Inc.
438 U.S. 1 (1978)

CAPSULE: The media have no right of access to inmates and prisons be-yond that given to the general public.

FACTS: KQED, a television station, reported the suicide of a prisoner in the Greystone area of the Santa Rita Jail on March 31, 1975. The report included two statements, one from a psychiatrist who said that the conditions at the Greystone facility caused the illnesses of his patient-prisoners there. The other statement was from Sheriff Houchins, who denied that prison conditions were responsible for the prisoners' illnesses. KQED then asked to inspect and take pictures in the Greystone facility. Permission was refused and KQED and the Alameda and Oakland branches of the NAACP filed suit under 42 U.S.C.

§1983. They alleged that Houchins had violated the First Amendment by denying media access to his jail and by failing to provide an effective means whereby the public could be informed of conditions in the Greystone facility or learn of prisoners' grievances.

At the time of the suit, there was no formal policy regarding public access to the jail. On July 8, 1975, Sheriff Houchins announced a program of regular monthly tours and invited all interested persons to make arrangements for the tours. The news media were given notice in advance of the public. On July 14, 1975, the first tour was conducted, which included a KQED reporter. Each tour allowed a maximum of 25 persons and access to the jail was limited.

KQED and the NAACP contended that these tours failed to provide adequate access to the jail for two reasons: (1) once the scheduled tours had been filled, media representatives who had not signed up were excluded and therefore unable to cover newsworthy events at the jail; and (2) the prohibition on photography and tape recordings, the exclusion of portions of the jail from the tours, and the practice of keeping inmates generally removed from view substantially reduced the usefulness of such tours to the media. Houchins asserted that unregulated access to the jail by the media would infringe on the inmates' right to privacy and that it would create jail celebrities who would undermine jail security. The Sheriff also contended that unscheduled media tours would cause jail operations to be disrupted. He asserted that information concerning the jail could reach the public through current mail, visitation, and phone call regulations.

ISSUE: Does the Alameda County Jail policy regarding public access to the jail violate constitutional rights under the First Amendment? NO.

DECISION: The Constitution does not guarantee the media a right of access to prisons or inmates beyond that given to the general public. Whether the government should open penal institutions in the way asserted by KQED and the NAACP is a matter for legislative, not judicial, resolution.

REASON: "The public importance of conditions in penal facilities and the media's role of providing information afford no basis for reading into the Constitution a right of the public or the media to enter these institutions, with camera equipment, and take moving and still pictures of inmates for broadcast purposes. This Court has never intimated a First Amendment guarantee of a right of access to all sources of information within governmental control. Nor does the rationale of the decisions upon which respondents rely lead to the implication of such a right.

"A number of alternatives are available to prevent problems in penal facilities from escaping public attention . . . Citizen task forces and prison visitation committees continue to play an important role in keeping the public informed of deficiencies in prison systems and need for reforms. Grand juries, with the potent subpoena power—not available to the media—traditionally concern themselves with conditions in public institutions: a prosecutor or judge may initiate similar inquiries, and the legislative power embraces an arsenal of weapons for inquiry relating to tax-supported institutions. In each case, these public bodies are generally compelled to publish their findings and, if they default, the power of the media is always available to generate public pressure for disclosure. But the choice as to the most effective and appropriate method is a policy decision to be resolved by legislative decision. We must not confuse what is 'good,' 'desirable,' or 'expedient' with what is constitutionally commanded by the First Amendment. To do so is to trivialize constitutional adjudication . . . We, therefore, reject the Court of Appeals' conclusory assertion that the public and the media have a First Amendment right to government information regarding the conditions of jails and their inmates and presumably all other public facilities such as hospitals and mental institutions.

"Petitioner cannot prevent respondents from learning about jail conditions in a variety of ways, albeit not as conveniently as they might prefer. Respondents have a First Amendment right to receive letters from inmates criticizing jail officials and reporting on conditions. Respondents are free to interview those who render the legal assistance to which inmates are entitled. They are also free to seek out former inmates, visitors to the prison, public officials, and institutional personnel, as they sought out complaining psychiatrists here.

"Neither the First Amendment nor the Fourteenth Amendment mandates a right of access to government information or sources of information with the government's control. Under our holdings in *Pell v. Procunier, supra*, and *Saxbe v. Washington Post Co., supra*, until the political branches decree otherwise, as they are free to do, the media has no special right of access to the Alameda County Jail different from or greater than that accorded the public generally."

CASE SIGNIFICANCE: This case followed two 1974 cases, *Pell v. Procunier* and *Saxbe v. Washington Post Co.*, which also stated that there is no constitutional right of access to prisons or their inmates on the part of the media beyond that afforded the general public. In both cases, prison regulations that prevented media interviews with inmates were challenged, as was part of the basis of this challenge. In this case, the U.S. Supreme Court again reiterated that there is no "right" guaranteed under the First Amendment for the press to be able to interview prisoners under all circumstances. In deciding that a sheriff can restrict press access to physical parts of a jail, the Court further restricted freedom of the press. An important reason the Court decided this case the way it did was the presence of "access alternatives" made available by Sheriff Houchins to the press. As long as these alternatives were available, freedom of the press was not violated, although the degree of access given by the sheriff was not as extensive as that sought by the press. What prison authorities cannot do is deny access completely; such would be viewed differently by the Court.

R. Protection of Inmates from Injury

DeShaney v. Winnebago County Department of Social Services
57 L.W. 4218 (1989)

CAPSULE: The state has no duty to protect individuals who are not in state custody from harm by private persons. (This implies that the state may be held liable if the individual is under its custody, as when in prison.)

FACTS: Four-year-old Joshua DeShaney was beaten and permanently injured by his father, to whose custody he was awarded after a divorce. The county department of social services and several social workers received several complaints that the child was being abused by his father. Over a period of time, they took various steps to protect the boy, but they did not remove him from his father's custody. Subsequently, the child was beaten by the father so severely he suffered permanent brain damage and was rendered severely retarded. He is expected to spend the rest of his life confined to an institution. His father was tried and convicted of child abuse. The mother, acting for and as guardian of the child, later sued the officials of the County Department of Social Services under 42 U.S.C. §1983, charging that county officials violated the child's constitutional right to due process by failing to intervene to protect him against his father's violence. The District Court decided for the county; the Court of Appeals affirmed.

ISSUE: Does the state have the duty to protect individuals who are not in state custody from harm by a private person? NO, with some exceptions.

DECISION: The Fourteenth Amendment due process clause does not impose an affirmative duty on the state to protect individuals who are not in state custody from harm by private persons. The county social services agency and the officers who failed to protect the child from severe beatings by the father did not violate the child's due process rights and could not be held civilly liable even though they had knowledge of such abuse and had continuing contact with the family.

REASON: "The Due Process Clause of the Fourteenth Amendment provides that '[n]o State shall . . . deprive any person of life, liberty, or property, without due process of law.' Petitioners contend that the State deprived Joshua of his liberty interest in 'free[dom] from . . . unjustified intrusions on personal security,' by failing to provide him with adequate protection against his father's violence. The claim is one invoking the substantive rather than procedural component of the Due Process Clause; petitioners do not claim that the State denied Joshua protection without according him appropriate procedural safeguards, but that it was categorically obligated to protect him in these circumstances.

"But nothing in the language of the Due Process Clause itself requires the State to protect the life, liberty, and property of its citizens against invasion by private actors. The Clause is phrased as a limitation on the State's power to act, not as a guarantee of certain minimal levels of safety and security. It forbids the State itself to deprive individuals of life, liberty, or property without 'due process of law,' but its language cannot fairly be extended to impose an affirmative obligation on the State to ensure that those interests do not come to harm through other means . . . Its purpose was to protect the people from the State, not to ensure that the State protected them from each other. The Framers were content to leave the extent of governmental obligation in the latter area to the democratic political processes.

"Consistent with these principles, our cases have recognized that the Due Process Clauses generally confer no affirmative right to governmental aid, even where such aid may be necessary to secure life, liberty, or property interests of which the government itself may not deprive the individual.

"If the Due Process Clause does not require the State to provide its citizens with particular protective services, it follows that the State cannot be held liable under the Clause for injuries that could have been averted had it chosen to provide them. As a general matter, then, we conclude that a State's failure to protect an individual against private violence simply does not constitute a violation of the Due Process Clause.

"That the State once took temporary custody of Joshua does not alter the analysis, for when it returned him to his father's custody, it placed him in no worse position than that in which he would have been had it not acted at all; the State does not become the permanent guarantor of an individual's safety by having once offered him shelter. Under these circumstances, the State has no constitutional duty to protect Joshua."

CASE SIGNIFICANCE: This is an important case because for the first time the Court addressed the issue of the civil liability of public officials for failure to protect a member of the public from harm or injury inflicted by a third person (not a government official). The Court decided that there is no constitutional right on the part of the public to be protected from such harm, and therefore failure to protect does not result in civil damages against the state and its officers.

Although not a prison law case, this case is important and is briefed here because of what the Court said about the responsibility of the state to protect prisoners and detainees from harm. After discussing previously decided cases, the Court concluded: "Taken together, they stand only for the proposition that when the State takes a person into its custody and holds him there against his will, the Constitution imposes upon it a corresponding duty to assume some responsibility for his safety and well-being."

Quoting *Youngberg v. Romeo* (457 U.S. 307 [1982]), the Court said: "When a person is institutionalized—and wholly dependent on the State . . . a duty to provide certain services and care does exist." The Court then added: "The rationale for this principle is simple enough: when the State by the affirmative exercise of its power so restrains an individual's liberty that it renders him unable to care for himself, and at the same time fails to provide for his basic human needs—e.g., food, clothing, shelter, medical care, and reasonable safety—it transgresses the substantive limits on state action set by the Eighth Amendment and the Due Process Clause." Clearly, therefore, the state has a responsibility to protect prisoners from injury or harm while in state custody. A breach of that duty constitutes a violation of the ban against cruel and unusual punishment and the right of due process, and subjects the state and its officers to liability.

Farmer v. Brennan
55 Cr. L. 2135 (1994)

CAPSULE: A prison official is not liable under the Eighth Amendment for injury inflicted on an inmate by other inmates "unless the official knows of and disregards an excessive risk of harm to an inmate." It is not enough for liability that "the risk was so obvious that a reasonable person should have noticed it."

FACTS: Farmer, a preoperative transsexual, was transferred from a federal correctional institution to a state penitentiary, where he was placed in the general population. Farmer has the appearance and demeanor of a woman, enhanced by silicone breast implants and female hormones, but he had male sex organs. He was serving a 20-year term for credit card fraud in a federal prison for men.

Farmer was beaten and raped by another inmate after transfer to the state penitentiary. He filed an action seeking damages and an injunction barring future confinement in any penitentiary. The inmate alleged that prison officials had acted with deliberate indifference to his safety, in violation of the Eighth Amendment, by placing him in a penitentiary that they knew had a violent environment and a history of inmate assaults, and that they knew that he would be vulnerable to sexual attack.

ISSUE: May prison officials be held liable under the Eighth Amendment for unsafe conditions of confinement if they know that inmates face a substantial risk of serious harm and disregard that risk by failing to take reasonable measures to abate it? YES.

DECISION: Prison officials are not liable under the Eighth Amendment for injury inflicted on an inmate by other inmates unless the official was aware of and disregarded an excessive risk of harm to the inmate. However, it is not enough for liability that the risk was so obvious that a reasonable person should have noticed.

REASON: "Our cases have held that a prison official violates the Eighth Amendment only when two requirements are met. First, the deprivation alleged must be, objectively, 'sufficiently serious,' *Wilson, supra*, at 298 . . . The second requirement follows from the principle that 'only unnecessary and wanton infliction of pain implicates the Eighth Amendment.' *Wilson*, 501 U.S. at 297 . . . In prison condition cases that state of mind is one of 'deliberate indifference' to inmate health or safety, *Wilson, supra*, at 302-303 . . .

"We reject petitioner's invitation to adopt an objective test for deliberate indifference. We hold instead that a prison official cannot be found liable under the Eighth Amendment for denying an inmate humane conditions of confinement unless the official knows of and disregards an excessive risk to inmate health or safety; the official must both be aware of facts from which the inference could be drawn that a substantial risk of serious harm exists, and he must also draw the inference. This approach comports best with the text of the Amendment as our cases have interpreted it.

"Under the test we adopt today, an Eighth Amendment claimant need not show that a prison official acted or failed to act believing that harm would befall an inmate: it is enough that the official acted or failed to act despite his knowledge of a substantial risk of serious harm. . . . Nor may a prison official escape liability for deliberate indifference by showing that, while he was aware of an obvious, substantial risk to inmate safety, he did not know that the complainant was especially likely to be assaulted by the specific prisoner who eventually committed the assault . . . and it does not matter whether the risk comes from a single source or multiple sources, any more than it matters whether a prisoner faces an excessive risk of an attack for reasons personal to him or because all prisoners in his situation face such risk."

CASE SIGNIFICANCE: This case defines the standard for liability of prison officials under the Eighth Amendment in inmate-on-inmate assault cases. The facts indicate that Farmer was a transsexual who was transferred from a federal to a state prison. Given his demeanor and appearance, it was predictable that he would be sexually assaulted in prison—and he was. He then filed a Section 1983 case alleging violation of his constitutional right against cruel and unusual punishment. The Court held that for prison officials to be liable, the official must have "knowingly disregarded an excessive risk of harm." It is not enough that the official "should have known that harm was inevitable because the risk was so obvious that a reasonable person should have noticed it." Under the standard proposed by the inmate, prison officials would have been held liable because the facts of the case indicated that risk to the inmate was obvious.

This decision makes it difficult for inmates to hold prison officials liable in inmate-on-inmate assault cases. The standard of "knowingly disregarded an excessive risk of harm" is a high standard for inmates to establish. The word "knowingly" indicates that prison officials who are unaware of the risk cannot be held liable. It is difficult for inmates to establish in court that prison officials knew harm was imminent and yet disregarded it. Whether this standard applies to assaults on inmates by correctional officers remains to be seen.

S.   Freedom of Religion

Cruz v. Beto
405 U.S. 319 (1972)

CAPSULE: Inmates must be given reasonable opportunities to exercise their religious beliefs.

FACTS: Cruz, a member of the Buddhist faith and a prisoner in the Texas Department of Corrections, was not allowed to use the prison chapel, nor to correspond with his religious advisor in the Buddhist sect. He was placed in solitary confinement on a diet of bread and water for two weeks because he shared his Buddhist religious materials with other inmates. While he was in solitary confinement, he was not allowed access to newspapers, magazines, or other sources of news.

Cruz filed suit under 42 U.S.C. §1983, alleging that he was denied his First Amendment right to freedom of religion, claiming that Texas encouraged participation in other faiths by providing chaplains for those of the Catholic, Jewish, and Protestant faiths. Texas also provided copies of the Jewish and Christian

Bibles and conducted weekly Sunday school classes and services. Cruz alleged that points of good merit were given to inmates as a reward for participation in the Protestant, Jewish, and Catholic faiths and that these points enhanced an inmate's eligibility for promotions in class, job assignments, and early parole consideration.

ISSUE: Must inmates with unconventional religious beliefs be given a reasonable opportunity to exercise those beliefs, comparable to the opportunities offered to those with conventional religious beliefs? YES.

DECISION: The Texas Department of Corrections discriminated against inmate Cruz by denying him reasonable opportunity to pursue his Buddhist faith comparable to opportunities offered to other inmates of conventional religious beliefs.

REASON: "Federal courts sit not to supervise prisons but to enforce the constitutional rights of all 'persons,' including prisoners. We are not unmindful that prison officials must be accorded latitude in the administration of prison affairs, and that prisoners necessarily are subject to appropriate rules and regulations. But persons in prison, like other individuals, have a right to petition the Government for redress of grievances which, of course, includes 'access of prisoners to the courts for the purpose of presenting their complaints.' *Johnson v. Avery*, 393 U.S. 483, 485; *Ex parte Hull*, 312 U.S. 546, 549 . . . Even more closely in point is *Cooper v. Pate*, 378 U.S. 546, where we reversed a dismissal of a complaint brought under 42 U.S.C. Section 1983.

"If Cruz was a Buddhist and if he was denied a reasonable opportunity of pursuing his faith comparable to the opportunity afforded fellow prisoners who adhere to conventional religious precepts, then there was palpable discrimination by the State against the Buddhist religion, established 600 B.C., long before the Christian era. The First Amendment, applicable to the States by reason of the Fourteenth Amendment, *Torcaso v. Watkins*, 367 U.S. 488, 492-493, prohibits government from making a law 'prohibiting the free exercise' of religion. If the allegations of this complaint are assumed to be true, as they must be on the motion to dismiss, Texas has violated the First and Fourteenth Amendments."

CASE SIGNIFICANCE: This case is considered a landmark case because it clarified the right of an inmate to practice religious beliefs even if those beliefs were not considered a part of mainstream and "traditional" religions. The Supreme Court rejected the federal district court's decision that a complaint involving freedom of religion should be left "to the sound discretion of prison administration." In essence, the Court said that freedom of religion in prisons applies to all religions and not just to those with many adherents in American society. What is important, however, is access to worship and religious observance rather than equal treatment for all religions. A prison does not have to build a chapel for every religious faith; instead, what is required is that the chapel be available for use by various religious groups or individuals in prison.

O'Lone v. Estate of Shabazz
482 U.S. 342 (1987)

CAPSULE: Prison policies that in effect prevented inmates from exercising freedom of religion are constitutional because they are reasonably related to legitimate penological interests.

FACTS: Inmates in a New Jersey state prison brought suit under 42 U.S.C. §1983, claiming that two prison policies violated their free exercise rights under the First Amendment. The inmates were of the Islamic faith and were prevented from attending Jumu'ah, a religious service held on Friday afternoons. The first policy required that inmates who were classified as "gang minimum" work outside the buildings where they were housed and where Jumu'ah was held. The second policy prohibited inmates who worked outside from returning to these buildings during the day, for security reasons. The Federal District Court held that no constitutional violations had occurred. The Court of Appeals vacated and remanded. It ruled that the prison policies could be sustained only if the State showed that the challenged regulations were intended to and did serve the penological goal of security, and that no reasonable method existed by which prisoners' religious rights could be accommodated without creating bona fide security problems.

ISSUE: Do the prison policies requiring inmates to work outside and preventing them from returning to the building during the day violate the inmates' freedom of religion? NO.

DECISION: The prison policies do not violate inmate constitutional rights because they are reasonably related to legitimate penological interests.

REASON: "By placing the burden on prison officials to disprove the availability of alternatives, the approach articulated by the Court of Appeals fails to reflect the respect and deference that the United States Constitution allows for the judgment of prison administrators . . . the findings of the District Court establish clearly that prison officials acted in a reasonable manner. *Turner v. Safley*, *supra*, drew upon our previous decisions to identify several factors relevant to this reasonableness determination. First, a regulation must have a logical connection to legitimate governmental interests invoked to justify it. The policies at issue here clearly meet that standard. The requirement that full minimum and gang minimum prisoners work outside the main facility was justified by concerns of institutional order and security . . . The subsequent policy prohibiting returns to the institution during the day also passes muster under this standard.

"While we in no way minimize the central importance of Jumu'ah to respondents, we are unwilling to hold that prison officials are required by the Constitution to sacrifice legitimate penological objectives to that end . . . These concerns of prison administrators [the effect this would have on other inmates, on prison personnel, and on allocation of prison resources generally] provide adequate support for the conclusion that the accommodations of respondents' request to attend Jumu'ah would have undesirable results in the institution."

CASE SIGNIFICANCE: In *Turner v. Safley* (482 U.S. 78 [1987]), decided one week earlier, the Court held that "a prison regulation that impinges on inmates' constitutional rights is valid if it is reasonably related to legitimate penological interests." In this case, the Court applied that test to freedom of religion cases.

Freedom of religion is a preferred constitutional right and therefore enjoys utmost protection from the courts. In this case, the inmates alleged that the two prison regulations violated the Free Exercise Clause of the First Amendment because the regulations prohibited them from doing what their religion allows them to do—which is attending a congregational service held on Friday afternoons. In previous cases, the Court used the "compelling state interest" test to determine the constitutionality of prison rules impinging on inmates' freedom of religion. Under that test, the Court determined whether there was any compelling state interest that justified either regulating or prohibiting the exercise of such right. The compelling state interest test was difficult for prison administrators to establish, thus affording inmates more religious freedom. The *Turner* test gives prison administrators greater authority because all they have to do is prove that the prison regulation that impinges on religious freedom is "reasonably related to legitimate penological interests." This new test limited inmates' rights to religious freedom by giving prison authorities more power to issue regulations in the name of a legitimate penological interest such as prison order and security.

The *Turner* test (that a prison regulation impinging on inmates' constitutional rights is valid if "reasonably related to a legitimate penological interest") has been replaced, however, by a federal law. The Religious Freedom Restoration Act (RFRA), passed by Congress in 1993, provides that the government "shall not substantially burden a person's exercise of religion even if the burden results from a rule of general applicability. . . ." The only exception is (1) if the government demonstrates that the application of the burden is in furtherance of a compelling governmental interest, and (2) is the least restrictive means of furthering that compelling governmental interest." This law was passed by Congress to undo the effect of several U.S. Supreme Court decisions that made it easier for the government to limit any citizen's freedom of religion. The American Corrections Association tried, but failed, to exempt prisons and jails from the law's coverage. Unless amended, the RFRA is the test courts all over the country use to determine whether prison regulations impinge on an inmate's freedom of religion. The provisions of this law prevail over the standard set by the Court in the *Turner v. Safley* case. The provisions of RFRA have already been the basis of numerous lawsuits filed by prisoners seeking to invalidate prison regulations that limit their religious freedom.

T. Searches and Seizures

Stone v. Powell
428 U.S. 465 (1976)

CAPSULE: A habeas corpus petition in federal court will not be granted based on an alleged violation of the Fourth Amendment right if the same allegation was raised and rejected earlier in state court during the criminal trial.

FACTS: Two state prisoners sought release from prison in a habeas corpus case filed in federal district court. One inmate was convicted of murder in state court, in part on the basis of testimony concerning a pistol taken from him when he was arrested for violating a vagrancy ordinance. The prisoner sought exclusion of the evidence during trial in a state court, alleging that the ordinance was unconstitutional, hence the arrest was invalid. The state trial court rejected the prisoner's contention; the appellate court affirmed the lower court's ruling. The other inmate was also convicted of murder in a state court, based in part on evidence seized pursuant to a warrant that the inmate claimed was invalid. The trial court denied the motion to suppress, and the denial was upheld by the appellate court. In both cases, the inmates sought relief in federal court in a habeas corpus action, seeking exclusion of the evidence obtained and admitted during trial in state courts.

ISSUE: May habeas corpus be granted in federal court to a prisoner who alleges that his constitutional rights were violated when evidence obtained in an unconstitutional search and seizure was introduced and admitted at trial? NO.

DECISION: A state prisoner cannot be granted habeas corpus relief (meaning release) by a federal court on the ground that evidence obtained through an unconstitutional search and seizure was introduced at trial, if the state has provided an opportunity to the inmate during that criminal trial for a full and fair consideration of the Fourth Amendment claim.

REASON: "Evidence obtained by police officers in violation of the Fourth Amendment is excluded at trial in the hope that the frequency of future violations will decrease. Despite the absence of supportive empirical evidence, we have assumed that the immediate effect of exclusion will be to discourage law enforcement officials from violating the Fourth Amendment by removing the incentive to disregard it. More importantly, over the long term, this demonstration that our society attaches serious consequences to violation of constitutional rights is thought to encourage those who formulate law enforcement policies, and the officers who implement them, to incorporate Fourth Amendment ideals into their value system.

"We adhere to the view that these considerations support the implementation of the exclusionary rule at trial and its enforcement on direct appeal of state-court convictions. But the additional contribution, if any, of the consideration of search-and-seizure claims of state prisoners on collateral review is small in relation to the costs. To be sure, each case in which such claim is considered may add marginally to an awareness of the values protected by the Fourth Amendment. There is no reason to believe, however, that the overall educative effect of the exclusionary rule would be appreciably diminished if search-and-seizure claims could not be raised in federal habeas corpus review of state convictions. Nor is there reason to assume that any specific disincentive already created by the risk of exclusion of evidence at trial or the reversal of convictions on direct review would be enhanced if there were the future risk that a conviction obtained in state court and affirmed on direct review might be overturned in collateral proceedings often occurring years after the incarceration of the defendant. The view that the deterrence of Fourth Amendment violations would be furthered rests on the dubious assumption that law enforcement authorities would fear that federal habeas review might reveal flaws in a search or seizure that went undetected at trial and on appeal. Even if one rationally could assume that some additional incremental deterrent effect would be presented in isolated cases, the resulting advance of the legitimate goal of furthering Fourth Amendment rights would be outweighed by the acknowledged costs to other values vital to a rational system of criminal justice.

"In sum, we conclude that where the State has provided an opportunity for full and fair litigation of a Fourth Amendment claim, a state prisoner may not be granted federal habeas corpus relief on the ground that evidence obtained in an unconstitutional search or seizure was introduced at his trial. In this context the contribution of the exclusionary rule, if any, to the effectuation of the Fourth Amendment is minimal, and the substantial societal costs of application of the rule persist with special force."

CASE SIGNIFICANCE: Decided by the Court in 1976, this case represents one of the earliest efforts on the part of the Court to cut down on the number of habeas corpus cases reaching federal courts from state prisoners. In this case, the prisoners alleged that the refusal of the state trial courts to exclude evidence that they alleged was obtained in violation of the Fourth Amendment, violated their constitutional rights. The claims for exclusion of the evidence were raised during trial and rejected by the trial courts for various reasons. There was, therefore, full and fair consideration of these allegations by the state trial court. The decisions to admit the evidence in both cases were affirmed by the state appellate courts. The prisoners then sought relief in federal courts. On appeal to the Supreme Court, the Court said that the relief sought could not be granted because there was in fact no violation of a constitutional right because the same issues had been resolved in the state courts.

In deciding this case, the Court went into a discussion of the exclusionary rule (the rule that states that evidence obtained as a result of an illegal search or seizure is not admissible in a court of law), saying that the "primary justification for the exclusionary rule then is the deterrence of police conduct that violates Fourth Amendment rights." The immediate question—whether state prisoners who have been given the opportunity to litigate the exclusion claim at trial and on direct review should be allowed to raise the question again on a federal habeas corpus proceeding—is to be decided "by weighing the utility of the exclusionary rule against the costs of extending it to collateral review of the Fourth Amendment claims." The Court concluded that the contribution of the rule, "if any, to the effectuation of the Fourth Amendment was minimal compared to the substantial societal costs of applying the rule" in a collateral proceeding in federal court. In sum, once an issue has been resolved by state courts, the federal courts should not relitigate the same issue in a habeas corpus case. This gives finality to state court decisions, at least on the issue of whether evidence obtained by the police should be admitted at trial.

Hudson v. Palmer
468 U.S. 517 (1984)

CAPSULE: A prison cell may be searched without a warrant or probable cause because a prison cell is not protected by the Fourth Amendment.

FACTS: Palmer was an inmate at the Bland Correctional Center in Virginia, serving sentences for forgery, uttering a forged instrument, grand larceny, and bank robbery convictions. Hudson, an officer at the Correctional Center, conducted a shakedown search of Palmer's prison locker and cell, together with another officer. The officers discovered a ripped pillow case in the trash basket near his bunk. Palmer was charged with destroying state property. He was found guilty at a prison disciplinary hearing, and was ordered to reimburse the state for the cost of the pillow case. Additionally, a reprimand was entered on Palmer's prison record.

Palmer brought a pro se action in United States District Court under 42 U.S.C. §1983, claiming that Hudson had conducted the shakedown search of his cell and had brought a false charge for the sole purpose of harassing him. Palmer also claimed that Hudson had intentionally destroyed certain items of his noncontraband personal property during the search, in violation of his Fourteenth Amendment right not to be deprived of property without due process of law.

ISSUES:
1. Does a prison inmate have a reasonable expectation of privacy in his prison cell, entitling him to the protection of the Fourth Amendment against unreasonable searches and seizures? NO.

2. Should the due process clause of the Fourteenth Amendment apply to intentional deprivations of property? NO.

DECISIONS:
1. A prisoner has no reasonable expectation of privacy in his prison cell, entitling him to the protection of the Fourth Amendment against unreasonable searches.
2. Destruction of Palmer's personal property during the search, even if intentional, did not violate the due process clause of the Fourteenth Amendment because Palmer had adequate post-deprivation remedies under Virginia law for any loss suffered.

REASON: "We have repeatedly held that prisons are not beyond the reach of the Constitution. No 'iron curtain' separates one from the other. *Wolff v. McDonnell*, 418 U.S. 539, 555 (1974). Indeed, we have insisted that prisoners be accorded those rights not fundamentally inconsistent with imprisonment itself or incompatible with the objectives of incarceration.

"However, while persons imprisoned for crime enjoy many protections of the Constitution, it is also clear that imprisonment carries with it the circumscription or loss of many significant rights. *See Bell v. Wolfish*, 441 U.S., at 545.

These constraints on inmates, and in some cases the complete withdrawal of certain rights, are 'justified by the considerations underlying our penal system.' *Price v. Johnston*, 334 U.S. 266, 285 (1948).

"Notwithstanding our caution in approaching claims that the Fourth Amendment is inapplicable in a given context, we hold that society is not prepared to recognize as legitimate any subjective expectation of privacy that a prisoner might have in his prison cell and that, accordingly, the Fourth Amendment proscription against unreasonable searches does not apply within the confines of the prison cell. The recognition of privacy rights for prisoners in their individual cells simply cannot be reconciled with the concept of incarceration and the needs and objectives of penal institutions.

"The administration of a prison, we have said, is 'at best an extraordinarily difficult undertaking.' *Wolff v. McDonnell*, 418 U.S., at 566; *Hewitt v. Helms*, 459 U.S. 460, 467 (1983). But it would be literally impossible to accomplish the prison objectives identified above if inmates retained a right of privacy in their cells. Virtually the only place inmates can conceal weapons, drugs, and other contraband is in their cells. Unfettered access to these cells by prison officials, thus, is imperative if drugs and contraband are to be ferreted out and sanitary surroundings are to be maintained.

"Our holding that respondent does not have a reasonable expectation of privacy enabling him to invoke the protections of the Fourth Amendment does not mean that he is without a remedy for calculated harassment unrelated to prison needs. Nor does it mean that prison attendants can ride roughshod over inmates' property rights with impunity. The Eighth Amendment always stands as a protection against 'cruel and unusual punishments.' By the same token, there are adequate state tort and common law remedies available to respondent to redress the alleged destruction of his personal property. See discussion *infra*, at 534-536.

"If negligent deprivations of property do not violate the due process clause because predeprivation process is impracticable, it follows that intentional deprivations do not violate that Clause provided, of course, that adequate state postdeprivation remedies are available. Accordingly, we hold that an unauthorized intentional deprivation of property by a state employee does not constitute a violation of the procedural requirements of the Due Process Clause of the Fourteenth Amendment if a meaningful postdeprivation remedy for the loss is available. For intentional, as for negligent deprivations of property by state employees, the state's action is not complete until and unless it provides or refuses to provide a suitable postdeprivation remedy."

CASE SIGNIFICANCE: This case followed the precedent set in *Parratt v. Taylor*, 451 U.S. 527 (1981), decided three years earlier. The Supreme Court again ruled that depriving an inmate of personal property is not a violation of the due process clause of the Fourteenth Amendment where state post-deprivation remedies are available (usually a tort action under state law). The Court made clear that an inmate has no reasonable expectation of privacy in his or her cell. This means that prison authorities may search an inmate's cell at any time without a warrant or probable cause as long as the search does not constitute harassment. There is no need for a warrant or probable cause. Once again, the Court balanced institutional needs with an inmate's constitutional rights and decided in favor of the institution, saying that "it would be impossible to accomplish the prison objectives of preventing the introduction of weapons, drugs, and other contraband into the premises if inmates retained the right to privacy in their cells." The Court also rejected the prisoner's claim that the destruction of his personal property constituted an unreasonable seizure, saying that prison officials "must be free to seize from cells any articles which, in their view, disserve legitimate institutional interests." Furthermore, the intentional destruction of that personal property did not violate the due process clause of the Constitution because the inmate had remedies under state law.

U. Administrative Segregation

Hewitt v. Helms
459 U.S. 460 (1983)

CAPSULE: A formal hearing is not required to place an inmate in administrative segregation; an informal evidentiary review is sufficient.

FACTS: In December of 1978, a prison riot erupted at the State Correctional Institution in Huntingdon, Pennsylvania. It was quelled with the assistance of state police units, local law enforcement officers, and off-duty correctional officers. Inmate Helms was removed from his cell and the general prison population after the riot ended. He was questioned by the state police and placed in restrictive confinement while the police and prison authorities investigated his role in the riot. The following day, Helms was given a "Misconduct Report" that charged him with assaulting correctional officers and "conspiracy to disrupt normal institution routine by forcefully taking over the control center." Four days later, a hearing committee considered his case and decided that Helms' restricted confinement would be continued although the committee did not find him guilty, due to insufficient evidence.

A second misconduct report charged Helms with assaulting a second officer during the riot. Helms and one correctional officer testified at the subsequent hearing. The Hearing Committee found Helms guilty of the second misconduct charge and ordered him confined in administrative segregation for six months. The Committee also decided to drop the first misconduct charge without determining guilt. Helms sued in the United States District Court, alleging that his confinement in administrative segregation violated his rights under the due process clause of the Fourteenth Amendment.

ISSUE: Is a formal hearing required in order to place an inmate in administrative segregation? NO.

DECISION: Formal hearings like those used in prison disciplinary cases (*Wolff v. McDonnell*, 418 U.S. 539 [1974]) are not required for placing inmates in administrative segregation. An informal, non-adversary evidentiary review is sufficient both for the decision that the inmate represents a security risk and the decision to confine the inmate to administrative segregation pending completion of the investigation of the alleged misconduct. An inmate must merely receive notice of the charges against him and be given an opportunity to present his views to the prison official who will decide whether to transfer him to administrative segregation.

REASON: "We have repeatedly said both that prison officials have broad administrative and discretionary authority over the institutions they manage and that lawfully incarcerated persons retain only a narrow range of protected liberty interests . . . Accordingly, administrative segregation is the sort of confinement that inmates would reasonably anticipate receiving at some point in their incarceration. This conclusion finds ample support in our decisions regarding parole and good-time credits. Both of these subjects involve release from institutional life altogether, which is a far more significant change in a prisoner's freedoms than that at issue here, yet in *Greenholtz* and *Wolff* we held that neither situation involved an interest independently protected by the Due Process Clause. These decisions compel an identical result here.

"But on balance we are persuaded that the repeated use of explicitly mandatory language in connection with requiring specific substantive predicates demands a conclusion that the State has created a protected liberty interest. That being the case, we must then decide whether the process afforded respondent satisfied the minimum requirements of the Due Process Clause. We think that it did. The requirements imposed by the Clause are, of course, flexible and variable dependent upon the particular situation being examined. E.g., *Greenholtz v. Nebraska Penal Inmates*, 442 U.S., at 12, *Morrissey v. Brewer*, 408 U.S. 471, 481 (1972). In determining what is 'due process' in the prison context, we are reminded that 'one cannot automatically apply procedural rules designed for free citizens in an open society . . . to the very different situation presented by a disciplinary proceeding in a state prison.' *Wolff v. McDonnell*, 418 U.S., at 560.

'Prison administrators . . . should be accorded wide-ranging deference in the adoption and execution of policies and practices that in their judgment are needed to preserve internal order and discipline and to maintain institutional security.' *Bell v. Wolfish*, 441 U.S. 520, 547 (1979). These conditions convince us that petitioners were obligated to engage only in an informal, nonadversary review of the information supporting respondent's administrative confinement, including whatever statement respondent wished to submit, within a reasonable time after confining him to administrative segregation."

CASE SIGNIFICANCE: This case addresses the issue of what rights inmates are entitled to, if any, prior to being placed in administrative segregation. There is a difference between administrative segregation and punitive segregation, in that administrative segregation is primarily for prisoner protection, and punitive segregation is imposed to punish the inmate. While both actions involve isolation from the general inmate population, the Court in this case said that a formal process such as that prescribed for inmates facing punitive segregation (as required in *Wolff v. McDonnell*, 418 U.S. 539 [1974]) is not required for administrative segregation. All that is required is that the inmate receive notice of the charges and an opportunity to present his or her views to the prison officials who are to decide whether to transfer the inmate to administrative segregation. Justifications for the decision are: (1) prison officials have broad administrative and discretionary authority over the institutions they manage, and (2) administrative segregation is the sort of confinement that inmates should reasonably anticipate receiving at some point during their incarceration.

V. Punitive Segregation

Hutto v. Finney
437 U.S. 678 (1978)

CAPSULE: Courts can set time limitations on solitary confinement (punitive segregation); they can also order that plaintiff's attorney's fees be paid from Department of Correction funds.

FACTS: In 1970, a District Court found that conditions in the Arkansas penal system constituted cruel and unusual punishment in violation of the Eighth Amendment. In 1976, after several hearings to check on the progress of prison administrators' improvements to the system, the court concluded that the constitutional violations it identified had not been remedied. The court issued an order placing limits on the number of inmates that could be confined in one cell. It also required that each inmate have a bunk, discontinued the "gruel" diet, which was a poor nutritional mixture, and set 30 days as the maximum isolation sentence. The District Court also considered the matter of fees and expenses. It found that prison officials had acted in bad faith and awarded a counsel fee of $20,000 to the plaintiffs, to be paid by funds from the Arkansas Department of Correction.

Hutto, the Commissioner of Correction, and members of the Arkansas Board of Correction appealed the following: (1) the order placing a limit of 30 days on confinement in punitive isolation; and (2) the award of attorney's fees based on the finding that they had acted in bad faith in failing to cure the previously identified problems in the prison system. Hutto and members of the Board argued that indeterminate sentences of punitive isolation do not always constitute cruel and unusual punishment in violation of the Eighth Amendment. They also alleged that the District Court's award of attorney's fees violated the Eleventh Amendment's prohibition against such.

ISSUES:
1.   Was the District Court's imposition of a 30-day limit on punitive isolation in the Arkansas Department of Correction constitutional? YES.

2.   Was the District Court's award of attorney's fees to be paid out of Department of Correction funds constitutional? YES.

DECISIONS:
1.   The District Court did not err in including the 30-day limit on sentences of isolation as part of its comprehensive remedy to correct violations of constitutional rights.

2.   The District Court's award of attorney's fees to be paid out of Department of Correction funds is adequately supported by its finding that petitioners had acted in bad faith, and does not violate the Eleventh Amendment.

REASON: "Confinement in a prison or in an isolation cell is a form of punishment subject to scrutiny under Eighth Amendment standards . . . [P]etitioners single out the portion of the District Court's most recent order that forbids the Department to sentence inmates to more than 30 days in punitive isolation. Petitioners assume that the District Court held that indeterminate sentences to punitive isolation always constitute cruel and unusual punishment. This assumption misreads the District Court's holding. Read in its entirety, the District Court's opinion made it abundantly clear that the length of isolation sentences was not considered in a vacuum. In the court's words, punitive isolation 'is not necessarily unconstitutional, but it may be, depending on the duration of the confinement and the conditions thereof.' 410 F. Supp., at 275.

"In fashioning a remedy, the District Court had ample authority to go beyond earlier orders and to address each element contributing to the violation. The District Court had given the Department repeated opportunities to remedy the cruel and unusual conditions in the isolation cells. If petitioners had fully complied with the court's earlier orders, the present time limit might well have been unnecessary. But taking the long and unhappy history of the litigation into account, the court was justified in entering a comprehensive order to insure against the risk of inadequate compliance.

"The order is supported by the interdependence of the conditions producing the violation. The vandalized cells and the atmosphere of violence were attributable, in part, to overcrowding and to deep-seated enmities growing out of months of constant daily friction. The 30-day limit will help to correct these conditions. Moreover, the limit presents little danger of interference with prison administration, for the Commissioner of Correction himself stated that prisoners should not ordinarily be held in punitive isolation for more than 14 days. Id. at 278.

"Like the Court of Appeals, we find no error in the inclusion of a 30-day limitation on sentences to punitive isolation as a part of the District Court's comprehensive remedy.

"In exercising their prospective powers under *Ex parte Young* and *Edelman v. Jordan*, federal courts are not reduced to issuing injunctions against state officers and hoping for compliance. Once issued, an injunction may be enforced. Many of the court's most effective enforcement weapons involve financial penalties.

"In this case, the award of attorney's fees for bad faith served the same purpose as a remedial fine imposed for civil contempt. It vindicated the District Court's authority over a recalcitrant litigant . . . We see no reason to distinguish this award from any other penalty imposed to enforce a prospective injunction. Hence the substantive protections of the Eleventh Amendment do not prevent an award of attorney's fees against the Department's officers in their official capacities.

"Petitioners, as the losing litigants in the Court of Appeals, were ordered to pay an additional $2,500 to counsel for the prevailing parties 'for their services on this appeal.' 548 F.2d, at 743. The order does not expressly direct the Department of Correction to pay the award, but since petitioners are sued in their official capacities, and since they are represented by the Attorney General, it is obvious that the award will be paid by state funds. It is also clear that this order is not supported by any finding of bad faith. It is founded instead on the provisions of the Civil Rights Attorney's Fees Awards Act of 1976. Pub. L. No. 94-559, 90 Stat. 2641, 42 U.S.C. §1988 (1976 ed.). The Act declares that, in suits under 42 U.S.C. §1983 and certain other statutes, federal courts may award prevailing parties reasonable attorney's fees 'as part of the costs.'

"There is no indication in this case that the named defendants litigated in bad faith before the Court of Appeals. Consequently, the Department of Correction is the entity intended by Congress to bear the burden of the counsel-fees award."

CASE SIGNIFICANCE: This was one of the first cases appealed to the Supreme Court in which an entire state prison system was declared unconstitutional by a state district court and ordered to institute massive reform. The prison authorities in this case tested the limits of the power of a district court judge to order reforms. The power of the judge to set a limit on the length of punitive isolation of inmates was questioned; so was his power to award attorney's fees. The Court upheld the power of the judge in both instances, implying that the discretion of a trial court judge in prison cases is not narrowly circumscribed.

The 30-day limitation on punitive segregation was deemed valid because of the past record of the Department of Correction in failing to correct constitutional violations. Said the Court: "Where the question before the court was whether past constitutional violations had been remedied, it was entitled to consider the severity of the violations in assessing the constitutionality of conditions in the isolation cells, the length of time each inmate spent in isolation being simply one consideration among many."

The award of $20,000 to inmates' counsel from the Department of Correction funds was also held valid in accordance with the Civil Rights Attorney's Fees Award Act of 1976. This act states that in civil rights cases the federal courts may award prevailing parties reasonable attorney's fees. Corrections officials had argued that such an award was unconstitutional because under the Eleventh Amendment Arkansas enjoys immunity. The Court replied that "costs have traditionally been awarded against States without regard for the States' Eleventh Amendment immunity, and it is much too late to single out attorney's fees as the one kind of litigation cost whose recovery may not be authorized by Congress without an express statutory waiver of States' immunity."

W. Transfer

Meachum v. Fano
427 U.S. 215 (1976)

CAPSULE: Inmates are not entitled to due process when transferred intra-state (meaning from one prison to another within the state), even if conditions in one prison are less favorable than in another.

FACTS: There were nine serious fires during a two-and-one-half month period at the Massachusetts Correctional Institution at Norfolk, a medium-security institution. After a hearing, the Classification Board recommended that inmate Royce be placed in administrative segregation for 30 days because of his involvement with the fires. Inmates Fano, Dussault, and McPhearson were to be transferred to Walpole, a maximum-security institution with living conditions that were substantially less favorable than those at Norfolk. Inmates DeBrosky and Hathaway were to be transferred to Bridgewater, which had both maximum- and medium-security facilities.

The recommendations of the Board were reviewed by the Acting Deputy Commissioner for Classification and Treatment and by the Commissioner of Corrections. They accepted the recommendations with respect to Fano, Dussault, Hathaway, and McPhearson, and ordered DeBrosky and Royce to be transferred to Walpole.

The inmates brought an action under 42 U.S.C. §1983, alleging that they were being deprived of liberty without due process of law because the petitioners had ordered them transferred to an institution where conditions were less favorable, without an adequate fact-finding hearing.

ISSUE: Does the due process clause of the Fourteenth Amendment entitle a state prisoner to a hearing when he or she is transferred to a prison where conditions are less favorable? NO.

DECISION: The due process clause of the Fourteenth Amendment does not protect a prisoner against transfer from one prison to another. The fact that conditions in one prison are less favorable than in another also does not mean that a Fourteenth Amendment liberty interest is violated if a prisoner is transferred there.

REASON: "The initial inquiry is whether the transfer of the inmates from Norfolk to Walpole and Bridgewater infringed or implicated a 'liberty' interest of the respondents within the meaning of the Due Process Clause. Contrary to the

Court of Appeals, we hold that it did not. We reject at the outset the notion that any grievous loss visited upon a person by the State is sufficient to invoke the procedural protections of the Due Process Clause.

"Similarly, we cannot agree that any change in the conditions of confinement having a substantial adverse impact on the prisoner involved is sufficient to invoke the protections of the Due Process Clause. The Due Process Clause by its own force forbids the State from convicting any person of crime and depriving him of his liberty without complying fully with the requirements of the Clause. But given a valid conviction, the criminal defendant has been constitutionally deprived of his liberty to the extent that the State may confine him and subject him to the rules of its prison system so long as the conditions of confinement do not otherwise violate the Constitution. The Constitution does not require that the State have more than one prison for convicted felons; nor does it guarantee that the convicted prisoner will be placed in any particular prison if, as is likely, the State has more than one correctional institution.

"Neither, in our view, does the Due Process Clause in and of itself protect a duly convicted prisoner against transfer from one institution to another within the state prison system. Confinement in any of the State's institutions is within the normal limits or range of custody which the conviction has authorized the State to impose. That life in one prison is much more disagreeable than in another does not in itself signify that a Fourteenth Amendment liberty interest is implicated when a prisoner is transferred to the institution with the more severe rules.

"Here, Massachusetts law conferred no right on the prisoner to remain in the prison to which he was initially assigned, defeasible only upon proof of specific acts of misconduct. Insofar as we are advised, transfers between Massachusetts prisons are not conditioned upon the occurrence of specified events. On the contrary, transfer in a wide variety of circumstances is vested in prison officials. The predicate for invoking the protection of the Fourteenth Amendment as construed and applied in *Wolff v. McDonnell* is totally nonexistent in this case.

"A prisoner's behavior may precipitate a transfer; and absent such behavior, perhaps transfer would not take place at all. But, as we have said, Massachusetts prison officials have the discretion to transfer prisoners for any number of reasons. Their discretion is not limited to instances of serious misconduct. As we understand it no legal interest or right of these respondents under Massachusetts law would have been violated by their transfer whether or not their misconduct had been proved in accordance with procedures that might be required by the Due Process Clause in other circumstances.

"Holding that arrangements like this are within reach of the procedural protections of the Due Process Clause would place the Clause astride the day-to-day functioning of state prisons and involve the judiciary in issues and discretionary decisions that are not the business of federal judges. We decline to so

interpret and apply the Due Process Clause. The federal courts do not sit to su-
pervise state prisons, the administration of which is of acute interest to the
States. *Preiser v. Rodriguez*, 411 U.S. 475, 491-492 (1973); *Cruz v. Beto*, 405
U.S. 319, 321 (1972); *Johnson v. Avery*, 393 U.S. 483, 486 (1969)."

CASE SIGNIFICANCE: In this case, the Court refused to extend due process
protection to the transfer of an inmate from one prison to another within the
state. The inmates here alleged that their transfer to a less favorable institution
(from a medium-security institution to a maximum-security institution where the
living conditions were not as good), without an adequate fact-finding hearing,
violated their right to due process. They maintained that such a transfer could be
made only if they were given due process rights. The Court disagreed, saying
that "would subject to judicial review a wide spectrum of discretionary actions
that traditionally have been the business of prison administrators rather than of
the federal courts." The Court added that "whatever expectation the prisoner
may have in remaining at a particular prison so long as he behaves himself, it is
too ephemeral and insubstantial to trigger procedural due process protections as
long as prison officials have discretion to transfer him for any reasons whatsoever or for no reason at all." In sum, the Court decided that as long as the transfer of such prisoners is discretionary under state law or agency policy, there was
no need to give inmates a hearing or other due process rights.

Montanye v. Haymes
427 U.S. 236 (1976)

**CAPSULE: A prisoner is not entitled to a hearing before being transferred
to another prison facility within the state even if the reason for the transfer
was disciplinary or punitive.**

FACTS: Haymes, an inmate at the Attica Correctional Facility in the State of
New York, was removed from his assignment as a clerk in the law library. That
afternoon he was observed circulating a petition signed by 82 other inmates,
complaining that each of them had been deprived of legal assistance as a result
of the removal of Haymes and another inmate from the prison law library. The
following day, Haymes was advised that he would be transferred to the Clinton
Correctional Facility which, like Attica, was a maximum-security facility. He
was transferred the next day with no loss of good time, segregated confinement,
loss of privileges, or any other disciplinary measures.

Haymes filed a petition with the United States District Court seeking relief
against Montanye, who was then the Superintendent of Attica. Haymes complained that the seizure and retention of his petition not only violated Adminis-

trative Bulletin No. 20, which allegedly made any communication to a court privileged and confidential, but also infringed on his federally guaranteed right to petition the court for redress of grievances. He further alleged that his removal to Clinton was to prevent him from continuing his legal remedies and in reprisal for his legal assistance to various prisoners, as well as for seeking to petition the court.

ISSUE: Does the due process clause of the Fourteenth Amendment require that a hearing be held if a state prisoner is to be transferred to another institution in the state whether or not this is a disciplinary or punitive transfer? NO.

DECISION: The due process clause of the Fourteenth Amendment does not require a hearing if a prisoner is to be transferred to another facility in the state whether or not such transfer resulted from the prisoner's misbehavior or was disciplinary or punitive.

REASON: "As long as the conditions or degree of confinement to which the prisoner is subjected is within the sentence imposed upon him and is not otherwise violative of the Constitution, the Due Process Clause does not in itself subject an inmate's treatment by prison authorities to judicial oversight. The Clause does not require hearings in connection with transfers whether or not they are the result of the inmate's misbehavior or may be labeled as disciplinary or punitive.

"We also agree with the State of New York that under the law of that State Haymes had no right to remain at any particular prison facility and no justifiable expectation that he would not be transferred unless found guilty of misconduct. Under New York law, adult persons sentenced to imprisonment are not sentenced to particular institutions, but are committed to the custody of the Commissioner of Corrections . . . [T]he Commissioner is empowered by statute to 'transfer inmates from one correctional facility to another.' N.Y. Correc. Law, Section 23(1) (McKinney Supp. 1975-1976)."

CASE SIGNIFICANCE: This case is significant in light of *Meachum v. Fano*, 427 U.S. 215 (1976), which was heard at the same time. Because the Court decided in the *Meachum* case that a prisoner was not entitled to have a hearing if he was being transferred from one prison to another within the state, even if to a less desirable prison, it would make sense that the Court would also rule that a transfer to the same type of prison would not require a hearing even if such transfer was for purposes of punishment. In essence, the Court ruled that, in the absence of prohibition under state law, prison officials can transfer prisoners from one prison to another without giving them due process—thus affording prison officials discretion in the transfer of prisoners intrastate.

Vitek v. Jones
445 U.S. 480 (1980)

CAPSULE: **Inmates are entitled to due process in involuntary transfers from prison to a mental hospital.**

FACTS: Jones, a Nebraska prison inmate convicted of robbery, was transferred to the penitentiary hospital seven months after he was sentenced to prison. After two days in the hospital he was placed in solitary confinement. While there, he set his mattress on fire, severely burning himself. The burn unit of a private hospital treated him and he was then transferred to the security unit of the Lincoln Regional Center, a state mental hospital that was run by the Department of Public Institutions. Jones was transferred to the mental hospital under Nebraska statute §831-180, which stated that when a designated physician or psychologist finds that a prisoner "suffers from a mental disease or defect" and "cannot be given proper treatment in that facility," the Director of Corrections may transfer him for examination, study, and treatment to another institution whether it is within the Department of Correctional Services or not. Jones was found to be suffering from a mental illness or defect and he could not receive proper treatment in the penal complex; thus the transfer was ordered.

Jones then intervened in this case, which was brought by other prisoners against the appropriate state officials, including Vitek, the Director of Corrections. The case challenged the Nebraska statutes that permitted transfers of prisoners from the prison complex to a mental hospital without procedural due process, as a violation of the Fourteenth Amendment. Jones was subsequently paroled, violated his parole, and returned to prison before the U.S. Supreme Court heard the case.

ISSUE: Are inmates entitled to due process rights when being involuntarily transferred from prison to a mental hospital? YES.

DECISION: The involuntary transfer of a prisoner to a mental hospital implicates a liberty interest that is protected by the due process clause of the Fourteenth Amendment. Although a conviction and sentence extinguish an individual's right to freedom for the term of his sentence, they do not authorize the state to classify him as mentally ill and subject him to involuntary psychiatric treatment without affording him additional due process protections. These protections include:
1.   written notice to the prisoner that such a transfer is being considered;

2.   a full hearing held after a reasonable period has passed to allow the pris-
     oner to prepare for it;

3.   an opportunity for the prisoner to present witnesses at his hearing and,
     when feasible, the opportunity to cross-examine witnesses called by the
     state;

4.   an independent decisionmaker to preside over the hearing;

5.   a written statement to the prisoner citing the evidence and reasons for the
     transfer; and

6.   prisoners must be advised of all their procedural rights.

REASON: "We have repeatedly held that state statutes may create liberty interests that are entitled to the procedural protections of the Due Process Clause of
the Fourteenth Amendment . . . We think the District Court properly understood
and applied these decisions. Section 83-180(1) provides that if a designated
physician finds that a prisoner 'suffers from a mental disease or defect' that
'cannot be given proper treatment' in prison, the Director of Correctional Services may transfer a prisoner to a mental hospital . . . This 'objective expectation,
firmly fixed in state law and official Penal Complex practice,' that a prisoner
would not be transferred unless he suffered from a mental disease or defect that
could not be adequately treated in the prison, gave Jones a liberty interest that
entitled him to the benefits of appropriate procedures in connection with determining the conditions that warranted his transfer to a mental hospital.

"In *Morrissey, Gagnon,* and *Wolff,* the States had adopted their own procedures for determining whether conditions warranting revocation of parole, probation, or good-time credits had occurred; yet we held that those procedures
were constitutionally inadequate. In like manner, Nebraska's reliance on the
opinion of a designated physician or psychologist for determining whether the
conditions warranting a transfer exist neither removes the prisoner's interest
from due process procedures nor answers the question of what process is due
under the Constitution.

"Were an ordinary citizen to be subjected involuntarily to these consequences, it is undeniable that protected liberty interests would be unconstitutionally infringed absent compliance with the procedures required by the Due
Process Clause. We conclude that a convicted felon also is entitled to the benefit
of procedures appropriate in the circumstances before he is found to have a
mental disease and transferred to a mental hospital.

"A criminal conviction and sentence of imprisonment extinguish an individual's right to freedom from confinement for the term of his sentence, but
they do not authorize the State to classify him as mentally ill and to subject him
to involuntary psychiatric treatment without affording him additional due process protections.

"In light of the findings made by the District Court, Jones' involuntary transfer to the Lincoln Regional Center pursuant to Section 83-180, for the purpose of psychiatric treatment, implicated a liberty interest protected by the Due Process Clause . . . Because prisoners facing involuntary transfer to a mental hospital are threatened with immediate deprivation of liberty interests they are currently enjoying and because of the inherent risk of a mistaken transfer, the District Court properly determined that procedures similar to those required by the Court in *Morrissey v. Brewer*, 408 U.S. 471 (1972), were appropriate in the circumstances present here."

CASE SIGNIFICANCE: This case gives procedural due process rights to prisoners being transferred from a penal institution to a state mental hospital. The case follows the trend toward recognizing due process rights for the convicted. The first case was *Morrissey v. Brewer* in 1972, which extended due process rights to parole revocation hearings. This was followed by *Gagnon v. Scarpelli* in 1973, giving due process rights in probation revocation hearings; and *Wolff v. McDonnell* in 1974, which required due process in prison disciplinary hearings. The Court noted in this case that due process procedures are necessary for two reasons: (1) although conviction and sentencing mean that a person's freedom can be extinguished, they do not authorize the prison authorities to classify the inmate as mentally ill and subject to psychiatric treatment, and (2) the subjection of inmates to mandatory behavior modification as treatment for mental illness constitutes the kind of action that requires due process protection. The court said that the severity of the effects of such transfer and the stigma it carries require protection under the due process clause.

X. Union Membership and Activities

Jones v. North Carolina
Prisoners' Labor Union Inc.
433 U.S. 119 (1977)

CAPSULE: A ban on prison union membership and activities is valid. Prisoners do not retain First Amendment rights that are inconsistent with their prison status or with the legitimate objectives of the corrections system.

FACTS: The North Carolina Prisoners' Labor Union was incorporated in 1974 with several goals, including: (1) to promote charitable labor union purposes; (2) to form a prisoners' labor union at every prison and jail in North Carolina to improve working conditions through collective bargaining; (3) to work toward the alteration or elimination of practices and policies of the Department of Correction of which it did not approve; and (4) to serve as a vehicle for the presentation and resolution of inmates' grievances. In 1975, there were approximately 2,000 members of this union in 40 prison units throughout the state. The State of North Carolina decided to prevent inmates from effectively forming or operating a union. The state allowed individual membership or belief in the union but prohibited the following: inmate solicitation of other inmates, meetings between union members, and bulk mailings concerning the union from outside sources.

The North Carolina Prisoners' Labor Union, Inc., brought suit under 42 U.S.C. §1983, alleging that its First Amendment and equal protection rights under the Fourteenth Amendment were violated by the Department of Correction's regulations, which had not yet gone into effect. The First Amendment claim was based on the no-meeting and no-solicitation rules. The Fourteenth Amendment claim was based on deprivation of equal protection of the laws, because Alcoholics Anonymous and the Jaycees were permitted to have meetings and other organizational rights, which included distribution of bulk mailing materials. The union sought a declaratory judgment and injunction against the state's policies as well as substantial damages.

ISSUE: Do regulations that prohibit inmate solicitation of other inmates, meetings of union members, and bulk mailings concerning the union, violate the First or Fourteenth Amendment? NO.

DECISION:

1. Prisoners' First Amendment rights have not been violated by the ban on membership, solicitation, and group meetings, because inmates do not retain First Amendment rights that are inconsistent with their prison status or with legitimate objectives of the corrections system. Restrictions imposed on union activities are reasonable and consistent with the legitimate operational considerations of the institution.

2. The prohibition against the receipt by and distribution to the inmates of bulk mail from the union as well as the prohibition of union meetings among inmates do not violate the equal protection clause. Prison officials are entitled to conclude that organizations such as Alcoholics Anonymous and the Jaycees serve a rehabilitative purpose and as such their activities are desirable, unlike the prisoners' union, which not only pursues an adversary relationship with prison officials, but also has an illegal purpose under North Carolina Law.

REASON: "The fact of confinement and the needs of the penal institution impose limitations on constitutional rights, including those derived from the First Amendment, which are implicit in incarceration . . . Because the realities of running a penal institution are complex and difficult, we have also recognized the wide-ranging deference to be accorded the decisions of prison administrators . . . It is in this context that the claims of the Union must be examined.

"It is clearly not irrational to conclude that individuals may believe what they want, but that concerted group activity, or solicitation therefor, would pose additional and unwarranted problems and frictions in the operation of the State's penal institutions. The ban on inmate solicitation and group meetings, therefore, was rationally related to the reasonable, indeed to the central, objectives of prison administration.

"An examination of the potential restrictions on speech or association that have been imposed by the regulations under challenge, demonstrates that the restrictions imposed are reasonable, and are consistent with the inmates' status as prisoners and with the legitimate operational considerations of the institution. To begin with, First Amendment speech rights are barely implicated in this case . . . Since other avenues of outside informational flow by the Union remain available, the prohibition on bulk mailing, reasonable in the absence of First Amendment considerations, remains reasonable.

"The case of a prisoners' union, where the focus is on the presentation of grievances to, and encouragement of adversary relations with, institution officials surely would rank high on anyone's list of potential trouble spots. If the appellants' views as to the possible detrimental effects of the organizational activities of the Union are reasonable, as we conclude they are, then the regulations are drafted no more broadly than they need to be to meet the perceived threat—which stems directly from group meetings and group organizational activities of the Union. When weighed against the First Amendment rights asserted, these institutional reasons are sufficiently weighty to prevail.

"Prison administrators may surely conclude that the Jaycees and Alcoholics Anonymous differ in fundamental respects from appellee Union, a group with no past to speak of, and with the avowed intent to pursue an adversary relationship with prison officials. Indeed, it would be enough to distinguish the Union from Alcoholics Anonymous to note that the chartered purpose of the Union, apparently pursued in the prison, was illegal under North Carolina law.

"It is precisely in matters such as this, the decision as to which of many groups should be allowed to operate within the prison walls, where, confronted with claims based on the Equal Protection Clause, the courts should allow the prison administrators full latitude of discretion, unless it can be firmly stated that the two groups are so similar that discretion has been abused. That is surely not the case here."

CASE SIGNIFICANCE: This is the only case decided by the Court involving prisoners' unions. In this case, the prisoners alleged violations of First Amendment and Fourteenth Amendment rights. The Court rejected both contentions, saying in essence that prison officials enjoy a great deal of discretion in regulating the conduct of inmates. The Court concluded that First Amendment rights were not "unduly abridged," stating that the finding by prison authorities that "the presence of a prisoners' union would be detrimental to prison order and security has not been conclusively shown to be wrong." As for the equal protection challenge, the Court said that prison officials do not have to treat all organizations equally, adding that they have the power to determine which organizations are desirable or undesirable.

Decided in 1977, this case did not prescribe clear guidelines as to how alleged First Amendment violations are to be resolved. If this case were decided today, the standard used would be whether the regulations questioned are "reasonably related to legitimate penological interests," as prescribed in *Turner v. Safley*, 482 U.S. 78 (1987).

Y. Visitation

Block v. Rutherford
468 U.S. 576 (1984)

CAPSULE: Prisoners have no constitutional right to contact visits or to observe shakedown searches of their cells.

FACTS: Pretrial detainees at the Los Angeles County Central Jail brought a class action under 42 U.S.C. §1983 against the County Sheriff, certain administrators of the Central Jail, and the County Board of Supervisors. This jail, with a capacity of over 5,000, had a policy of denying pretrial detainees contact visits with their spouses, relatives, children, and friends. The jail also had a practice of conducting random "shakedown" searches of cells while the detainees were away at meals, recreation, or other activities. The detainees challenged these two policies, claiming that the policies deprived them of liberty without due process in violation of the Fourteenth Amendment.

ISSUE: Do pretrial detainees have a constitutional right to contact visits and to observe shakedown searches of their cells by jail officials? NO.

DECISION:

1. The jail's blanket prohibition on contact visits is an entirely reasonable, nonpunitive response to legitimate security concerns, consistent with the Fourteenth Amendment.

2. The jail's practice of conducting random, irregular "shakedown" searches of cells in the absence of the cell occupants is also a reasonable response by jail officials to legitimate security concerns.

REASON: "The question before us, therefore, is narrow: whether the prohibition of contact visits is reasonably related to legitimate governmental objectives. More particularly, because there is no dispute that internal security of detention facilities is a legitimate governmental interest, our inquiry is simply whether petitioners' blanket prohibition on contact visits at Central Jail is reasonably related to the security of that facility.

"That there is a valid, rational connection between a ban on contact visits and internal security of a detention facility is too obvious to warrant extended discussion. The District Court acknowledged as much. Contact visits invite a host of security problems. They open the institution to the introduction of drugs, weapons, and other contraband. Visitors can easily conceal guns, knives, drugs, or other contraband in countless ways and pass them to an inmate unnoticed by even the most vigilant observers. And these items can readily be slipped from the clothing of an innocent child, or transferred by other visitors permitted close contact with inmates.

"Contact visitation poses other dangers for a detention facility, as well. Detainees—by definition persons unable to meet bail—often are awaiting trial for serious, violent offenses, and many have prior criminal convictions. Exposure of this type of person to others, whether family, friends, or jail administrators, necessarily carries with it risks that the safety of innocent individuals will be jeopardized in various ways.

"The District Court and Court of Appeals held that totally disallowing contact visits is excessive in relation to the security and other interests at stake. We reject this characterization. There are many justifications for denying contact visits entirely, rather than attempting the difficult task of establishing a program of limited visitation such as that imposed here.

"The burdens of identifying candidates for contact visitation—glossed over by the District Court—are made even more difficult by the brevity of detention and the constantly changing nature of the inmate population. Or a complete prohibition could reasonably be thought necessary because selectively allowing contact visits to some—even if feasible—could well create tension between those allowed contact visits and those not.

"Thus, contrary to respondents' suggestion, we have previously considered not only a Fourth Amendment challenge but also a due process challenge to a room search procedure almost identical to that used at Central Jail, and we sustained the practice on both scores. We have no reason to reconsider that issue; the identical arguments made by respondents here were advanced by the respondents in *Wolfish*. The security concerns that we held justified the same restriction in *Wolfish*, see id., at 555, n. 36, are no less compelling here. Moreover, we could not have been clearer in our holding in *Wolfish* that this is a matter lodged in the sound discretion of the institutional officials. We reaffirm that 'proper deference to the informed discretion of prison authorities demands that they, and not the courts, make the difficult judgments which reconcile conflicting claims affecting the security of the institution, the welfare of the prison staff, and the property rights of the detainees.' Id., at 557, n. 38."

CASE SIGNIFICANCE: This case was the second Supreme Court case that addressed the rights of pretrial detainees, the first being *Bell v. Wolfish*, 441 U.S. 520 (1979). The Supreme Court continued the legacy of *Wolfish* in this decision. Relying heavily on *Wolfish*, the Court once again came up with a conservative decision that favors penal administrators. It found that denying contact visits and not allowing detainees to observe cell searches was reasonably related to a legitimate governmental interest.

The Court quoted the *Wolfish* case, saying: "[P]rison administrators [are to be] accorded wide-ranging deference in the adoption and execution of policies and practices that in their judgment are needed to preserve internal order and discipline and to maintain institutional security." 441 U.S. at 547. What this case also says is that there is no difference in the standard used for the constitutionality of regulations involving pretrial detainees and convicts—despite the presumption of innocence for pretrial detainees.

Chapter 2—Probation

Ex parte United States (Killits)
37 S. Ct. 72 (1916)

CAPSULE: A federal district court does not have the legal authority to place a convicted felon on probation.

FACTS: Killits pleaded guilty to an indictment charging him with several counts of embezzling the money of a national bank of which he was an officer, and making false entries in its books. He was sentenced to five years imprisonment. The federal district court ordered that the execution of his sentence be suspended for five years, dependent upon his good behavior. The United States District Attorney moved to set aside this order on the ground that it was not a temporary suspension to enable legal proceedings pending or contemplated to be revised, or an application for pardon to be made, or any other legal relief against the sentence. Instead, it was a permanent suspension based upon considerations extraneous to the legality of the conviction and it was equivalent to a refusal to carry out the statute governing sentencing in such cases.

ISSUE: Does common law allow the courts to suspend a sentence permanently? NO.

DECISION: Common law does not give a court discretion to permanently decline to enforce the law by suspending its application. What the court did in this case was therefore illegal.

REASON: "While it may not be doubted under the common law as thus stated that courts possessed and asserted the right to exert judicial discretion in the enforcement of the law to temporarily suspend either the imposition of sentence or its execution when imposed to the end that pardon might be procured, or that a violation of law in other respects might be prevented, we are unable to perceive any ground for sustaining the proposition that, at common law, the courts possessed or claimed the right which is here insisted upon. No elaboration could make this plainer than does the text of the passages quoted.

"Nor from the fact that common-law courts possessed the power by recognizance to secure good behavior, that is, to enforce the law, do we think any support is afforded for the proposition that those courts possessed the arbitrary discretion to permanently decline to enforce the law . . . So far as the courts of the United States are concerned it suffices to say that we have been referred to no opinion maintaining the asserted power, and, on the contrary, in the opinion in the only case in which the subject was considered, it was expressly decided the power was wanting. *United States v. Wilson*, 46 F. 748 (1891).

". . . [S]o far as the future is concerned, that is, the causing of the imposition of penalties as fixed to be subject, by probation legislation or such other means as the legislative mind may devise, to such judicial discretion as may be adequate to enable courts to meet, by the exercise of an enlarged but wise discretion, the infinite variations which may be presented to them for judgment, recourse must be had to Congress, whose legislative power on the subject is, in the very nature of things, adequately complete."

CASE SIGNIFICANCE: This case holds that courts do not have the authority under common law to suspend a sentence for five years, which was the same imprisonment time imposed by law on the offender. Such act in effect negates the penalty imposed by the legislature and is unauthorized.

The power to impose punishment is derived by the courts from the legislature, which imposes punishment categories through the penal code. In this case, the court in effect suspended the sentence permanently. Authority for this act was not given by statute; however, the judge sought to justify it under common law. The Supreme Court concluded that even under common law no such authority for the judge's action existed.

This case was decided in 1916 and was perhaps the first case ever to be brought to the Supreme Court involving probation, hence its significance. The Court did not say that probation could not be granted; what it said was that this type of sentence could not be granted under common law and without any legislative authorization. The implication is that probation is a valid punishment, but it must be granted by law. Without statutory authorization, the granting of probation is questionable, particularly if the law specifies that judges do not possess discretion in imposing sentences.

Mempa v. Rhay
389 U.S. 128 (1967)

CAPSULE: A defendant has a constitutional right to a lawyer during probation revocation that is followed by sentencing (as opposed to probation revocation after the probationer has been sentenced).

FACTS: Mempa pleaded guilty, on the advice of his attorney, to the offense of "joyriding," and was placed on probation for 10 years. The imposition of sentence was deferred under Washington law and the defendant was placed on probation. About four months later, the prosecutor moved to have Mempa's probation revoked due to his apparent involvement in a burglary. At the revocation hearing, Mempa was not represented by counsel, nor asked if he wanted counsel. He admitted to being involved in the burglary. Without further questioning, the court revoked Mempa's probation and, in accordance with state law, imposed the maximum sentence of 10 years. The court stated that it would recommend to the parole board that Mempa serve only one year. While serving his sentence, Mempa filed a writ of habeas corpus, seeking release from an unconstitutional confinement, claiming that he had been denied his right to counsel at a hearing in which his probation was revoked and sentence imposed.

ISSUE: Does a defendant have a constitutional right to counsel during a probation revocation hearing that is followed by the imposition of a deferred sentence? YES.

DECISION: The Sixth Amendment requires that counsel be afforded to a felony defendant in a probation revocation proceeding that is followed by the imposition of a deferred sentence.

REASON: "It is true that sentencing in Washington offers fewer opportunities for the exercise of judicial discretion than in many other jurisdictions. The applicable statute requires the trial judge in all cases to sentence the convicted person to the maximum term provided by law for the offense of which he was convicted. The actual determination of the length of time to be served is to be made by the Board of Prison Terms and Paroles within six months after the convicted person is admitted to prison.

"Even more important in a case such as this is the fact that certain legal rights may be lost if not exercised at this stage. For one, Washington law provides that an appeal in a case involving a plea of guilty followed by probation can only be taken after sentence is imposed following revocation of probation. Therefore in a case where an accused agreed to plead guilty, although he had a valid defense, because he was offered probation, absence of counsel at the imposition of the deferred sentence might well result in loss of the right to appeal. While ordinary appeals from a plea of guilty are less frequent than those following a trial on the merits, the incidence of improperly obtained guilty pleas is not so slight as to be capable of being characterized as de minimis."

CASE SIGNIFICANCE: Probation generally implies that a probationer will remain in the community unless he or she commits a major violation. To protect the probationer's interest in liberty, the Supreme Court has recognized some procedural due process rights at this stage of the criminal process. *Mempa v. Rhay* was the first of several cases that provided procedural safeguards in revocation hearings. The Court ruled that a probationer is entitled to counsel in a probation revocation hearing in cases in which a sentence has been deferred. By contrast, the Court in *Gagnon v. Scarpelli*, 411 U.S. 778 (1973), held that whether a probationer is entitled to a lawyer during probation revocation must be decided on a case-by-case basis. The difference in these two decisions lies in the fact that *Mempa* involved the revocation of a suspended sentence in the course of which the defendant was placed on probation, while *Gagnon* involved regular probation in which the defendant had been found guilty and then placed on probation. What *Mempa* implies is that the right to counsel must be provided during sentencing (even if it is preceded by probation, as in the case of suspended sentences), but that the right to counsel during probation revocation is not a constitutional right. It may, however, be given by state law.

Gagnon v. Scarpelli
411 U.S. 778 (1973)

CAPSULE: **Probationers are entitled to certain due process rights before probation can be revoked.**

FACTS: Scarpelli, a felony probationer, was arrested after committing a burglary. At first he admitted involvement in the crime, but later claimed that his admission was made under duress and thus was invalid. His probation was revoked without a hearing and without a lawyer present. After serving three years of his sentence, Scarpelli filed for a writ of habeas corpus, claiming denial of due process because his probation was revoked without a hearing or counsel.

ISSUES:
1. Is a probationer entitled to due process rights in a revocation proceeding? YES.
2. Is a probationer constitutionally entitled to be represented by counsel in a probation revocation hearing? NO.

DECISIONS:
1. Probationers, like parolees, are entitled to the following due process rights prior to probation revocation:
   A. Preliminary and final revocation hearings
   B. Other due process rights, such as:
      1. Written notice of the alleged probation violation;
      2. Disclosure to the probationer of the evidence of violation;
      3. Opportunity to be heard in person and to present evidence as well as witnesses;

4. Right to confront and cross-examine adverse witnesses, unless good cause can be shown for not allowing this confrontation;
5. Right to judgment by a detached and neutral hearing body;
6. Written statement of reasons for revoking probation, as well as of the evidence used in arriving at that decision.

2. The right to counsel during probation revocation should be decided on a case-by-case basis. Although the state is not constitutionally obliged to provide counsel in all cases, it should do so where the indigent probationer or parolee may have difficulty in presenting his or her version of disputed facts without the examination or cross-examination of witnesses or the presentation of complicated documentary evidence. The grounds for refusal to provide counsel must be stated in the record.

REASON: "Of greater relevance is our decision last Term in *Morrissey v. Brewer*, 408 U.S. 471 (1972). There we held that the revocation of parole is not a part of a criminal prosecution. Parole arises after the end of the criminal prosecution, including imposition of sentence. Revocation deprives an individual, not of the absolute liberty to which every citizen is entitled, but only of the conditional liberty properly dependent on observance of special parole restrictions.

"Even though the revocation of parole is not part of the criminal prosecution, we held that the loss of liberty entailed is a serious deprivation requiring that the parolee be accorded due process. Specifically, we held that a parolee is entitled to two hearings, one a preliminary hearing at the time of his arrest and detention to determine whether there is probable cause to believe he has committed a violation of his parole, and the other a somewhat more comprehensive hearing prior to the making of the final revocation decision.

"Petitioner does not contend that there is any difference relevant to the guarantee of due process between the revocation of parole and the revocation of probation, nor do we perceive one. Probation revocation, like parole revocation, is not a stage of a criminal prosecution, but does result in a loss of liberty. Accordingly, we hold that a probationer, like a parolee, is entitled to a preliminary and a final revocation hearing, under the conditions specified in *Morrissey v. Brewer*."

CASE SIGNIFICANCE: This case was decided one year after *Morrissey v. Brewer*, 408 U.S. 471 (1972), a parole revocation case in which the Supreme Court held that parolees were entitled to certain due process rights prior to parole revocation. The Court in *Gagnon v. Scarpelli* extended the due process rights given to parolees in *Morrissey v. Brewer* to probationers, reasoning that in both cases revocation resulted in loss of liberty, which is a "grievous loss." The rights enumerated by the Court in this case must be given to probationers prior to revocation, otherwise due process is violated. The Court, however, refused to require the presence of counsel in every probation revocation proceeding, holding that, as in parole, the right to counsel must be decided by the hearing judge or body on a case-by-case basis.

In both *Morrissey v. Brewer* (parole revocation) and *Gagnon v. Scarpelli* (probation revocation), the Court prescribed a two-step procedure for revocation, consisting of: (1) the preliminary hearing, and (2) the final hearing. In subsequent cases, however, the Supreme Court and lower courts have not adhered strictly to these requirements, holding instead that there need not be two separate proceedings as long as some type of hearing is afforded. In a number of jurisdictions, there is only one hearing given to a parolee or probationer prior to revocation. This hearing should, however, feature all the rights given to probationers and parolees in the *Gagnon* and *Morrissey* cases.

Cabell v. Chavez-Salido
454 U.S. 432 (1982)

CAPSULE: Requiring American citizenship to become a probation officer is constitutional.

FACTS: A California statute requires that public employees declared by law to be peace officers must be United States citizens. In the state of California, probation officers are "peace officers" and therefore must be American citizens. This requirement was challenged by a class of lawfully admitted permanent resident aliens after having been denied positions as Deputy Probation Officers in Los Angeles County because they were not American citizens.

ISSUE: Is a state law requiring U.S. citizenship for peace officer positions constitutional? YES.

DECISION: A state law requiring U.S. citizenship for public officers or employees, including probation officers, declared by law to be peace officers, is valid and constitutional. Because probation officers take part in the exercise of coercive power by the sovereign over the individual, the citizenship requirement is justified.

REASON: "The cases through *Graham* dealt for the most part with attempts by the States to retain certain economic benefits exclusively for citizens. Since *Graham*, the Court has confronted claims distinguishing between the economic and sovereign functions of government. This distinction has been supported by the argument that although citizenship is not a relevant ground for the distribution of economic benefits, it is a relevant ground for determining membership in the political community. 'We recognize a State's interest in establishing its own form of government, and in limiting participation in that government to those who are within 'the basic conception of a political community.' *Sugarman v. Dougall*, 413 U.S., at 642. While not retreating from the position that restrictions on lawfully resident aliens that primarily affect economic interests are subject to heightened judicial scrutiny, we have concluded that strict scrutiny is out of place when the restriction primarily serves a political function: '[O]ur scrutiny will not be so demanding where we deal with matters resting firmly within a State's constitutional prerogatives [and] constitutional responsibility for the establishment and operation of its own government, as well as the qualifications of an appropriately designated class of public office holders.' *Sugarman v. Dougall, supra,* at 648. We have thus 'not abandoned the general principle that some state functions are so bound up with the operation of the State as a governmental entity as to permit the exclusion from those functions of all persons who have not become part of the process of self-government.' *Ambach v. Norwick,* 441 U.S., at 73-74. And in those areas the State's exclusion of aliens need not 'clear the high hurdle of 'strict scrutiny,' because [that] would 'obliterate all the distinctions between citizens and aliens, and thus depreciate the historic value of citizenship." *Foley v. Connelie,* 435 U.S., at 295.

"The exclusion of aliens from basic governmental processes is not a deficiency in the democratic system but a necessary consequence of the community's process of political self-definition. Self-government, whether direct or through representatives, begins by defining the scope of the community of the governed and thus of the governors as well: Aliens are by definition those outside of this community. Judicial incursions in this area may interfere with those aspects of democratic self-government that are most essential to it. This distinction between the economic and political functions of government has, therefore, replaced the old public/private distinction. Although this distinction rests on firmer foundations than the old public/private distinction, it may be difficult to apply in particular cases.

"Looking at the functions of California probation officers, we conclude that they, like the state troopers involved in *Foley*, sufficiently partake of the sovereign's power to exercise coercive force over the individual that they may be limited to citizens. Although the range of individuals over whom probation officers exercise supervisory authority is limited, the powers of the probation officer are broad with respect to those over whom they exercise that authority. The probation officer has the power both to arrest, and to release those over whom he has jurisdiction. He has the power and the responsibility to supervise probationers and insure that all the conditions of probation are met and that the probationer accomplishes a successful reintegration into the community. With respect to juveniles, the probation officer has the responsibility to determine whether to release or detain offenders, and whether to institute judicial proceedings or take other supervisory steps over the minor.

"From the perspective of the probationer, his probation officer may personify the State's sovereign powers; from the perspective of the larger community, the probation officer may symbolize the political community's control over, and thus responsibility for, those who have been found to have violated the norms of social order. From both of these perspectives, a citizenship requirement may seem an appropriate limitation on those who would exercise and, therefore, symbolize this power of the political community over those who fall within its jurisdiction."

CASE SIGNIFICANCE: This case addresses the question of whether resident aliens can be disqualified from certain public positions through a state law that requires U.S. citizenship for these positions. The Court answered yes, saying that "a citizenship requirement is an appropriate limitation on those who exercise and, therefore, symbolize this power of the political community over those who fall within its jurisdiction." Said the Court:

> The exclusion of aliens from basic governmental processes is not a deficiency in the democratic system but a necessary consequence of the community's process of political self-definition. Self-government, whether direct or through representatives, begins by defining the scope of the community of the governed and thus of the governors as well: Aliens are by definition those outside of this community.

This decision does not mean that resident aliens may, by law, be disqualified from any and all public positions by requiring U.S. citizenship as a condition for employment. Such a law would be unconstitutional as overinclusive, meaning that it would disqualify individuals without justification. Citizenship can be required only in certain public positions. "Looking at the functions of California probation officers," the Court said, "we conclude that they, like state troopers . . . sufficiently partake of the sovereign's power to exercise coercive force over the individual that they may be limited to citizens." The implication is that public positions that do not "sufficiently partake of the sovereign's power to exercise coercive force over the individual" cannot be limited to American citizens.

Bearden v. Georgia
461 U.S. 660 (1983)

CAPSULE: **It is unconstitutional to revoke probation based on failure to pay a fine or restitution if the probationer is indigent.**

FACTS: Bearden pleaded guilty in state court to burglary and theft by receiving stolen goods. He was a first-time offender and under Georgia statute was given probation on the condition that he pay a $500 fine and $250 in restitution, with $100 payable that day, $100 the next day, and the balance within four months. Bearden borrowed money and paid off the first $200 but was laid off from his job about one month later. He tried to find other work but was unsuccessful. Shortly before the $550 balance became due, he notified the probation office that his payment was going to be late. Bearden's probation was revoked because of nonpayment and he was sent to prison.

ISSUE: Can probation be revoked based on the failure to pay a fine and restitution if the probationer does not have the resources to pay? NO.

DECISION: A judge cannot constitutionally revoke probation because of failure to pay a fine or restitution in the absence of evidence and a finding that the probationer was somehow responsible for the failure or that alternative forms of punishment were inadequate to meet the state's interest in punishment and deterrence.

REASON: "This Court has long been sensitive to the treatment of indigents in our criminal justice system. Over a quarter-century ago, Justice Black declared that 'there can be no equal justice where the kind of trial a man gets depends on the amount of money he has.' (*Griffin v. Illinois*, 351 U.S. 12, [1956]). *Griffin*'s principle of 'equal justice,' which the Court applied there to strike down a state practice of granting appellate review only to persons able to afford a trial transcript, has been applied in numerous other contexts. *See e.g., Douglas v. California*, 372 U.S. 353 (1963) (indigent entitled to counsel on first direct appeal); *Roberts v. LaVallee*, 389 U.S. 40 (1967) (indigent entitled to free transcript of preliminary hearing for use at trial); *Mayer v. Chicago*, 404 U.S. 189 (1971) (indigent cannot be denied an adequate record to appeal a conviction under a fine-only statute). Most relevant to the issue here is the holding in *Williams v. Illinois*, 399 U.S. 235 (1970), that a State cannot subject a certain class of convicted defendants to a period of imprisonment beyond the statutory maximum solely because they are too poor to pay a fine."

CASE SIGNIFICANCE: This case reiterates the principle enunciated in previous Supreme Court cases, that "there can be no equal justice where the kind of trial a man gets depends on the amount of money he has." To revoke the probation of an indigent probationer would be to violate the equal protection clause of the Constitution because the only reason the probationer would then be sent to prison is that he or she is too poor to pay. Note the following points, however, in connection with this case:

1. The decision states that "a sentencing court cannot properly revoke a defendant's probation for failure to pay a fine and make restitution, absent evidence and findings that he was somehow responsible for the failure . . ." A distinction must be made between failure to pay because of indigency and refusal to pay even if resources are available. Failure to pay because of indigency cannot lead to revocation because such revocation would violate the equal protection clause of the Constitution; refusal to pay, however, can result in a valid revocation because there is no equal protection issue.

2. The decision also states that "a sentencing court cannot properly revoke a defendant's probation without ascertaining that alternative forms of punishment were inadequate to meet the State's interest in punishment and deterrence . . ." The Court rules out an automatic probation revocation without first determining whether other, alternative forms of punishment are in fact adequate to satisfy the state's purpose of punishment and deterrence. *Bearden* does not categorically say that failure to pay because of indigency can never lead to revocation under any circumstance. Revocation can be resorted to even in cases of indigency as long as the judge first determines that "alternative forms of punishment were inadequate to meet the State's interest in punishment and deterrence . . ." In reality, however, it is difficult to imagine instances in which alternative forms of punishment (such as community service) would not suffice as an alternative form of punishment to fine or restitution, hence effectively ruling out imprisonment resulting from revocation in indigency cases.

Minnesota v. Murphy
465 U.S. 420 (1984)

CAPSULE: **Statements made by a probationer to his probation officer during interrogation while not in custody are admissible in a subsequent criminal trial.**

FACTS: Murphy was prosecuted for criminal sexual conduct and pleaded guilty to the lesser charge of false imprisonment. He received a suspended prison sentence and was placed on probation for three years. The terms of Murphy's probation provided that he participate in a treatment program for sexual offenders, report to his probation officer as directed, and be truthful with the probation officer "in all matters." Murphy was told that failure to comply with the conditions of his probation could result in probation revocation.

Murphy's probation officer learned from one of the counselors at the treatment facility that Murphy had confessed to a rape and murder in 1974. Armed with this information, the probation officer met with Murphy and confronted him with the information from the counselor. After further questioning by the probation officer, Murphy admitted his involvement in the 1974 rape and murder.

Murphy was charged with first degree murder. During the trial he attempted to suppress the confession made to the probation officer on the ground that it was obtained in violation of the Fifth and Fourteenth Amendments. The trial court admitted the evidence, ruling that Murphy was not "in custody" when he confessed to the probation officer and that the confession was neither compelled nor involuntary despite the absence of *Miranda* warnings.

ISSUE: Is a statement made by a probationer to his probation officer without the *Miranda* warnings admissible in a subsequent criminal trial? YES.

DECISION: Incriminating evidence revealed to a probation officer by a probationer who is not in custody and who does not assert the Fifth Amendment privilege is admissible as evidence in a subsequent criminal trial.

REASON: "The general obligation to appear before his probation officer and answer questions truthfully did not in itself convert respondent's otherwise voluntary statements into compelled ones.

"A witness confronted with questions that the government should reasonably expect to elicit incriminating evidence ordinarily must assert the Fifth Amendment privilege rather than answer if he desires not to incriminate himself. If he chooses to answer rather than assert the privilege, his choice is considered to be voluntary since he was free to claim the privilege and would suffer no penalty as a result of his decision to do so.

"Respondent cannot claim the benefit of the 'in custody' exception to the general rule that the Fifth Amendment privilege is not self-executing. It is clear that respondent was not 'in custody' for purposes of receiving *Miranda* protection since there was no formal arrest or restraint on freedom of movement of the degree associated with formal arrest. The fact that the probation officer could compel respondent's attendance and truthful answers and consciously sought incriminating evidence, that respondent did not expect questions about prior criminal conduct and could not seek counsel before attending the meeting, and that there were no observers to guard against abuse or trickery, neither alone nor in combination, are sufficient to excuse respondent's failure to claim the privilege in a timely manner."

CASE SIGNIFICANCE: This case answers a question probation officers face whenever they ask questions of or are interviewing probationers. The question is: Should the *Miranda* warnings be given by the probation officer when asking questions of a probationer? The answer is complex and may be presented in a chart as follows:

	A. Evidence to be used in a Revocation Proceeding	B. Evidence to be used in a Criminal Trial
I. If probationer is not in custody	No.	No, unless probationer asserts right (this situation is the *Murphy* case).
II. If probationer is in custody.	Some states say no; others, yes. Depends upon statutory or case law.	Yes.

As the above chart shows, it is important to know whether the evidence obtained is to be used in a revocation proceeding or in a criminal trial, and whether the probationer is in custody or not in custody. Evidence obtained by probation officers is usually used in probation revocation proceedings, which are administrative proceedings. There are instances, however, when the evidence obtained by the probation officer might be needed by the prosecutor in a subsequent criminal trial of that offender. In these cases, the *Miranda* warnings must be given if the evidence is to be used in a criminal trial and if the probationer is in custody.

The important question is: When is a probationer in custody or not in custody? Jurisdictions differ, but the general rule is this: If the probation officer will allow the probationer to leave after the interrogation, then chances are that the probationer is not in custody. Conversely, if the probation officer knows he or she will not allow the probationer to leave after the interrogation, then the probationer is in custody. Under this test, asking routine questions during a routine visit with a probationer is considered non-custodial; however, asking the probationer to come to the office after the officer receives information from the police and the officer asking the police to take the probationer into custody after the interrogation, imply that the probationer is in custody. Although this case involves a probationer, there is every reason to believe that the same rules outlined above also apply to parolees who, like probationers, are under supervision but are not in custody.

Black v. Romano
471 U.S. 606 (1985)

CAPSULE: A sentencing judge does not have to indicate that he or she considered alternatives to incarceration before revoking probation.

FACTS: Black, after pleading guilty to two counts of transferring and selling controlled substances, was placed on probation for five years and given suspended prison sentences. Two months later he was arrested and charged with leaving the scene of an automobile accident. At Black's probation revocation hearing, he offered no explanation of his involvement in the accident. The judge found that Black had violated the conditions of his probation by committing a felony; Black's probation was revoked.

ISSUE: Does the due process clause of the Constitution require that a sentencing court indicate that it considered alternatives to incarceration before revoking probation? NO.

DECISION: The due process clause of the Fourteenth Amendment does not require that the sentencing judge indicate consideration of alternatives to incarceration before probation can be revoked.

REASON: "The Due Process Clause of the Fourteenth Amendment does not generally require a sentencing court to indicate that it has considered alternatives to incarceration before revoking probation. The procedures for revocation of probation—written notice to the probationer of the claimed probation violations, disclosure of the evidence against him, an opportunity for the probationer to be heard in person and to present witnesses and documentary evidence, a neutral hearing body, a written statement by the factfinder as to the evidence relied on and the reasons for revoking probation, the right to cross-examine adverse witnesses unless the hearing body finds good cause for not allowing confrontation, and the right to assistance of counsel—do not include an express statement by the factfinder that alternatives to incarceration were considered and rejected. The specified procedures adequately protect the probationer against revocation of probation in a constitutionally unfair manner."

CASE SIGNIFICANCE: This case further explores the limits of due process guarantees available to probationers during the revocation hearing. In *Gagnon v. Scarpelli*, 411 U.S. 778 (1973), the Court said that probationers are entitled to the following due process rights at revocation: (1) written notice to the probationer of the claimed violations; (2) disclosure of the evidence against the probationer; (3) an opportunity for the probationer to be heard in person and to present witnesses and documentary evidence; (4) a neutral hearing body; (5) a written statement by the factfinder as to the evidence relied on and the reasons for revoking probation; (6) the right to cross-examine adverse witnesses unless the hearing body finds good cause for not allowing confrontation; and (7) the right to assistance of counsel, as decided on a case-by-case basis. In this case, the probationer sought to add to these rights, saying that the due process clause requires a sentencing court to indicate that alternatives to incarceration were considered by the judge before revoking probation. The Supreme Court disagreed, saying that the rights guaranteed in *Gagnon* ensured fairness in the revocation proceedings. Aside from refusing to add to a probationer's due process rights beyond those enumerated in *Gagnon v. Scarpelli*, the Court in this case basically reiterates the generally accepted legal principle that probation is a privilege and not a right. This means that probation may be given or withheld by the court and the court may refuse to extend probation to a defendant even if other non-incarceration alternatives are available.

Griffin v. Wisconsin
483 U.S. 868 (1987)

CAPSULE: The search of a probationer's home without a warrant and based on reasonable grounds (which is a lower standard than probable cause) is valid.

FACTS: In 1980, Griffin, who had a prior criminal record, was convicted in state court of resisting arrest, disorderly conduct, and obstructing an officer. He was placed on probation.

Probationers in Wisconsin are subject to conditions set by the court as well as by rules and regulations established by the State Department of Health and Social Services. One of the Department's regulations permits any probation officer to search a probationer's home without a warrant upon supervisory approval, and as long as there are "reasonable grounds" to believe the probationer is in possession of contraband.

The supervisor of Griffin's probation officer received information from a detective that there were or might be guns in Griffin's apartment. Probation officers searched the apartment and discovered a handgun. Griffin was tried and convicted of the charge of possession of a firearm by a convicted felon and was sentenced to two years imprisonment.

ISSUE: Is the warrantless search based on "reasonable grounds" (which is a lower standard than probable cause) of a probationer's home by probation officers constitutional? YES.

DECISION: The warrantless search of a probationer's home based on reasonable grounds (and not probable cause) is constitutional if conducted pursuant to a regulation that is itself a reasonable response to the "special needs" of a probation system.

REASON: "A state's operation of a probation system, like its operation of a school, government office or prison, or its supervision of a regulated industry, likewise presents 'special needs' beyond normal law enforcement that may justify departures from the usual warrant and probable cause requirements.

"We think it clear that the special needs of Wisconsin's probation system make the warrant requirement impracticable and justify replacement of the standard of probable cause by 'reasonable grounds' as defined by the Wisconsin Supreme Court."

CASE SIGNIFICANCE: The Fourth Amendment generally requires that searches and seizures be made with probable cause and a warrant. This case is significant because it holds that searches and seizures involving probationers may be made based on "reasonable grounds" (lower than probable cause) and without a warrant. These lower standards are justified by the "special needs" of probation supervision and also by the fact that probationers, having been convicted of a crime, enjoy diminished constitutional rights. This does not mean, however, that searches of probationers by probation officers based on reasonable grounds are automatically valid. What it means is that such searches are allowed by the Constitution if authorized by state law or agency policy. If state law or agency policy provides for probable cause, such must be followed. In the absence of a state statute or agency policy, case law governs the issue of what quantum of certainty is required to make a search by probation officers legal.

Forrester v. White
108 S. Ct. 538 (1988)

CAPSULE: Judges do not enjoy absolute immunity when not performing judicial or adjudicative acts. The act performed by the judge in this case was administrative, not judicial or adjudicative.

FACTS: Forrester, a former probation officer, filed a lawsuit seeking damages from White, a state court judge. Under Illinois law, a judge had authority to appoint and discharge a probation officer. Forrester alleged that White demoted and later discharged her from her duties on account of her sex, in violation of the equal protection clause of the Fourteenth Amendment. The jury decided in Forrester's favor. However, the district court ruled that the judge had absolute immunity from a civil damages suit.

ISSUE: Does a state court judge have absolute immunity from damages in a §1983 (civil rights) suit for a decision to demote and dismiss a subordinate? NO.

DECISION: A judge's decisions to demote and dismiss a probation officer are not judicial acts and therefore do not enjoy absolute immunity in a §1983 suit.

REASON: "Respondent's decisions to demote and discharge petitioner were administrative rather than judicial or adjudicative in nature. Such decisions are indistinguishable from those of an executive branch official responsible for making similar personnel decisions, which, no matter how crucial to the efficient operation of public institutions, are not entitled to absolute immunity from liability in damages under Section 1983. The Court of Appeals reasoned that the threat of vexatious lawsuits by disgruntled ex-employees could interfere with the quality of the judge's decisions. However true this may be, it does not serve to distinguish judges from other public officials who hire and fire subordinates. In neither case is the danger that officials will be deflected from the effective performance of their duties great enough to justify absolute immunity."

CASE SIGNIFICANCE: Judges enjoy absolute immunity when performing judicial acts. This means that, if sued, the lawsuit will be dismissed because of such immunity. Absolute immunity for judges, however, is limited to instances when the judge performs a "judicial or adjudicative" act. This case is significant because the Court said that the demotion and dismissal of a probation officer (who, in many states, is "hired and fired" by a judge) is not a judicial act, but is instead an administrative act for which the judge does not enjoy absolute immunity. Probation officers are thus afforded better protection under this case against capricious and arbitrary administrative actions of a judge.

Although the Court is aware that government officials must have some protection in order to fulfill their duties, the Court also recognizes that these officials should not be totally exempt from accountability for their acts. The Court examines the functions with which a particular official or class of officials has been lawfully entrusted and "evaluates the effect that exposure to particular forms of liability would likely have on the appropriate exercise of those duties."

Immunity for judicial acts is justified and defined by the functions it protects, but there is a significant distinction between judicial acts and the administrative, legislative, or executive functions that judges often perform. In this case, the judge was acting in an administrative capacity, hence his actions did not enjoy absolute immunity from liability under §1983.

Chapter 3—Parole

Morrissey v. Brewer
408 U.S. 471 (1972)

CAPSULE: A parolee must be given six basic due process rights prior to parole revocation

FACTS: Morrissey pleaded guilty to, and was convicted of false drawing or uttering of checks. He was paroled from the Iowa State Penitentiary in 1988. Seven months later, Morrissey's parole was revoked for violating the conditions of his parole by buying a car under an assumed name and operating it without permission, giving false statements to the police concerning his address and insurance company after a minor accident, obtaining credit under an assumed name, and failing to report his residence to his parole officer. The parole officer's report also showed that Morrissey had been interviewed, had admitted to the violations, and could not explain why he had not contacted his parole officer.

ISSUE: Does the due process clause of the Fourteenth Amendment afford a parolee due process rights prior to parole revocation? YES.

DECISION: Although parole revocation does not require the application of all of the rights due a defendant in a criminal proceeding, a revocation represents a "grievous loss" of liberty and therefore a parolee is entitled to certain due process rights prior to revocation. There must be a revocation hearing that is to be conducted reasonably soon after the parolee's arrest. In these hearings, the parolee is entitled to the following due process rights:

1. "written notice of the claimed violations of parole;
2. "disclosure to the parolee of evidence against him;
3. "opportunity to be heard in person and to present witnesses and documentary evidence;
4. "the right to confront and cross-examine adverse witnesses (unless the hearing officer specifically finds good cause for not allowing confrontation);
5. "a 'neutral and detached' hearing body such as a traditional parole board, members of which need not be judicial officers or lawyers; and
6. "a written statement by the factfinders as to the evidence relied on and reasons for revoking parole."

REASON: "We begin with the proposition that the revocation of parole is not part of a criminal prosecution and thus the full panoply of rights due a defendant in such a proceeding does not apply to parole revocations. Cf. *Mempa v. Rhay,*

389 U.S. 128 (1967). Parole arises after the end of the criminal prosecution, including imposition of sentence. Supervision is not directly by the court but by an administrative agency, which is sometimes the arm of the court and sometimes of the executive. Revocation deprives an individual, not of absolute liberty to which every citizen is entitled, but only of the conditional liberty properly dependent on observance of special parole restrictions.

"The liberty of a parolee, although indeterminate, includes many of the core values of unqualified liberty and its termination inflicts a 'grievous loss' on the parolee and often on others. It is hardly useful any longer to try to deal with this problem in terms of whether a parolee's liberty is a 'right' or a 'privilege.' By whatever name, the liberty is valuable and must be seen as within the protection of the Fourteenth Amendment. Its termination requires some orderly process.

". . . [M]ost States have recognized that there is no interest on the part of the State in revoking parole without any procedural guarantees at all. What is needed is an informal hearing structured to assure that the finding of a parole violation will be based on verified facts and that the exercise of discretion will be informed by an accurate knowledge of the parolee's behavior."

CASE SIGNIFICANCE: This case is significant because, for the first time, the Court decided that parolees are entitled to some form of due process, at least in the parole revocation process. Relying on previous non-parole cases, the Court said that "whether any procedural protections are due depends on the extent to which an individual will be 'condemned to suffer grievous loss.' " Revoking parole signifies a "grievous loss" that triggers due process guarantees.

Morrissey is also significant because it has been used as precedent by offenders to claim similar due process rights in such proceedings as the decision to release or not release an inmate on parole (*Greenholtz v. Nebraska Penal Inmates*, 442 U.S. 1, [1979]); probation revocation (*Gagnon v. Scarpelli*, 411 U.S. 778, [1973]); and prison disciplinary proceedings (*Wolff v. McDonnell*, 418 U.S. 539 [1974]). The Court has decided that offenders are entitled to *Morrissey* due process rights in probation revocation and prison disciplinary proceedings, but not in the decision to release or not to release an inmate on parole. The standard used in these cases by the Court has been whether the offender will "suffer grievous loss" from such proceedings.

Aside from the six due process rights given by the Court to parolees in parole revocation proceedings, *Morrissey* also said that there are two important stages in the typical process of parole revocation: (1) the arrest of the parolee and the preliminary hearing, and (2) the revocation hearing. In both stages, the parolee is entitled to the due process rights enumerated above. Some writers interpret *Morrissey* to mean that parolees are also constitutionally entitled to a two-stage hearing process prior to revocation. There is nothing in the *Morrissey* case to indicate that a two-stage hearing process is constitutionally required. Many jurisdictions in effect have only one hearing in both probation and parole revocation, with the six due process rights enumerated above being given. Although not decided by the U.S. Supreme Court, most lower courts have considered these merged proceedings constitutional.

Moody v. Daggett
429 U.S. 78 (1976)

CAPSULE: An incarcerated parolee has no constitutional right to a prompt judicial hearing after a detainer is issued against him.

FACTS: Moody was convicted in 1962 of rape on an Indian reservation. He received a 10-year sentence, but was paroled in 1966. While on parole, Moody shot and killed two people on the Fort Apache Indian Reservation. He was found guilty of one count of manslaughter and one count of second-degree murder. He received concurrent 10-year sentences for these two offenses. Commission of these offenses violated Moody's 1966 parole. The United States Board of Parole issued, but did not execute, a parole violator warrant soon after Moody was incarcerated for the two homicides. The warrant was lodged with prison officials as a "detainer" (defined as "an instrument issued by a competent officer, authorizing the keeper of a prison to keep in custody a person therein named"). Moody asked that the warrant be executed immediately so that any imprisonment imposed for violating his earlier parole could run at the same time with the homicide sentences. The Board rejected the request, saying that the warrant would be executed only upon Moody's release from his second sentence. Moody brought suit against the Board, asking for dismissal of the parole violator warrant, alleging that he had been denied a prompt hearing at which the pending parole revocation issues could be examined.

ISSUE: Is a federal parolee, imprisoned for a crime committed while on parole, constitutionally entitled to a prompt revocation hearing when a detainer is issued and lodged with the institution where he is serving time? NO.

DECISION: An incarcerated parolee is deprived of no constitutionally protected rights simply by the issuance of a parole violator warrant. An adversary parole hearing need not take place until such time as the individual is taken into custody as a parole violator by execution of the warrant.

REASON: "Petitioner's present confinement and consequent liberty loss derive not in any sense from the outstanding parole violator warrant, but from his two

1971 homicide convictions. Issuance of the warrant and notice of that fact to the institution of confinement did no more than express the Board's intent to defer consideration of parole revocation to a later time. Though the gravity of petitioner's subsequent crimes places him under a cloud, issuance of the warrant was not a determination that petitioner's parole under his 1962 rape conviction will be revoked; the time at which the Commission must make that decision has not yet arrived. With only a prospect of future incarceration which is far from certain, we cannot say that the parole violator warrant has any present or inevitable effect upon the liberty interests which Morrissey sought to protect.

"The other injuries petitioner claims to suffer either do not involve a loss of protected liberty or have not occurred by reason of the warrant and detainer. His real complaint is that he desires to serve his sentence for the 1982 rape conviction concurrently with his sentences for two 1971 homicides. But, as we have noted, even after completion of the homicide sentences the Commission retains full discretion to dismiss the warrant or decide, after hearing, that petitioner's parole need not be revoked. If revocation is chosen, the Commission has power to grant, retroactively, the equivalent of concurrent sentences and to provide for unconditional or conditional release upon completion of the subsequent sentence.

"The statutory hearing to which petitioner will be entitled upon his application for release on parole will give him the same full opportunities to persuade the Commission that he should be released from federal custody as would an immediate hearing on the parole violator warrant. Whether different issues would be presented by the prospect of adverse action by different and autonomous parole authorities, we need not consider."

CASE SIGNIFICANCE: The *Moody* case answers the following question: Is an incarcerated parolee entitled to a prompt hearing after a detainer is issued against him? The Supreme Court said no. It found no liberty loss simply because the parole board wished to defer revocation consideration, stating that the parolee's present confinement was for crimes committed while on parole and not due to the detainer.

The federal parolee in this case argued that he was constitutionally entitled to an immediate parole revocation hearing when the parole violator warrant was issued and lodged with the institution as a detainer, but which the institution did not execute. The parolee was hoping that, if the warrant was issued, he could serve his new homicide sentences and his parole revocation simultaneously. The Court added that "as a practical matter, in cases such as this, in which the parolee has been convicted of an offense plainly constituting a parole violation, a decision to revoke parole would often be foreordained, so that given the predictive nature of parole revocation hearings, it is appropriate that such a hearing be held at the time at which prediction as to the parolee's ability to live in society without committing anti-social acts is both relevant and most accurate—at the expiration of the parolee's intervening sentence."

The Court did not wish to interfere with the parole board's powers and stated that the parolee would be given a statutory hearing at the parole board's discretion, at which time he would be given an opportunity to persuade the board that any sentence he received if parole was revoked should be retroactive.

What if the parolee is in confinement not because of the conviction for a new offense (as in this case), but solely because of a detainer? The Court has not addressed this, but chances are that a prompt hearing would be required because the detainer alone would have caused the parolee to suffer loss of liberty.

Greenholtz v. Nebraska Penal Inmates
442 U.S. 1 (1979)

CAPSULE: Inmates are not entitled to due process rights under the Constitution in discretionary parole release determinations.

FACTS: Inmates at the Nebraska Penal and Correctional Complex who had been denied parole brought a class action against the Nebraska Parole Board, claiming that they had been denied procedural due process. Under Nebraska statute, a prison inmate becomes eligible for discretionary parole when his minimum term, minus good-time credits, has been served. Each case is decided through a two-stage hearing in the form of: (1) an initial review hearing, and (2) a final parole hearing. Each inmate receives an initial review at least once a year. During the review the Parole Board does the following: (1) examines the inmate's pre-confinement and post-confinement record, (2) interviews the inmate, and (3) considers any documentation presented in support of a claim for release. If it is determined that the inmate is not yet a good risk for release, the Board denies parole, stating why release was not granted. If it is determined that the inmate is a good risk, a final hearing is scheduled, at which time the following rights are given: the inmate may (1) present evidence; (2) call witnesses; (3) be represented by counsel; and (4) be given a written statement of the reasons if parole is denied. The State of Nebraska, therefore, gave inmates statutory rights prior to parole revocation. Despite these rights, inmates filed suit, claiming more rights than those provided by Nebraska statute and claiming that their due process rights were being denied. They wanted the same rights given to parolees prior to parole revocation, as given in the case of *Morrissey v. Brewer.*

ISSUES:

1. Does the due process clause of the Fourteenth Amendment apply to discretionary parole release determinations made by the Nebraska Parole Board? NO.
2. If Nebraska inmates are not entitled to due process under the Constitution prior to discretionary parole release determinations, are they nonetheless entitled to due process because of the way the Nebraska law is worded? YES.
3. If the answer to (2) is yes, did the Nebraska law provide for sufficient due process rights? YES.

DECISIONS:

1. The mere possibility of discretionary parole release does not carry with it due process rights under the Constitution, hence inmates are not entitled to due process rights.
2. In the case of the Nebraska inmates, however, they are entitled to due process rights not because of the U.S. Constitution, but because the Nebraska statute is worded so as to create a "liberty interest" that entitles inmates to due process.
3. The rights given to inmates by the Nebraska statute, however, satisfy the due process requirements of the Constitution, thus inmates were afforded proper due process under Nebraska law.

REASONS:

1.   There is no constitutional or inherent right of a convicted person to be conditionally released before the expiration of a valid sentence. The natural desire of an individual to be released is indistinguishable from the initial resistance to being confined. But the conviction, with all its procedural safeguards, has extinguished the liberty right: '[G]iven a valid conviction, the criminal defendant has been constitutionally deprived of his liberty.' *Meachum v. Fano*, 427 U.S. 215, 224 (1976).

"A state may, as Nebraska has, establish a parole system, but it has no duty to do so. Moreover, to insure that the state-created parole system serves the public interest purposes of rehabilitation and deterrence, the state may be specific or general in defining the conditions for release and the factors that should be considered by the parole authority. It is thus not surprising that there is no prescribed or defined combination of facts which, if shown, would mandate release on parole. Indeed, the very institution of parole is still in an experimental stage . . .

"The fallacy in respondent's position is that parole release and parole revocation are quite different. There is a crucial distinction between being deprived of a liberty one has, as in parole, and being denied a conditional liberty that one desires.

"Respondents emphasize that the structure of the [Nebraska] provision together with the use of the word 'shall' binds the Board of Parole to release an inmate unless one of the four specifically designated reasons is found. In their view, the statute creates a presumption that parole release will be granted, and that this in turn creates a legitimate expectation of release absent the requisite finding that one of the justifications for deferral exists.

"We can accept respondents' view that the expectancy of release provided in this statute is entitled to some measure of constitutional protection.

2.   "Here, as we noted previously, the Parole Board's decision is subjective in part and predictive in part. Like most parole statutes, it vests very broad discretion in the Board. No ideal, error-free way to make parole-release decisions has been developed; the whole question has been and will continue to be the subject of experimentation involving analysis of psychological factors combined with fact evaluation guided by the practical experience of the actual parole decision-makers in predicting future behavior. Our system of federalism encourages this state experimentation. If parole determinations are encumbered by procedures that states regard as burdensome and unwarranted, they may abandon or curtail parole.

"At the Board's initial interview hearing, the inmate is permitted to appear before the Board and present letters and statements on his own behalf. He is thereby provided with an effective opportunity first, to insure that the records before the Board are in fact the records relating to his case; and second, to present any special considerations that demonstrate why he is an appropriate candidate for parole. Since the decision is one that must be made largely on the basis of the inmates' files, this procedure adequately safeguards against serious risks of error and thus satisfies due process.

"Next, we find nothing in the due process concepts as they have thus far evolved that requires the Parole Board to specify the particular 'evidence' in the inmate's file or at his interview on which it rests the discretionary determination that an inmate is not ready for conditional release. The Board communicates the reason for its denial as a guide to the inmate for his future behavior."

3.   "The Nebraska procedure affords an opportunity to be heard, and when parole is denied it informs the inmate in what respects he falls short of qualifying for parole; this affords the process that is due under these circumstances. The Constitution does not require more."

CASE SIGNIFICANCE: This case is perhaps the most significant case decided thus far by the Court on parole. The inmates argued that they were entitled to due process rights in the determination to release or not to release an inmate on parole. In the absence of such a constitutional right, they alternatively argued that the provisions of the Nebraska law created such a right.

The Court held that they were not entitled under the Constitution to due process in the decision to release or not to release on parole. Despite this, they were nonetheless entitled to some type of due process because of the wording of the Nebraska law. The way it was worded was such that it established a right (a state-created liberty interest protected by the Fourteenth Amendment) to due process where otherwise none was given by the Constitution. Having said that, however, the Court then held that the rights given under Nebraska law (see the FACTS section above) were sufficient to comply with the due process requirement. In short, the inmates won the battle but lost the war.

The Court in this case laid down three important constitutional principles on the granting or non-granting of parole:

1. "There is no constitutional or inherent right of a convicted person to be conditionally released before the expiration of a valid sentence." Simply stated, parole is a privilege and not a right, and thus may be granted or withheld by the state.

2. "A state may, as Nebraska has, establish a parole system, but it has no duty to do so." This means that parole is optional with the state. If a state wants to abolish parole it may do so without violating the constitutional rights of inmates. Again, parole is a privilege and not a right.

3. "There is a crucial distinction between being deprived of a liberty one has, as in parole, and being denied a conditional liberty one desires." The Court said this in response to inmate claims that parole release should be protected by the same due process rights given to parole revocation in *Morrissey v. Brewer*, 408 U.S. 471 (1972). The Court rejected such claim by articulating the distinction between parole revocation ("being deprived of a liberty one has") and parole release ("being denied a conditional liberty that one desires").

This case also illustrates the concept of the "state-created liberty interest." This is an often-misunderstood concept that essentially means that the constitutional right to due process may be given because of the way in which a state words its law or policy. The concept of the "state-created liberty interest" is best stated this way: "Where the government theoretically has complete discretion in a matter, but chooses, through statute, administrative rule, policy or similar sort of document, to limit its discretion in some way, then the state must follow some sort of procedural steps (due process) to assure that it is making the decision consistent with the limitations it has imposed on itself" (*Legal Responsibility and Authority of Correctional Officers*. American Correctional Association, 1987, at 40).

This case is a good illustration of the "state-created liberty interest" concept because the inmates argued that even if they were not entitled to due process under the Constitution, the way the Nebraska statute was worded created a "protectible expectation of parole." The section of the Nebraska law on which the inmates relied was worded as follows:

> Whenever the Board of Parole considers the release of a committed offender who is eligible for release on parole, it shall order his release unless it is of the opinion that his release should be deferred because:
> (a)   There is a substantial risk that he will not conform to the conditions of parole;
> (b)   His release would depreciate the seriousness of his crime or promote disrespect for law;
> (c)   His release would have a substantially adverse effect on institutional discipline; or
> (d)   His continued correctional treatment, medical care, or vocational or other training in the facility will substantially enhance his capacity to lead a law-abiding life when released at a later date. [Nebraska Revised Statutes, Section 88-1, 114 (1)].

The Court agreed that the above provision, as worded, created a due process right for the inmates, but the Court quickly added that the provisions of the Nebraska law (which gave inmates certain rights at the initial review hearing and the final hearing) complied with due process requirements, hence the inmates did not have any legal basis on which to base their claim of a denial of due process.

Martinez v. California
444 U.S. 275 (1980)

CAPSULE: A state law exempting parole officers from civil liability under state law is valid. The Court did not decide, however, whether that state law can be used to defeat a civil liability claim under Section 1983 (a federal law) against the same state officials.

FACTS: A parolee, Thomas, was convicted of rape in 1969 and sentenced to a term of one to 20 years, with a recommendation that he not be paroled. Prior to being sentenced to prison, Thomas had been committed to a state mental hospital as a "Mentally Disordered Sex Offender not amenable to treatment." After having served only five years, Thomas was paroled to the care of his mother. The California parole authorities were aware of Thomas' history and the likelihood that he would commit another violent crime. Five months after his release, Thomas tortured and killed a 15-year-old girl. The girl's survivors brought suit against state officials seeking damages under state law and 42 U.S.C. §1983, claiming that the state's action in releasing Thomas subjected the deceased to a deprivation of her life without due process of law.

ISSUES:
1. Are parole board officials liable under California law for the death of a person killed by a parolee five months after the parolee's release? NO.

2. Are parole board officials liable under 42 U.S.C. §1983 (a federal law) for the death of a person killed by a parolee five months after the parolee's release? NOT DECIDED.

DECISIONS:
1. Parole officials are not liable under California law for the death because state statute, declared by the Court to be valid, provides that "neither a public entity nor a public employee is liable for any injury resulting from determining whether to parole or release a prisoner or from determining the terms or conditions of his parole or release or from determining whether to revoke his parole or release." Such statute is constitutional and did not deprive the deceased of her right to due process.

2. Parole officials are not liable under federal law either because the action of the parolee, which took place five months after parolee's release, could not be characterized as "state action" (a requirement for liability under federal law).

REASON: "Like the California courts, we cannot accept the contention that this statute deprived Thomas' victim of her life without due process of law because it condoned a parole decision that led indirectly to her death. The statute neither authorized nor immunized the deliberate killing of any human being. It is not the equivalent of a death penalty statute which expressly authorizes state agents to take a person's life after prescribed procedures have been observed. This statute merely provides a defense to potential state tort-law liability. At most, the availability of such a defense may have encouraged members of the parole board to take somewhat greater risks of recidivism in exercising their authority to release prisoners than they otherwise might. But the basic risk that repeat offenses may occur is always present in any parole system. A legislative decision that has an incremental impact on the probability that death will result in any given situation—such as setting the speed limit at 55-miles-per-hour instead of 45—cannot be characterized as state action depriving a person of life just because it may set in motion a chain of events that ultimately leads to the random death of an innocent bystander.

"Appellants contend that the decedent's right to life is protected by the Fourteenth Amendment to the Constitution. But the Fourteenth Amendment protected her only from deprivation by the 'State . . . of life . . . without due process of law.' Although the decision to release Thomas from prison was action by the State, the actions of Thomas five months later cannot be fairly characterized as state action. Regardless of whether, as a matter of state tort law, the parole board could be said either to have had a 'duty' to avoid harm to his victim or to have proximately caused her death, see *Grimm v. Arizona Bd. of Pardons and Paroles*, 115 Ariz. 260, 564 P.2d 1227 (1977); *Palsgraf v. Long Island R. Co.*, 248 N.Y. 339, 162 N.E. 99 (1928), we hold that, taking these particular allegations as true, appellees did not 'deprive' appellants' decedent of life within the meaning of the Fourteenth Amendment.

"Her life was taken by the parolee five months after his release. He was in no sense an agent of the parole board. Cf. *Scheuer v. Rhodes*, 416 U.S. 232. Further, the parole board was not aware that appellants' decedent, as distinguished from the public at large, faced any special danger. We need not and do not decide that a parole officer could never be deemed to 'deprive' someone of life by action taken in connection with the release of a prisoner on parole. But we do hold that at least under the particular circumstances of this parole decision, appellants' decedent's death is too remote a consequence of the parole officers' action to hold them responsible under the federal civil rights law."

CASE SIGNIFICANCE: This is a civil liability case in which the family members of a murder victim sought monetary damages from state officials for their decision to parole a prisoner, alleging that the state officials were aware of the inmate's violent nature prior to release and were directly responsible for the parolee's act.

The Court addressed two issues. The first issue concerned the constitutionality of a state statute that exempts parole officials from liability in job-related decisions. The family members argued that such a law was unconstitutional when applied to defeat a tort claim arising under state law. The Court disagreed, saying that the law, which merely provides a defense to potential state tort law liability, did not deprive the 15-year-old girl of her life without due process of law because it condoned a parole decision that led indirectly to her death. The Court said that the statute was rational "because the California Legislature could reasonably conclude that judicial review of parole decisions 'would inevitably inhibit the exercise of discretion' and that this inhibiting effect could impair the State's ability to implement a parole program designed to promote rehabilitation of inmates as well as security within prisons by holding out a promise of potential rewards."

As to the second issue of possible liability under federal law (42 U.S.C. §1983), the Court did not address that issue head-on, stating instead that "although the decision to release Thomas from prison was action by the State, the action of Thomas five months later cannot be fairly characterized as state action." In view of this, the Court refused to decide whether the victim was deprived of a right secured by the Constitution and laws of the United States (a requirement for recovery under federal law). There are two requirements for a §1983 lawsuit to succeed: (1) the officer must have been acting under color of law (referring to some type of state action or state involvement), and (2) there must have been a violation of a constitutional right or of a right given by federal (not state) law. The action of the parolee here five months after release could not be attributed to the state and thus precluded recovery for damages.

The Court did not decide the issue whether state officials can be shielded from liability under federal law by a state law, such as the above, exempting state officials from liability both under state and federal law. The answer, however, would be that such a state law would not protect state officials from liability under federal law because in case of a conflict between state law (providing exemption from liability) and federal law (holding officials liable), federal law prevails.

Jago v. Van Curen
454 U.S. 14 (1981)

CAPSULE: An inmate does not have a due process right in the decision by a parole board to withdraw parole prior to the inmate's release.

FACTS: Van Curen pleaded guilty to a charge of embezzlement and was sentenced to not less than six nor more than 100 years in prison. Under Ohio law, he would have been eligible for parole in March 1976. In 1974, however, Ohio enacted a "shock parole" statute that provided for the early parole of first-time offenders who had served more than six months in prison for nonviolent offenses. Under this program, Van Curen was interviewed in 1974 by a panel representing the Ohio Adult Parole Authority. This panel recommended that Van Curen be paroled "on or after April 23, 1974." The parole authority approved the recommendation and the inmate was notified of its decision. Several days after Van Curen was interviewed, the Ohio Adult Parole Authority was informed that he had not been truthful during his interview nor in the parole plan that he submitted to his parole officers. Van Curen had told the panel that he had embezzled $1 million when in fact he had embezzled $6 million. In his parole plan, Van Curen stated that he would be living with his half-brother if paroled; it was discovered that Van Curen actually intended to live with his homosexual lover. The parole authorities rescinded the early parole decision as a result of these revelations and, at a later meeting, formally denied Van Curen parole. At no time was Van Curen granted a hearing to explain the false statements he had given the parole authorities. He brought suit against the Ohio Adult Parole Authority, claiming that the rescission of parole without a hearing violated his constitutional right to due process.

ISSUE: Does a parolee have a right to be heard in a parole rescission (withdrawal of parole prior to inmate release) proceeding? NO.

DECISION: The due process clause of the Fourteenth Amendment does not guarantee a hearing on the rescission of parole, nor did the Ohio statute create any protected "liberty" interest in early parole.

REASON: "We do not doubt that respondent suffered 'grievous loss' upon OAPA's rescission of his parole. But we have previously 'reject[ed] . . . the notion that any grievous loss visited upon a person by the State is sufficient to invoke the procedural protections of the Due Process Clause.' In this case, as in our previous cases, '[t]he question is not merely the weight of the individual's interest, but whether the nature of the interest is one within the contemplation of the liberty or property language of the Fourteenth Amendment.' *Morrissey v. Brewer*, 408 U.S. 471, 481 (1972).

"We would severely restrict the necessary flexibility of prison administrators and parole authorities were we to hold that any one of their myriad decisions with respect to individual inmates may, as under the general law of contracts, give rise to protected 'liberty' interests which could not thereafter be impaired without a constitutionally mandated hearing under the Due Process Clause."

CASE SIGNIFICANCE: In the case of *Morrissey v. Brewer*, 408 U.S. 471 (1972), the Court ruled that state parole statutes would have to be examined individually on the question of whether they created a protected "liberty" interest. The Court held that the Ohio statute created no such liberty interest, thus no process was required prior to parole rescission.

Parole decisions in Ohio are solely at the discretion of the state's parole authorities. Van Curen lied to the board during his interview and in the parole plan submitted to his parole officer. The Court ruled that the parole board was within its authority to rescind its earlier decision to parole Van Curen on the basis of his false statements and there were no due process violations in not affording Van Curen a hearing in which he could explain his actions. Van Curen was not entitled to a hearing, either under the Constitution or Ohio law, prior to being released on parole. The fact that he was scheduled for parole, but prior to actual release the board's decision was rescinded because of Van Curen's false statements, did not give Van Curen any constitutional right to a hearing. In effect, the Court said that parole rescission prior to release is not equivalent to parole revocation, in which due process rights must be given because of consequent "grievous loss" of liberty.

It is evident from this decision that the Court considers parole rescission to be in the same legal category as the decision to grant or to not grant parole, rather than the decision to revoke parole.

Connecticut Board of Pardons v. Dumschat
452 U.S. 458 (1981)

CAPSULE: Prior actions of the Board of Pardons in granting commutation of life sentences created no right nor entitlement to commutation. Inmates are not constitutionally entitled to reasons from the Board for rejecting their application for parole or commutation

FACTS: Dumschat was sentenced to life imprisonment for murder in 1964. Under Connecticut law, he was not eligible for parole until December 1983. In Connecticut, the Board of Pardons had authority to commute the sentences of life inmates by reducing the minimum prison term, thus accelerating eligibility for parole. Dumschat applied several times for a commutation of his sentence. The Board rejected each application without explanation. Dumschat sued the Board of Pardons under 42 U.S.C. §1983, alleging that the Board's failure to provide him with a written statement of reasons for denying commutation violated his rights guaranteed by the due process clause of the Fourteenth Amendment. Relying mainly on the fact that in the past the board had granted approximately three-fourths of all applications for commutation of life sentences, the federal district court held that all prisoners serving life sentences in Connecticut state prisons have a constitutionally protected "entitlement" to a statement of reasons why commutation is not granted, if their applications are denied.

ISSUE: Did the fact that the Connecticut Board of Pardons had, in the past, granted approximately three-fourths of the applications for commutation of life sentences create a constitutional "liberty interest" or "entitlement" in life-term inmates so as to require that the board explain its reasons for denying an application for commutation? NO.

DECISION: The mere existence of a power vested in the Connecticut Board of Pardons to commute sentences under state statute and the granting of commuta tion to many inmates confers no right or "entitlement" to inmates beyond the right to seek commutation. The Board did not have to give reasons for denying the applications.

REASON: "In terms of the Due Process Clause, a Connecticut felon's expectation that a lawfully imposed sentence will be commuted or that he will be pardoned is no more substantial than an inmate's expectation, for example, that he will be transferred to another prison; it is simply a unilateral hope.

"The Court of Appeals correctly recognized that Connecticut has conferred 'unfettered discretion' on its Board of Pardons, but—paradoxically—then proceeded to fetter the Board with a halter of constitutional 'entitlement.' The statute imposes no limit on what procedure is to be followed, what evidence may be considered, or what criteria are to be applied by the Board. Respondents challenge the Board's procedure precisely because of 'the absence of any apparent standards.' Brief for Respondents 28. We agree that there are no explicit standards by way of statute, regulation, or otherwise.

"This contrasts dramatically with the Nebraska statutory procedures in *Greenholtz*, which expressly mandated that the Nebraska Board of Parole 'shall' order an inmate's release 'unless' it decided that one of four specified reasons for denial was applicable. 442 U.S., at 11. The Connecticut statute, having no definitions, no criteria, and no mandated 'shalls,' creates no analogous duty or constitutional entitlement."

CASE SIGNIFICANCE: In this case, the inmate argued that the fact that in the past the board had granted approximately three-fourths of all applications for commutation of life sentences meant that a constitutional "entitlement" had been created by such practice so that inmates were now entitled to know the reasons for the rejection of their applications for commutation. The Court disagreed, saying that "no matter how frequently a particular form of clemency has been granted, the statistical probabilities generate no constitutional protections." This means that board or agency practice never rises to the level of a constitutional right and therefore parole boards may engage in release practices without having to be concerned that what they do may create a constitutional right that will limit their actions in the future.

Inmates are not constitutionally entitled either to reasons from the board for rejecting their application for parole or commutation of sentence. This is because the decision to grant parole or commutation is discretionary with the board. Parole is not a right, but is a privilege that may be given or withheld by the state.

California Department of Corrections v. Morales
57 Cr. L. 2021 (1995)

CAPSULE: A law decreasing the frequency of parole hearings for certain prisoners does not change the punishment for crimes already committed and, therefore, may be applied retrospectively without violating the ex post facto clause of the Constitution.

FACTS: Morales was twice convicted of murder, once in 1971 and once in 1980. In 1980, he was sentenced to a term of 15 years to life, but became eligible for parole beginning in 1990. In 1989, he had a hearing before the California Board of Prison Terms to determine his suitability for parole, in accordance with state law. At that time he was found to be unsuitable for parole for numerous reasons.

Under state law at the time Morales committed his second murder, he would have been entitled to subsequent suitability hearings on an annual basis. However, in 1981, the California legislature authorized the Board to defer subsequent suitability hearings for up to three years if the prisoner had been convicted of more than one offense that involved the taking of a life, and the Board found that it was not reasonable to expect that parole would be granted at a hearing during the following years and it stated the bases for the finding. The Board determined the above conditions in Morales' case and scheduled his next hearing for 1992. Morales filed a federal habeas corpus petition in U.S. District Court alleging that he was being held in custody in violation of the ex post facto clause of the Constitution.

ISSUE: Does the 1981 amendment to the California statutes in effect increase the punishment attached to Morales' crime, in violation of the ex post facto clause of the Constitution? NO.

DECISION: Application of the new California parole law to prisoners who committed their crimes before it was enacted does not violate the ex post facto clause of the Constitution.

REASON: "The amendment did not increase the 'punishment' attached to the respondent's crime. It left untouched his indeterminate sentence and the substantive formula for securing any reductions to the sentencing range. By introducing the possibility that the Board would not have to hold another parole hearing in the year or two after the initial hearing, the amendment simply alters the method to be followed in fixing a parole release date under identical substantive standards.

"Under respondent's expansive view, the Clause would forbid any legislative change that has any conceivable risk of affecting a prisoner's punishment. In contrast, this Court has long held that the question of what legislative adjustments are of sufficient moment to transgress the constitutional prohibition must be a matter of degree, and has declined to articulate a single 'formula' for making this determination. There is no need to do so here, either, since the amendment creates only the most speculative and attenuated possibility of increasing the measure of punishment for covered crimes, and such conjectural effects are insufficient under any threshold that might be established under the Clause. This amendment applies only to those who have taken more than one life, a class of prisoners for whom the likelihood of release on parole is quite remote. In addition, it affects the timing only of subsequent hearings, and does so only when the Board makes specific findings in the first hearing. Moreover, the Board has the authority to tailor the frequency of subsequent hearings."

CASE SIGNIFICANCE: This case decided that the new California parole law did not violate the ex post facto clause of the Constitution and therefore may be applied retrospectively. The new law merely altered the former system of mandatory annual parole hearings by providing the following: It "allowed the parole board, after it finds a prisoner unsuitable for parole at his initial hearing, to defer subsequent hearing for up to three years if the prisoner has been convicted of more than one offense involving the taking of life and the board determines that it is not reasonable to expect that the prisoner would be granted parole at a hearing within the intervening period, and the board states its reasons for that determination."

The Court held that this was not an ex post facto law because it merely decreased the frequency of parole hearings for certain prisoners. It did not change the punishment for crimes already committed, which in this case was 15 years to life. The purpose of the law was merely "to relieve the board of the need to conduct futile hearings for prisoners it determined had no reasonable chance for parole." As such, it may be applied retrospectively without running afoul of the ex post facto provision of the Constitution.

Lynce v. Mathis
No. 95-7452 (1997)

CAPSULE: A Florida statute canceling an inmate's provisional release is ex post facto if applied to a prisoner who was convicted before the law was in effect.

FACTS: Lynce was convicted of attempted murder in 1986 and sentenced to 22 years in a Florida prison. He was released in 1992 based on the Department of Corrections' determination that he had accumulated five different types of early release credits totaling 5,668 days, 1,860 of those days were provisional credits given as a result of prison overcrowding.

After the prisoner was released, the Florida State Attorney General issued an opinion that a 1992 statute retroactively canceled all provisional credits awarded to inmates convicted of murder or attempted murder. Lynce was rearrested and returned to custody. He filed a petition for a writ of habeas corpus, alleging that the retroactive cancellation of provisional credits violated the ex post facto clause of the Constitution.

ISSUE: Does the 1992 Florida statute canceling provisional credits for certain classes of offenders after they have been awarded violate the ex post facto clause of the Constitution? YES.

DECISION: The 1992 Florida statute canceling provisional release credits for certain classes of offenders after they have been awarded violates the ex post facto clause of the Constitution.

REASON: "To fall within the ex post facto prohibition, a law must be retrospective—that is, 'it must apply to events occurring before its enactment'—and it 'must disadvantage the offender affected by it' . . . by altering the definition of criminal conduct or increasing the punishment for the crime, see *Collins v. Youngblood*, 497 U.S. 37, 50 (1990). In this case, the operation of the 1992 statute to effect the cancellation of overcrowding credits and the consequent reincarceration of petitioner was clearly retrospective. The narrow issue that we must decide upon is thus whether those consequences disadvantaged petitioner by increasing his punishment.

"Respondents also argue that the retroactive cancellation of overcrowding credits is permissible because overcrowding gain-time—unlike the incentive gain-time at issue in *Weaver,* which is used to encourage good prison behavior and prison rehabilitation—'b[ears] no relationship to the original penalty assigned the crime or the actual penalty calculated under the sentencing guidelines' . . . As we recognized in *Weaver*, retroactive alteration of parole or early release provisions, like the retroactive application of provisions that govern initial sentencing, implicates the ex post facto clause because such credits are 'one determinant of petitioner's prison term . . . and . . . [the petitioner's] effective sentence is altered once this determinant is changed.' *Ibid.* We explained in *Weaver* that the removal of such provisions can constitute an increase in punishment . . .

"In this case, unlike in *Morales*, the actual course of events makes it unnecessary to speculate about what might have happened. The 1992 statute has unquestionably disadvantaged the petitioner because it resulted in his rearrest and prolonged his imprisonment. Unlike the California amendment at issue in *Morales*, the 1992 Florida statute did more than simply remove a mechanism that created an opportunity for early release for a class of prisoners whose release was unlikely; rather, it made ineligible for early release a class of prisoners who were previously eligible—including some, like petitioner, who had actually been released."

CASE SIGNIFICANCE: This case prohibits the retroactive application of laws that disadvantage an inmate when obtaining parole. Parole is a privilege, hence it may be granted or not granted by the state. Once granted, however, it becomes an entitlement, meaning it cannot be taken away without giving the inmate certain basic due process guarantees.

This case addresses a slightly different issue: may a state take away early release credits through a statute that cancels provisional credits awarded to inmates convicted of and already serving time? The Court said no, saying that such a statute violates the ex post facto clause when applied to an inmate who had already earned the credits before the law was passed. The law could be applied to inmates who had not yet earned the credits, but not to inmates who had already earned them.

This case is significant for parole in that it limits the impact of newly enacted restrictive parole laws on inmates. The public has become weary of parole and wants to limit it. That can be done, but any new restrictive law would apply only to inmates who have not as yet earned parole credits. It cannot apply to all inmates in the prison population.

This case differs from *California Department of Corrections v. Morales*, 57 Cr. L. 2021 (1995), in that the *Morales* case merely involved a procedure whereby an inmate was considered for parole by providing that the parole hearing could be deferred for up to three years instead of a mandatory annual parole hearing. *Morales* did not affect the length of the punishment being served. In contrast, in *Lynce,* prison time was in effect extended by the statute that retroactively canceled all provisional credits the inmate had already earned.

Young v. Harper
No. 95-1598 (1997)

CAPSULE: Oklahoma's pre-parole release program was equivalent to parole and therefore released prisoners under pre-parole were entitled to due process rights prior to being brought back to prison.

FACTS: The State of Oklahoma has a Pre-parole Conditional Supervision Program (Pre-parole or Program). That is, when Oklahoma's prisons become overcrowded, the Pardon and Parole Board (Board) is authorized to conditionally release prisoners before the expiration of their sentences. Upon the determination of the Board, an inmate could be placed on pre-parole after serving 15 percent of his sentence. An inmate became eligible for parole only after one-third of his sentence had elapsed. The Governor granted parole on the Board's recommendation. Both Program participants and parolees were released subject to similar constraints. The Board reviewed Harper's criminal record and prison conduct and simultaneously recommended him for parole and released him under the Pre-parole Program. At the time, he had served 15 years of a life sentence. After five months of Pre-parole Program release, the Governor denied Harper's parole. On March 14, 1991, he was ordered by his parole officer to, and did, report back to prison.

ISSUE: Is Oklahoma's Pre-parole Conditional Supervision Program sufficiently like parole to be protected under the Fourteenth Amendment? YES.

DECISION: The Program, as it existed when respondent was released, was equivalent to parole and, therefore was protected under the due process clause of the Fourteenth Amendment.

REASON: " 'The essence of parole is release from prison, before the completion of sentence, on the condition that the prisoner abide by certain rules during the balance of the sentence.' *Morrissey*, 408 U.S., at 477. In *Morrissey*, we described the 'nature of the interest of the parolee in his continued liberty: [H]e can be gainfully employed and is free to be with family and friends and to form the other enduring attachments of normal life. Though the State properly subjects him to many restrictions not applicable to other citizens, his condition is very different from that of confinement in a prison. . . . The parolee has relied on at least an implicit promise that parole will be revoked only if he fails to live up to the parole conditions.'

"This passage could just as easily have applied to respondent while he was on pre-parole. In compliance with state procedures, he was released from prison before the expiration of his sentence. He kept his own residence; he sought, obtained, and maintained a job; and he lived a life generally free from the incidents of imprisonment. To be sure, respondent's liberty was not unlimited. He was not permitted to use alcohol, to incur other than educational debt, or to travel outside the county without permission. And he was required to report regularly to a parole officer. The liberty of a parolee is similarly limited, but that did not in *Morrissey*, 408 U.S., at 478, render such liberty beyond procedural protection."

"Petitioners do not ask us to revisit *Morrissey*; they merely dispute that pre-parole falls within its compass. Our inquiry, they argue, should be controlled instead by *Meachum v. Fano,* 427 U.S. 215 (1976). There, we determined that the interest of a prisoner in avoiding an intrastate prison transfer was 'too ephemeral and insubstantial to trigger procedural due process protections as long as prison officials have discretion to transfer him for whatever reason or for no reason at all.' Petitioners contend that reincarceration of a pre-parolee was nothing more than a transfe[r] to a higher degree of confinement or a 'classification to a more supervised prison environment,' Brief for Petitioners 18, which, like transfers within a prison setting, involved a liberty interest."

CASE SIGNIFICANCE: This case dealt with the issue of whether the pre-parole release program used in the State of Oklahoma to relieve prison over-crowding was equivalent to parole. If so, then inmates who were released under the program were entitled to the procedural protections mandated by the Court in *Morrissey v. Brewer,* 408 U.S. 471 (1972). The Court said yes, holding that due process protections were needed prior to the inmate's being brought back to prison.

In this case, an inmate was released by the Oklahoma Pardon and Parole Board, but was denied parole by the Governor five "uneventful months later." He was ordered back to prison without being given due process rights, the assumption being he was still a prisoner and, technically, was not on parole.

Morrissey v. Brewer, 408 U.S. 471 (1972), provides that the following due process rights be given a parolee before parole is revoked:

1. written notice of the claimed violations of parole;
2. disclosure to the parolee of evidence against him;
3. opportunity to be heard in person and to present witnesses and documentary evidence;
4. the right to confront and cross-examine adverse witnesses;
5. a neutral and detached hearing body; and
6. a written statement by the factfinders as to the evidence relied on and reasons for revoking parole.

The Court concluded that there was no significant difference between pre-parole and parole under Oklahoma procedures, hence pre-parole comes under the *Morrissey* due process requirements.

Chapter 4—Death Penalty

Louisiana ex rel. Francis v. Resweber, 329 U.S. 459 (1947)
Furman v. Georgia, 408 U.S. 238 (1972)
Gregg v. Georgia, 428 U.S. 153 (1976)
Pulley v. Harris, 465 U.S. 37 (1984)
Ford v. Wainwright 106 S. Ct. 2595 (1986)
Lockhart v. McCree, 476 U.S. 162 (1986)
Tison v. Arizona, 481 U.S. 137 (1987)
McCleskey v. Kemp, 481 U.S. 279 (1987)
Sumner v. Shuman, 483 U.S. 66 (1987)
Penry v. Lynaugh, 109 S. Ct. 2934 (1989)
Whitmore v. Arkansas, 58 L.W. 4495 (1991)
Lankford v. Idaho, 59 L.W. 4434 (1990)
Payne v. Tennessee, 59 L.W. 4814 (1991)
Morgan v. Illinois, 60 L.W. 4541 (1992)
Graham v. Collins, 52 Cr. L. 2114 (1993)
Arave v. Creech, 52 Cr. L. 2373 (1993)
Johnson v. Texas, 53 Cr. L. 2257 (1993)
Simmons v. South Carolina, 114 S. Ct. 2187 (1994)
Tuilaepa v. California, 55 Cr. L. 2244 (1994)
Harris v. Alabama, 56 Cr. L. 2152 (1995)

Louisiana ex rel. Francis v. Resweber
329 U.S. 459 (1947)

CAPSULE: The carrying out of an execution after a failed first attempt does not violate the Constitution.

FACTS: Francis was convicted of murder and in 1945 was sentenced to death. Pursuant to a proper death warrant, Francis was placed in the official electric chair of the State of Louisiana and received through his body a current of electricity intended to cause death. The execution attempt failed due to a mechanical defect in the electric chair. Francis was removed from the chair and returned to prison. A new death warrant was issued.

ISSUE: Is the carrying out of the execution of a criminal, after a failed first attempt, a violation of the Constitution? NO.

DECISION: The carrying out of the execution of a convicted murderer, after the first execution attempt failed because of a mechanical defect in the electric chair does not constitute "double jeopardy," nor does it constitute "cruel and unusual punishment" and therefore is not forbidden by the Constitution.

REASON: "As this is a prosecution under state law, so far as double jeopardy is concerned, the *Palko* case is decisive. For we see no difference from a constitutional point of view between a new trial or error of law at the instance of the state that results in a death sentence instead of imprisonment for life and an execution that follows a failure of equipment. When an accident, with no suggestion of malevolence, prevents the consummation of a sentence, the state's subsequent course in the administration of its criminal law is not affected on that account by any requirement of due process under the Fourteenth Amendment. We find no double jeopardy here which can be said to amount to a denial of federal due process in the proposed execution.

"We find nothing in what took place here which amounts to cruel and unusual punishment in the constitutional sense. The case before us does not call for an examination into any punishments except that of death. *See Weems v. United States*, 217 U.S. 349. . . . The traditional humanity of modern Anglo-American law forbids the infliction of unnecessary pain in the execution of the death sentence. Prohibition against the wanton infliction of pain has come into our law from the Bill of Rights of 1688. The identical words appear in our Eighth Amendment. The Fourteenth would prohibit by its due process clause execution by a state in a cruel manner.

"Petitioner's suggestion is that because he once underwent the psychological strain of preparation for electrocution, now to require him to undergo this preparation again subjects him to a lingering or cruel and unusual punishment. Even the fact that petitioner has already been subjected to a current of electricity does not make his subsequent execution any more cruel in the constitutional sense than any other execution. The cruelty against which the Constitution protects a convicted man is cruelty inherent in the method of punishment, not the necessary suffering involved in any method employed to extinguish life humanely. The fact that an unforeseeable accident prevented the prompt consummation of the sentence cannot, it seems to us, add an element of cruelty to a subsequent execution.

"We cannot agree that the hardship imposed upon the petitioner rises to that level of hardship denounced as denial of due process because of cruelty."

CASE SIGNIFICANCE: This was the first case decided by the Supreme Court on the death penalty and it involved bizarre circumstances. The defendant was placed in the electric chair, received a current of electricity intended to cause death, but death did not occur due to a mechanical defect in the electric chair. He was returned to prison and given a new execution date. The defendant objected, claiming that the carrying out of a second execution attempt after a failed first attempt violated his protection from double jeopardy and cruel and unusual punishment.

The Court rejected both objections, holding that "when an accident, with no suggestion of malevolence, prevents the consummation of a sentence, the state's subsequent course in the administration of its criminal law is not affected on that account by any requirement of due process . . ." The Court added that it saw "no difference from a constitutional point of view between a new trial or error of law at the instance of the state that results in a death sentence instead of imprisonment for life and an execution that follows a failure of equipment." This statement refers to a case decided ten years before (*Palko v. Connecticut*, 302 U.S. 319, 1937) which held that the double jeopardy provision of the Fifth Amendment did not (at that time) apply to the states, thus Francis (a defendant in state court) was not protected by the due process guarantee.

As for the allegation of cruel and unusual punishment, the Court did not find the second attempt at execution as constituting a violation of this constitutional protection, saying that "even the fact that the petitioner has already been subjected to a current of electricity does not make his subsequent execution any more cruel in the constitutional sense than any other execution." The Court added that "the cruelty against which the Constitution protects a convicted man is cruelty inherent in the method of punishment, not the necessary suffering involved in any method employed to extinguish life humanely." In sum, the Court said that the taking of life itself does not constitute cruel and unusual punishment; what is prohibited instead is the method of punishment that may be cruel and unusual. It is ironic that the imposition of corporal punishment (such as public whipping) is considered cruel and unusual punishment, while the death penalty is not.

Furman v. Georgia
408 U.S. 238 (1972)

CAPSULE: The death penalty violates the equal protection clause of the Fourteenth Amendment and the prohibition against cruel and unusual punishment and is therefore unconstitutional.

FACTS: Furman attempted to enter a private home at night. He shot and killed the homeowner through a closed door. He was 26 years old and had a sixth-grade education. Prior to trial, Furman was committed to the Georgia Central State Hospital for a psychiatric examination on his plea of insanity. The hospital superintendent reported that the staff diagnosis concluded that "this patient should retain his present diagnosis of Mental Deficiency, Mild to Moderate, with Psychotic Episodes associated with Convulsive Disorder." The physicians added that although Furman was not psychotic at present, he was not capable of cooperating with his counsel in the preparation of his criminal defense and they believed he needed further treatment. The superintendent later amended the report by stating that Furman knew right from wrong and was capable of cooperating with counsel. Furman was tried and found guilty of the murder of the homeowner. A jury sentenced him to death.

ISSUE: Is the death penalty constitutional? NO.

DECISION: The death penalty violates provisions of the Constitution, particularly the "equal protection" clause and the prohibition against "cruel and unusual punishment."

REASON: "In a Nation committed to equal protection of the laws there is no permissible 'caste' aspect of law enforcement. Yet we know that the discretion of judges and juries in imposing the death penalty enables the penalty to be selectively applied, feeding prejudices against the accused if he is poor and despised, lacking political clout, or if he is a member of a suspect or unpopular minority, and saving those who by social position may be in a more protected position. In ancient Hindu law a Brahman was exempt from capital punishment, and in those days, '[g]enerally, in the law books, punishment increased in severity as social status diminished.' We have, I fear, taken in practice the same position, partially as a result of making the death penalty discretionary and partially as a result of the ability of the rich to purchase the services of the most respected and resourceful legal talent in the Nation.

"There are, then, four principles by which we may determine whether a particular punishment is 'cruel and unusual.' The primary principle, which I believe supplies the essential predicate for the application of the others, is that a punishment must not by its severity be degrading to human dignity. The paradigm violation of this principle would be the infliction of a tortuous punishment of the type that the Clause has always prohibited. Yet '[i]t is unlikely that any State at this moment in history,' *Robinson v. California*, 370 U.S., at 666, would pass a law providing for the infliction of such a punishment. Indeed, no such punishment has ever been before this Court. The same may be said of the other principles. It is unlikely that this Court will confront a severe punishment that is obviously inflicted in wholly arbitrary fashion; no State would engage in a reign of blind terror. Nor is it likely that this Court will be called upon to review a severe punishment that is clearly and totally rejected throughout society; no legislature would be able even to authorize the infliction of such a punishment. Nor, finally, is it likely that this Court will have to consider a severe punishment that is patently unnecessary; no State today would inflict a severe punishment knowing that there is no reason whatever for doing so. In short, we are unlikely to have occasion to determine that a punishment is fatally offensive under any one principle.

"In sum, the punishment of death is inconsistent with all four principles: Death is an unusually severe and degrading punishment; there is a strong probability that it is inflicted arbitrarily; its rejection by contemporary society is virtually total; and there is no reason to believe that it serves any penal purpose more effectively than the less severe punishment of imprisonment. The function of these principles is to enable a court to determine whether a punishment comports with human dignity. Death, quite simply, does not."

CASE SIGNIFICANCE: For the first time, the Court in *Furman v. Georgia* declared the death penalty unconstitutional, based on two constitutional provisions: the equal protection clause and the prohibition against cruel and unusual punishment. Had the five justices based their decision solely on a violation of the cruel and unusual punishment clause, the death penalty could never have been imposed. Only two justices, however (Brennan and Marshall), used this argument, while the three others based their decision on the manner in which death penalties were being implemented. Their objection was not to the death penalty itself but to the way it was being selectively enforced to discriminate against the poor and the powerless, thus violating the equal protection clause.

After the *Furman* decision, 35 states and the federal government revised their capital punishment statutes to eliminate equal protection problems. The revised statutes fell into two categories: those that made the death penalty mandatory for certain crimes and those that allowed the judge or jury to decide, under legislative guidelines, whether to impose the death penalty. Every state statute that carried the death penalty had to undergo review by the United States Supreme Court in a proper case to determine whether the revision removed equal protection (or procedural) problems. The stage was therefore set for *Gregg v. Georgia*, decided in 1976, in which the Court said that the death penalty was not *per se* cruel and unusual punishment and could be imposed if there were safeguards against arbitrary and capricious imposition.

Gregg v. Georgia
428 U.S. 153 (1976)

CAPSULE: **Death penalty statutes that contain sufficient safeguards against arbitrary and capricious imposition are constitutional.**

FACTS: Gregg and a companion were picked up by two motorists while hitchhiking in Florida. The bodies of the two motorists were later found beside a road near Atlanta, Georgia. The next day Gregg and his companion were arrested. A .25 caliber pistol was found in Gregg's possession and subsequently identified as the murder weapon. Gregg confessed to the robberies and murders but claimed self-defense. He was found guilty of all four counts and was sentenced to death.

The Georgia death penalty statute had the following features: (1) a bifurcated trial; (2) instructions from the judge to the jury on what penalties they could recommend; (3) consideration of mitigating and aggravating factors, of which they must agree that at least one aggravating factor exists if they wish to recommend death; and (4) an automatic appeal to the Georgia Supreme Court. Moreover, the Georgia Supreme Court was required to review each death sentence for evidence of passion, prejudice, or any other arbitrary factor; whether the evidence supports the finding of an aggravating circumstance; and whether the death penalty "is excessive or disproportionate to the penalty imposed in similar cases, considering both the crime and the defendant."

ISSUES:
1. Is the death penalty constitutional as a form of punishment? YES.
2. If the death penalty is constitutional, does the Georgia statute contain sufficient safeguards against arbitrary and capricious imposition? YES.

DECISIONS:
1. The death penalty is constitutional as a form of punishment.

2.   The Georgia law is constitutional because it contains sufficient safeguards against arbitrary and capricious imposition.

REASON: "Four years ago, the petitioners in *Furman* and its companion cases predicated their argument primarily upon the asserted proposition that standards of decency had evolved to the point where capital punishment no longer could be tolerated. The petitioners in those cases said, in effect, that the evolutionary process had come to an end, and that standards of decency required that the Eighth Amendment be construed finally as prohibiting capital punishment for any crime regardless of its depravity and impact on society. This view was accepted by two Justices. Three other Justices were unwilling to go so far; focusing on the procedures by which convicted defendants were selected for the death penalty rather than on the actual punishment inflicted, they joined in the conclusion that the statutes before the Court were constitutionally invalid.

"The petitioners in the capital cases before the Court today renew the 'standards of decency' argument, but developments during the four years since *Furman* have undercut substantially the assumptions upon which their argument rested. Despite the continuing debate, dating back to the nineteenth century, over the morality and utility of capital punishment, it is now evident that a large proportion of American society continues to regard it as an appropriate and necessary sanction.

"While *Furman* did not hold that the infliction of the death penalty per se violates the Constitution's ban on cruel and unusual punishments, it did recognize that the penalty of death is different in kind from any other punishment imposed under our system of criminal justice. Because of the uniqueness of the death penalty, *Furman* held that it could not be imposed under sentencing procedures that created a substantial risk that it would be inflicted in an arbitrary and capricious manner.

"The basic concerns of *Furman* centered on those defendants who were condemned to death capriciously and arbitrarily. Under the procedures before the Court in that case, sentencing authorities were not directed to give attention to the nature of the circumstances of the crime committed or the character or record of the defendant. Left unguided, juries imposed the death sentence in a way that could only be called freakish. The new Georgia sentencing procedures, by contrast, focus the jury's attention on the particularized nature of the crime and the particularized characteristics of the individual defendant. While the jury is permitted to consider any aggravating or mitigating circumstances, it must find and identify at least one statutory aggravating factor before it may impose a penalty of death. In this way the jury's discretion is channeled. No longer can a jury wantonly and freakishly impose the death sentence; it is always circumscribed by the legislative guidelines. In addition, the review function of the Supreme Court of Georgia affords additional assurance that the concerns that prompted our decision in *Furman* are not present to any significant degree in the Georgia procedure applied here."

CASE SIGNIFICANCE: *Gregg v. Georgia* is the most important case thus far decided by the Supreme Court on the death penalty. For the first time, a majority of the Court said that the death penalty is not *per se* unconstitutional and may therefore be imposed and carried out. *Gregg v. Georgia* therefore overrules *Furman v. Georgia*. This did not mean, however, that the statutes in the various states were automatically declared constitutional and that executions could commence. What it meant was that the Court could now examine each statute in an appropriate case to determine whether its provisions contained guarantees against arbitrary and capricious imposition.

In the years since *Gregg*, the Court has decided many cases upholding the constitutionality of various state statutes. As a result, executions have been undertaken in a number of states. Although there are many prisoners on death row, only a small number have been executed. The explanation may be twofold. First, there is hesitation by the public to carry out the death penalty despite its availability. It is easy to leave that ultimate penalty in our penal codes; it is difficult to implement it. Second, numerous appeals are available to capital offenders. This frustrates the public, which feels that justice is not served by repeated delays. There is no simple solution to the problem, except to realize that the wheels of justice usually turn slowly in a civilized and constitutional society, particularly when a life and death decision is involved.

Pulley v. Harris
465 U.S. 37 (1984)

CAPSULE: Proportionality review is not required in death penalty cases.

FACTS: Harris was convicted of capital murder in a California court. In a separate sentencing hearing, the jury found several aggravating factors and sentenced him to death. Harris challenged the sentence, claiming that the California capital punishment statute was unconstitutional because it failed to require the California Supreme Court to compare Harris' sentence with the sentences imposed in similar capital cases to determine if the sentence was proportionate.

ISSUE: In death penalty cases, does the Eighth Amendment require a state appellate court to compare the sentence in the case before it with the penalties imposed in similar cases? NO.

DECISION: The Eighth Amendment does not require, as an invariable rule in every case, that a state appellate court, before it affirms a death sentence, compare the sentence in the case before it with the sentence imposed in similar cases even if asked to do so by the prisoner.

REASON: "At the outset, we should more clearly identify the issue before us. Traditionally, 'proportionality' has been used with reference to an abstract evaluation of the appropriateness of a sentence for a particular crime. Looking to the gravity of the offense and the severity of the penalty, to sentences imposed for other crimes, and to sentencing practices in other jurisdictions, this Court has occasionally struck down punishments as inherently disproportionate, and therefore cruel and unusual, when imposed for a particular crime or category of crime. The death penalty is not in all cases a disproportionate penalty in this sense.

"In *Gregg*, six Justices concluded that the Georgia system adequately directed and limited the jury's discretion. The bifurcated proceedings, the limited number of capital crimes, the requirement that at least one aggravating circumstance be present, and the consideration of mitigating circumstances minimized the risk of wholly arbitrary, capricious, or freakish sentences. In the opinion announcing the judgment of the Court, three Justices concluded that sentencing discretion under the statute was sufficiently controlled by clear and objective standards. In a separate concurrence, three other Justices found sufficient reason to expect that the death penalty would not be imposed so wantonly, freakishly, or infrequently as to be invalid under *Furman*.

"Both opinions made much of the statutorily required comparative proportionality review. This was considered an additional safeguard against arbitrary or capricious sentencing. While the opinion of Justices Stewart, Powell, and Stevens suggests that some form of meaningful appellate review is required, those Justices did not declare that comparative review was so critical that without it the Georgia statute would not have passed constitutional muster.

"Any capital sentencing scheme may occasionally produce aberrational outcomes. Such inconsistencies are a far cry from the major systemic defects identified in *Furman*. As we have acknowledged in the past, 'there can be "no perfect procedure for deciding in which cases governmental authority should be used to impose death."' As we are presently informed, we cannot say that the California procedures provided Harris inadequate protection against the evil identified in *Furman*. The Court of Appeals therefore erred in ordering the writ of habeas corpus to issue."

CASE SIGNIFICANCE: The Supreme Court ruled in this case that state appellate courts are not constitutionally required to provide, upon request by the defendant, a "proportionality review" of death sentences in which the court would compare the sentence in the case before it with penalties imposed in similar cases in that state. Proportionality reviews are constitutional and are provided for by law or judicial practice in some states, but such reviews are not required by the Constitution. For example, the Court found the Texas death penalty statute to be constitutional even though neither the law nor judicial practice provide for any form of proportionality review. The Court did not completely close the door to a proportionality review, however, in some extreme cases. It said: "assuming that there could be a capital sentencing scheme so lacking in other checks or arbitrariness that it could not pass constitutional muster without comparative proportional review, the California statute involved here is not of that sort."

Ford v. Wainwright
106 S. Ct. 2595 (1986)

CAPSULE: An insane prisoner may not be executed.

FACTS: In 1974, Ford was found guilty of murder and sentenced to death. At no time during the commission of the offense, at his trial, or at sentencing, did Ford show signs of incompetency. Beginning in 1982, however, Ford exhibited incompetent behavior that rendered him incapable of communication.

Ford was seen separately by two psychologists over an extended period. He was diagnosed as suffering from "a severe, uncontrollable, mental disease which closely resembles 'Paranoid Schizophrenia with Suicide Potential,' " a mental disorder that would substantially limit Ford's ability to act in his own defense. Ford later regressed so severely that he could only communicate in an incomprehensible code.

The governor appointed three psychologists to determine whether Ford had the mental capacity to understand the death penalty and why it had been imposed on him. The psychologists spent 30 minutes with Ford and, although each of them concluded that Ford suffered from a mental disorder, all three agreed he was sane as defined by state law. Based on these reports and with no consideration of the opinions of the two previous psychologists, the governor signed a death warrant for Ford's execution.

ISSUES:
1. Does the Eighth Amendment prohibit the execution of a prisoner who is insane at the time of the scheduled execution? YES.
2. Are the procedures used by the State of Florida to determine the sanity of a person who is to be executed adequate? NO.

DECISIONS:
1. The Eighth Amendment prohibits a state from carrying out a sentence of death upon a prisoner who is insane.
2. Florida's procedures for determining the sanity of a person who has been sentenced to death are not "adequate to afford a full and fair hearing;" therefore, an evidentiary hearing to determine competency must be granted.

REASONS:
1. "The reasons at common law for not condoning the execution of the insane—that such an execution has questionable retributive value, presents no example to others and thus has no deterrence value, and simply offends humanity—have no less logical, moral, and practical force at present. Whether the aim is to protect the condemned from fear and pain without comfort of understanding, or to protect the dignity of society itself from the barbarity of exacting mindless vengeance, the restriction finds enforcement in the Eighth Amendment.
2. "The first defect in Florida's procedure is the failure to include the prisoner in the truth-seeking process. Any procedure that precludes the prisoner or his counsel from presenting material relevant to his sanity or bars consideration of that material by the factfinder is necessarily inadequate. A related flaw in the procedures is the denial of any opportunity to challenge or impeach the state-appointed psychiatrist's opinions, thus creating a significant possibility that the ultimate decision made in reliance on those experts will be distorted. And perhaps the most striking defect in the procedures is the placement of the ultimate decision wholly within the Executive Branch. The Governor, who appoints the experts and ultimately decides whether the State will be able to carry out the death sentence and whose subordinates have been responsible for initiating every stage of the prosecution, cannot be said to have the neutrality that is necessary for reliability in the factfinding proceedings."

CASE SIGNIFICANCE: In this case, the defendant was sane at the time of the commission of the offense, but later became insane. It therefore raises a different issue from that of insanity at the time of the commission of the crime. The rule is that a defendant is not guilty if he or she was insane at the time the crime was committed. What if the person is insane at the time of the trial? Courts have said that competence to stand trial is necessary before a defendant can be tried. This case goes a step beyond that, raising the issue of whether a defendant who was sane when the crime was committed can be executed if he or she later becomes insane.

The Court decided that an insane person cannot be executed. This raises interesting questions, such as: Why is it cruel and unusual punishment to execute an insane person (who presumedly does not know what is happening and therefore is not as traumatized) and not cruel and unusual punishment to execute a sane person? Should a psychiatrist or psychologist help restore the defendant to sanity so he or she can be executed? Who determines whether a person is "sane enough" to be executed? The latter question was raised in this case. The Court said that this determination is to be made by the court, giving the defendant an opportunity to present his or her side, and not solely by the Governor or prison officials.

Lockhart v. McCree
476 U.S. 162 (1986)

CAPSULE: Prospective jurors opposed to the death penalty may be disqualified.

FACTS: McCree was charged with capital felony murder. He was arrested when found driving a car that matched an eyewitness' description of a vehicle seen driving away from a gift shop/gas station where a robbery and murder of the owner had just taken place. McCree admitted to being in the shop at the time of the murder but claimed that a stranger had done the killing, using McCree's rifle. McCree said that the stranger then rode in McCree's car for a short time, got out, and walked away with the rifle. This story was refuted by eyewitnesses who had seen only one person in the car during the time in which McCree claimed he had a passenger. The rifle was located and ballistic tests identified it as the murder weapon.

During jury selection in McCree's trial, the judge removed for cause prospective jurors who stated that they could not vote for the imposition of the death penalty under any circumstances. The jury convicted McCree of capital felony murder but did not impose the death penalty as the state had requested. Instead, McCree was given life imprisonment without parole.

ISSUE: Does the Constitution allow the removal for cause, during the guilt phase of a capital trial, of prospective jurors whose opposition to the death penalty is so great as to substantially impair their performance as jurors at the sentencing phase of the trial? YES.

DECISION: Prospective jurors, whose opposition to the death penalty is so strong as to prevent or impair the performance of their duties as jurors at the sentencing phase of a trial, may be removed for cause from jury membership during the guilt phase of the trial, and not just during the sentencing phase.

REASON: " 'Death qualification' of a jury does not violate the fair cross-section requirement of the Sixth Amendment, which applies to jury panels or venires but does not require that petit juries actually chosen reflect the composition of the community at large. Even if the requirement were extended to petit juries, the essence of a fair cross-section claim is the systematic exclusion of a 'distinctive group' in the community—such as blacks, women, and Mexican-Americans—for reasons completely unrelated to the ability of members of the group to serve as jurors in a particular case. Groups defined solely in terms of shared attitudes that would prevent or substantially impair members of the group from performing one of their duties as jurors, such as the 'Witherspoon-excludables' at issue here, are not 'distinctive groups' for fair cross-section purposes. 'Death qualification' is carefully designed to serve the State's legitimate interest in obtaining a single jury that can properly and impartially apply the law to the facts of the case at both the guilt and sentencing phases of a capital trial."

CASE SIGNIFICANCE: All states that impose the death penalty use a two-step procedure: the guilt stage and, if guilty, the sentencing stage. In an earlier case, *Witherspoon v. Illinois*, 391 U.S. 510 (1968), the Supreme Court said that in choosing juries for sentencing (as opposed to determining guilt) defendants in capital cases, prosecutors may exclude for cause potential jurors who say they are unwilling to vote for a death sentence under any circumstance. This means that a juror who says he or she is unwilling to vote for the death sentence under any circumstance could not be excluded from the guilt stage, but could be excluded from the sentencing stage. This case goes further by saying that prospective jurors whose opposition to capital punishment is so strong as to lead them to say that they would never vote for imposing the death penalty may now be excluded not only from the sentencing stage but from the guilt stage as well. Note, however, that prospective jurors cannot be rejected from either stage merely because they are opposed to the death penalty. To be disqualified, these jurors must indicate that they would automatically vote against the death penalty irrespective of the facts of the case.

Tison v. Arizona
481 U.S. 137 (1987)

CAPSULE: The death penalty may be imposed on defendants who did not specifically intend to kill their victims.

FACTS: Brothers Ricky and Raymond Tison, along with other family members, planned and effected the escape of their father from a prison where he was serving a life sentence. Ricky and Raymond Tison entered the prison with an ice chest filled with guns, and armed their father and another convicted murderer. They later helped to abduct, detain, and rob a family of four, and watched their father and the other convict murder the members of that family with shotguns. Although the brothers later stated they were surprised by the killings, neither of them attempted to help the victims. Instead, they drove away in the victim's car along with the rest of the escape party. Ricky and Raymond Tison received the death penalty under Arizona's felony-murder and accomplice liability statutes. They appealed their death sentences, alleging that the Supreme Court decision in *Enmund v. Florida*, 458 U.S. 782 (1982) required reversal of their sentences because they were merely accomplices and not principals.

ISSUE: Is imposition of the death penalty on defendants who did not specifically intend to kill the victims or inflict the fatal wounds constitutional? YES.

DECISION: Defendants who took part in a felony-murder, but did not themselves intend to kill or commit the specific act leading to that result, may nonetheless be sentenced to death as long as their participation in the felony was major and their mental state was one of reckless indifference to the value of human life.

REASON: "Petitioners argue strenuously that they did not 'intend to kill' as that concept has been generally understood in the common law. We accept this as true. Traditionally, 'one intends certain consequences when he desires that his acts cause those consequences or knows that those consequences are substantially certain to result from his acts.' As petitioners point out, there is no evidence that either Ricky or Raymond Tison took any act which he desired to, or was substantially certain would, cause death.

"On the other hand, it is equally clear that petitioners also fall outside the category of felony murderers for whom *Enmund* explicitly held the death penalty disproportional: their degree of participation in the crimes was major rather than minor, and the record would support a finding of the culpable mental state of reckless indifference to human life.

"The issue raised by this case is whether the Eighth Amendment prohibits the death penalty in the intermediate case of the defendant whose participation is major and whose mental state is one of reckless indifference to the value of human life. *Enmund* does not specifically address this point.

"Like the *Enmund* Court, we find the state legislatures' judgment as to proportionality in these circumstances relevant to this constitutional inquiry. The largest number of States still fall into the intermediate categories discussed in

Enmund. Four States authorize the death penalty in felony-murder cases upon a showing of culpable mental state such as recklessness or extreme indifference to human life. Two jurisdictions require that the defendant's participation be substantial and the statutes of at least six more, including Arizona, take minor participation in the felony expressly into account in mitigation of the murder. These requirements significantly overlap both in this case and in general, for the greater the defendant's participation in the felony-murder, the more likely that he acted with reckless indifference to human life. At a minimum, however, it can be said that all these jurisdictions, as well as six States which *Enmund* classified along with Florida as permitting capital punishment for felony-murder *simpliciter*, and the three States which simply require some additional aggravation before imposing the death penalty upon a felony-murder, specifically authorize the death penalty in a felony-murder case where, though the defendant's mental state fell short of intent to kill, the defendant was a major actor in a felony in which he knew death was highly likely to occur."

CASE SIGNIFICANCE: The *Enmund* Court ruled that accomplices to a crime who participated in a minor role and had no prior knowledge that lethal force might be used in the commission of a felony could not be held responsible for that lethal force. It held that the punishment of death in such a case is disproportionate to the crime and thus is prohibited by the Eighth Amendment. The Tison brothers attempted to use that ruling to overturn their death sentences, claiming that the death penalty was disproportionate for their participation in the crime committed. The Court disagreed and concluded that the Tison brothers played a major role in the killing of four family members and that their actions during the commission of the crime also suggested a reckless indifference to life. Based on these findings the Court stated that it could not find fault with the sentences handed down by the trial court and that a survey of other state procedures in similar cases showed that society was also in agreement with severe punishments for accomplices who actively participated in violent crimes.

McCleskey v. Kemp
481 U.S. 279 (1987)

CAPSULE: **A statistical study suggesting racial discrimination in the imposition of death sentences does not make the sentence unconstitutional.**

FACTS: In 1978, McCleskey, a black man, was found guilty of the robbery of a store and the murder of a white police officer. After considering mitigating and aggravating circumstances, the jury imposed the death penalty.

McCleskey claimed that the Georgia capital-sentencing process was racially discriminatory, based on a statistical study (known as the Baldus study) that suggested that there was a disparity in the imposition of the death penalty in Georgia. The study indicates that black defendants who kill white victims have the greatest likelihood of receiving a death sentence.

ISSUE: Does a statistical study suggesting that racial considerations enter into capital sentencing determinations prove that Georgia's capital sentencing procedures are arbitrary, capricious, and in violation of the equal protection clause? NO.

DECISION: A statistical study suggesting that racial considerations enter into capital sentencing in Georgia does not establish racial discrimination or that the death sentence is applied in an arbitrary or capricious manner.

REASON: "To prevail under that Clause, petitioner must prove that the decisionmakers in his case acted with discriminatory purpose. Petitioner offered no evidence specific to his own case that would support an inference that racial considerations played a part in his sentence, and the Baldus study is insufficient to support an inference that any of the decisionmakers in his case acted with discriminatory purpose. This Court has accepted statistics as proof of intent to discriminate in the context of a State's selection of the jury venire and in the context of statutory violations under Title VII of the Civil Rights Act of 1964. However, the nature of the capital sentencing decision and the relationship of the statistics to that decision are fundamentally different from the corresponding elements in the venire-selection or Title VII cases. Petitioner's statistical proffer must be viewed in the context of his challenge to decisions at the heart of the State's criminal justice system. Because discretion is essential to the criminal justice process, exceptionally clear proof is required before this Court will infer that the discretion has been abused.

"There is no merit to petitioner's argument that the Baldus study proves that the State has violated the Equal Protection Clause by adopting the capital punishment statute and allowing it to remain in force despite its allegedly discriminatory application. For this claim to prevail, petitioner would have to prove that the Georgia Legislature enacted or maintained the death penalty statute because of an anticipated racially discriminatory effect. There is no evidence that the legislature either enacted the statute to further a racially discriminatory purpose, or maintained the statute because of the racially disportionate impact suggested by the Baldus study."

CASE SIGNIFICANCE: This case declares that in death penalty cases, statistical studies showing discrimination in the imposition of the penalty do not in themselves prove that the state has violated the equal protection clause of the Constitution. In order for a claim of discrimination to succeed, "petitioner must prove that decisionmakers in his case acted with discriminatory purpose." It is not enough to allege and prove through statistical study that a particular race has been discriminated against; the person alleging discrimination must prove that there was discrimination in his or her particular case.

The Court said that discretion is essential in criminal justice and that "exceptionally clear proof is required before this Court will infer that the discretion has been abused." That was not proved in this case. All the defendant proved was that there was discrimination against blacks in the imposition of the death penalty in Georgia, not that discretion was clearly abused. The Court added that defendant's claim, taken to its logical conclusion, "throws into serious question the principles that underlie the entire criminal justice system." Were the defendant to prevail, his claim could be extended "to apply to other types of penalties and to claims based on unexplained discrepancies correlating to membership in other minority groups and even to gender." Absolute parity in sentences is not required by the Constitution. What the Constitution prohibits is abuse of discretion that amounts to a violation of the equal protection clause.

Sumner v. Shuman
483 U.S. 66 (1987)

CAPSULE: A mandatory death penalty for inmates convicted of murder while in prison is unconstitutional.

FACTS: In 1958, Shuman was convicted of first-degree murder. He had been charged in the shooting death of a truck driver during a roadside robbery. Nevada statute provided the jury, in cases of first-degree murder, with sentencing options of the death penalty or life imprisonment with or without the possibility of parole. Shuman was sentenced to life imprisonment without possibility of parole.

In 1975, while incarcerated, Shuman was convicted of capital murder for the killing of another inmate. Under the revised Nevada law, Shuman's conviction mandated that he receive the death penalty.

ISSUE: Does a statute that requires the death penalty for a prison inmate who is convicted of murder while serving a life sentence constitute cruel and unusual punishment, in violation of the Eighth Amendment? YES.

DECISION: A mandatory death sentence for a prison inmate who is convicted of murder while serving a life sentence is unconstitutional. The sentencing authority must consider mitigating factors relating to the defendant and the offense.

REASON: "Under the individualized capital-sentencing doctrine, it is constitutionally required that the sentencing authority consider, as a mitigating factor, any aspect of the defendant's character or record and any circumstances of the particular offense.

"A statute that mandates the death penalty for a prison inmate who is convicted of murder while serving a life sentence without possibility of parole violates the Eighth and Fourteenth Amendments."

CASE SIGNIFICANCE: This case reiterates the Court's decision in *Gregg v. Georgia*, 428 U.S. 153 (1976), which states that mitigating circumstances must be taken into account to determine whether a defendant deserves the death penalty. The Court feels that this requirement minimizes, and in some cases eliminates, arbitrary and capricious imposition of the death penalty. Taken together, these two decisions declare unconstitutional any statute that automatically imposes the death penalty. States may impose the death penalty, but must require that surrounding circumstances be considered in imposing the penalty. Regardless of the gravity of the offense, automatic imposition of the death penalty without consideration of these circumstances will be declared unconstitutional by the Supreme Court. Judges must instruct the jury, during the sentencing stage, that mitigating circumstances, if any, must be considered in deciding whether to impose death or life imprisonment on a person convicted of a capital offense.

Penry v. Lynaugh
109 S. Ct. 2934 (1989)

CAPSULE: A mentally retarded defendant may be given the death penalty.

FACTS: Penry was charged with capital murder in Texas state court. He raised the insanity defense. Evidence during the trial showed that Penry had an IQ of 54 and the mental age of six and one-half years. He also had the social maturity of a nine- or 10-year-old. He was 22 years old at the time the crime was committed. The jury found Penry competent to stand trial and he was found guilty.

Texas law provides that during the penalty phase of a capital trial, the jury must consider three special issues: (1) whether petitioner's conduct was committed deliberately and with the reasonable expectation that death would result; (2) whether there was a probability that he would be a continuing threat to society; and (3) whether the killing was unreasonable in response to any provocation by the victim. A request by Penry for specific jury instructions defining the terms used in the special issues and a grant of mercy based on the existence of mitigating circumstances was rejected. The jury answered "yes" to all of the special issues and, as required by Texas law, Penry was sentenced to death.

ISSUES:
1.   Does the Constitution prohibit the execution of a person who is mentally retarded? NO.
2.   Should the jury be instructed, upon request, to consider mental retardation as a mitigating circumstance during the sentencing stage of a death penalty case? YES.

DECISIONS:
1.   The execution of a mentally retarded person who has the ability to reason is not cruel and unusual punishment.
2.   When a request is made by the defense to instruct the jury concerning the mitigating evidence of mental retardation and child abuse, the request must be granted.

REASON: "The Eighth Amendment's categorical prohibition upon the infliction of cruel and unusual punishment applies to practices condemned by the common law at the time the Bill of Rights was adopted, as well as to punishments which offend our society's evolving standards of decency as expressed in objective evidence of legislative enactments and the conduct of sentencing juries. Since the common law prohibited the punishment of 'idiots'—which term was generally used to describe persons totally lacking in reason, understanding, or the ability to distinguish between good and evil—it may indeed be 'cruel and unusual punishment' to execute persons who are profoundly or severely retarded and wholly lacking in the capacity to appreciate the wrongfulness of their actions. Such persons, however, are not likely to be convicted or face the prospect of punishment today, since the modern insanity defense generally includes 'mental defect' as part of the legal definition of insanity, and since *Ford v. Wainright, supra,* prohibits the execution of persons who are unaware of their punishment and why they must suffer it. Moreover, petitioner is not such a person, since the jury (1) found him competent to stand trial and therefore to have a rational as well as factual understanding of the proceedings; and (2) rejected his insanity defense, thereby reflecting the conclusion that he knew his conduct was wrong and was capable of conforming it to the requirements of law. Nor is there sufficient objective evidence today of a national consensus against executing mentally retarded capital murderers, since petitioner has cited only one state statute that explicitly bans that practice and has offered no evidence of the general behavior of juries in this regard. Opinion surveys indicating strong public opposition to such executions do not establish a social consensus, absent some legislative reflection of the sentiment expressed therein.

"Mental retardation is a factor that may well lessen a defendant's culpability for a capital offense. But we cannot conclude today that the Eighth Amendment precludes the execution of any mentally retarded person of Penry's ability convicted of a capital offense simply by virtue of their mental retardation alone. So long as sentencers can consider and give effect to mitigating evidence of mental retardation in imposing sentence, an individualized determination of whether 'death is an appropriate punishment' can be made in each particular case."

CASE SIGNIFICANCE: In *Thompson v. Oklahoma*, 487 U.S. 815 (1988), the Court held that the execution of a person who was under the age of 16 at the time of the commission of the offense constituted cruel and unusual punishment. In *Stanford v. Kentucky*, 109 S. Ct. 2969 (1988), the Court held that the death penalty was not cruel and unusual punishment for an offender who committed murder at age 16 or 17. The issue in the *Penry* case was different: whether a mentally retarded offender can be sentenced to death. The Court answered in the affirmative, stating that, "The Eighth Amendment does not categorically prohibit the execution of mentally retarded capital murderers of petitioner's reasoning ability."

Despite this ruling, Penry's life was spared because the judge did not instruct the jury that it could consider and give effect to Penry's mitigating evidence of mental retardation and abuse, hence depriving the jury of a vehicle for expressing its "reasoned moral response" to these circumstances. In this case, although the defendant's lawyer was permitted to introduce and argue the significance of this mitigating evidence to the jury, the judge's instruction to the jury did not permit the jury to give effect to the evidence in answering the three special issues. In sum, the *Penry* case says that mentally retarded capital offenders can be sentenced to death as long as the jury is instructed to consider evidence of mental retardation and an abused background during the sentencing phase of the case.

Whitmore v. Arkansas
58 L.W. 4495 (1990)

CAPSULE: A third party cannot challenge the validity of a death sentence.

FACTS: Ronald Gene Simmons was convicted of capital murder and sentenced to death on two separate occasions for two separate sets of criminal charges. In both instances, Simmons made a statement under oath that he wanted no action taken on his behalf to appeal or in any way change the sentences. In both cases, the trial court conducted a hearing concerning Simmons' competence to waive further proceedings, and concluded that his decision was knowing and intelligent. Arkansas law does not require a mandatory appeal in all death penalty cases. Whitmore, another death row inmate in Arkansas, however, intervened in the case both individually and as "next friend" of Simmons and sought to appeal the conviction and sentence.

ISSUE: Does a third party have standing to challenge the validity of a death sentence imposed on a defendant who elected to forgo his right of appeal? NO.

DECISION: A state death row inmate lacks standing, either in a personal capacity or as "next friend," to seek review by the U.S. Supreme Court of a death sentence imposed upon a fellow inmate who has knowingly, intelligently, and voluntarily waived the right to pursue an appeal.

REASON: "Petitioner Whitmore asks this Court to hold that despite Simmons' failure to appeal, the Eighth and Fourteenth Amendments require the State of Arkansas to conduct an appellate review of his conviction and sentence before it can proceed to execute him. It is well established, however, that before a federal court can consider the merits of a legal claim, the person seeking to invoke the jurisdiction of the court must establish the requisite standing to sue. Article III, of course, gives the federal courts jurisdiction over only 'cases and controversies,' and the doctrine of standing serves to identify those disputes which are appropriately resolved through the judicial process.

"As we understand Whitmore's claim of standing in his individual capacity, he alleges that the State has infringed rights that the Eighth Amendment grants to him personally and to the subject of the impending execution, Simmons. He therefore rests his claim to relief both on his own asserted legal right to a system of mandatory appellate review and on Simmons' similar right. Under either theory, Whitmore must establish Article III standing and we find that his allegations fall short of doing so.

"As an alternative basis for standing to maintain this action, petitioner purports to proceed as 'next friend of Ronald Gene Simmons.' Although we have never discussed the concept of 'next friend' standing at length, it has long been an accepted basis for jurisdiction in certain circumstances. Most frequently, 'next friends' appear in court on behalf of detained prisoners who are unable, usually because of mental incompetence or inaccessibility, to seek relief themselves.

"Whitmore, of course, does not seek a writ of habeas corpus on behalf of Simmons. He desires to intervene in a state court proceeding to appeal Simmons' conviction and death sentence. Under these circumstances, there is no federal statute authorizing the participation of 'next friends.' The Supreme Court of Arkansas recognizes, apparently as a matter of common law, the availability of 'next friend' standing in the Arkansas courts but declined to grant it to Whitmore. Without deciding whether a 'next friend' may ever invoke the jurisdiction of a federal court absent congressional authorization, we think the scope of any federal doctrine of 'next friend' standing is no broader that what is permitted by the habeas corpus statute, which codified the historical practice. And in keeping with the ancient tradition of the doctrine, we conclude that one necessary condition for 'next friend' standing in federal court is a showing by the proposed 'next friend' that the real party in interest is unable to litigate his own cause due to mental incapacity, lack of access to court, or other similar disability."

CASE SIGNIFICANCE: The Supreme Court ruled in this case that Whitmore lacked standing, either in a personal capacity or as "next friend" to appeal the death sentence imposed on inmate Ronald Gene Simmons. This is significant because it means that a third party cannot initiate an appeal for a defendant who refuses to do so. This is bad news for organizations and individuals who espouse anti-death penalty causes. The Court said that to be able to appeal, an individual must clearly demonstrate that he or she suffered "injury in fact" and that such injury "can be fairly traced to the challenged action," and "is likely to be redressed by a favorable decision."

The Court held that Whitmore's personal interest in having Simmons' case reviewed was too remote to warrant Article III protection and that the State of Arkansas had taken every precaution necessary to ensure that Simmons "knowingly, intelligently, and voluntarily" waived his right to appeal. The Court did not, however, address the issue of whether a defendant can waive his or her right to appellate review of a death sentence or whether such review is mandatory. Those issues were not raised in this case.

Lankford v. Idaho
59 L.W. 4434 (1991)

CAPSULE: Lack of adequate notice during the sentencing hearing that the defendant might be given the death penalty violates due process if the judge later imposes the death penalty.

FACTS: On December 1, 1983, Bryan Lankford was charged with first-degree murder. Identical charges were also filed against Lankford's older brother, Mark. At the arraignment, the trial judge advised Bryan Lankford that "the maximum punishment that you may receive if you are convicted on either of the two charges is imprisonment for life or death." During plea negotiations, the prosecutor became convinced that Lankford's older brother Mark was primarily responsible for the crimes and was the actual killer of both victims. The parties agreed on an indeterminate sentence with a 10-year minimum in exchange for a guilty plea, subject to a commitment from the trial judge that he would impose the sentence. The trial judge refused to make the commitment and the case went to trial. A jury found Bryan Lankford guilty on both counts of first-degree murder. Prior to the sentencing hearing, the court ordered the State to provide notice of whether it would seek the death penalty, and if so, to file a statement of the aggravating circumstances on which it intended to rely. The state filed a negative response, and there was no discussion of the death penalty as a possible sentence at the sentencing hearing. Rather, both the defense counsel and the prosecutor argued the merits of concurrent or consecutive, and fixed or indeterminate, sentence terms. At the hearing's conclusion, the trial judge indicated a disbelief in Lankford's testimony, stating that the crime's seriousness warranted punishment more severe than what the state had recommended, and mentioned the possibility of death as a sentencing option. The trial judge later sentenced Lankford to death based on five specific aggravating circumstances.

ISSUE: Did the sentencing process in this case satisfy the requirements of the due process clause of the Fourteenth Amendment? NO.

DECISION: The sentencing process in this case violated the Due Process Clause of the Fourteenth Amendment because at the time of the sentencing hearing, Lankford and his counsel did not have adequate notice that the judge might sentence him to death.

REASON: "The presentencing order entered by the trial court requiring the State to advise the court and the defendant whether it sought the death penalty, and if so, requiring the parties to specify the aggravating and mitigating circumstances on which they intended to rely, was comparable to a pretrial order limiting the issues to be tried. The purpose of such orders is to eliminate the need to address matters that are not in dispute, and thereby to save the valuable time of judges and lawyers. For example, if the State had responded in the affirmative and indicated an intention to rely on only three aggravating circumstances, the defense could reasonably have assumed that the evidence to be adduced would relate only to those three circumstances, and therefore, the defense could have limited its preparation accordingly. Similarly, in this case, it was surely reasonable for the defense to assume that there was no reason to present argument or evidence directed at the question whether the death penalty was either appropriate or permissible. Orders that are designed to limit the issues would serve no purpose if counsel acted at their peril when they complied with the order's limitations.

"It is, of course, true that this order did not expressly place any limits on counsel's preparation. The question, however, is whether it can be said that counsel had adequate notice of the critical issue that the judge was actually debating. Our answer to that question must reflect the importance that we attach to the concept of fair notice as the bedrock of any constitutionally fair procedure.

"If defense counsel had been notified that the trial judge was contemplating a death sentence based on five specific aggravating circumstances, presumably she would have advanced arguments that addressed these circumstances; however, she did not make these arguments because they were entirely inappropriate in a discussion about the length of petitioner's possible incarceration.

"At the very least, this is a case in which reasonable judges might differ concerning the appropriateness of the death sentence. It is therefore a case in which some of the reasoning that motivated our decision in *Gardner v. Florida*, 430 U.S. 349 (1977), is applicable. In that case, relying partly on the Due Process Clause of the Fourteenth Amendment and partly on the Eighth Amendment's prohibition against cruel and unusual punishment, the Court held that a procedure for selecting people for the death penalty that permits consideration of secret information about the defendant is unacceptable. The plurality opinion, like the opinion concurring in the judgment, emphasized the special importance of fair procedure in the capital sentencing context. We emphasized that 'death is a different kind of punishment from any other which may be imposed in this country.' We explained:

> From the point of view of the defendant, it is different in both its severity and its finality. From the point of view of society, the action of the sovereign in taking the life of one of its citizens also differs dramatically from any other legitimate state action. It is vitally important to the defendant and to the community that any decision to impose the death sentence be, and appear to be, based on reason rather than caprice or emotion.

"Although the trial judge in this case did not rely on secret information, his silence following the State's response to the presentencing order had the practical effect of concealing from the parties the principal issue to be decided at the hearing. Notice of issues to be resolved by the adversary process is a fundamental characteristic of fair procedure.

"Without such notice, the Court is denied the benefit of the adversary process. As we wrote in *Strickland v. Washington*, 466 U.S. 668 (1984):

> A capital sentencing proceeding like the one involved in this case . . . is sufficiently like a trial in its adversarial format and in the existence of standards for decision . . . that counsel's role in the proceeding is comparable to counsel's role at trial—to ensure that the adversarial testing process works to produce a just result under the standards governing decision.

Earlier in *Gardner*, we had described the critical role that the adversary process plays in our system of justice:

> Our belief that debate between adversaries is often essential to the truth-seeking function of trials requires us also to recognize the importance of giving counsel an opportunity to comment on facts which may influence the sentencing decision in capital cases.

If notice is not given, and the adversary process is not permitted to function properly, there is an increased chance of error, and with that, the possibility of an incorrect result. *See, e.g., Herring v. New York*, 422 U.S. 853, 862 (1975) ('The very premise of our adversary system of criminal justice is that partisan advocacy on both sides of a case will best promote the ultimate objective that the guilty be convicted and the innocent go free'). Petitioner's lack of adequate notice that the judge was contemplating the imposition of the death sentence created an impermissible risk that the adversary process may have malfunctioned in this case."

CASE SIGNIFICANCE: This is an important case on the issue of what constitutes "fair notice" in death penalty cases. After the jury found the defendant guilty, the judge ordered the state to provide notice of whether it would seek the death penalty and, if the state wanted to do that, to list the aggravating circumstances it intended to rely upon, in accordance with state law, for seeking the death penalty. The state filed a negative response and there was no mention of the death penalty at the sentencing hearing. Nonetheless, the judge imposed the death penalty, saying that he did not believe the defendant's testimony. Moreover, the judge based the death sentence on five specific aggravating circumstances.

On appeal, the Court declared the procedure unconstitutional, concluding that "if defense counsel had been notified that the trial judge was contemplating a death sentence based on five specific aggravating circumstances, presumably she would have advanced arguments that addressed these circumstances; however, she did not make these arguments because they were entirely inappropriate in a discussion about the length of petitioner's possible incarceration." The Court added: "Although the trial judge in this case did not rely on secret information, his silence following the State's response to the presentencing order had the practical effect of concealing from the parties the principal issue to be decided at the hearing." The Court concluded by saying that "notice of issues to be resolved by the adversary process is a fundamental characteristic of fair procedure," and that "without such notice, the Court is denied the benefit of the adversary process."

This case points to the importance of giving the defendant in a death penalty case fair notice of anything and everything that happens in the case, including the issues that are to be raised in the sentencing phase. Not to do so is to violate a defendant's right to due process, as this case illustrates. Had there been fair notice that the death penalty might be imposed, counsel for the defendant could have introduced evidence in court to rebut the five specific aggravating circumstances used by the judge, hence making the death penalty inappropriate. Denial of the opportunity for the defense counsel to be able to do so violates due process.

Payne v. Tennessee
59 L.W. 4814 (1991)

CAPSULE: A victim impact statement is admissible in the sentencing phase of death penalty cases.

FACTS: Payne was convicted of the first-degree murders of Charisse Christopher and her two-year-old daughter, and of the first-degree assault with intent to murder of Charisse's three-year-old son, Nicholas. During the sentencing phase of the trial, Payne called his parents, his girlfriend, and a clinical psychologist on his behalf. They testified to various mitigating aspects of Payne's background and character. The state called Nicholas' grandmother, who testified that the child missed his mother and baby sister. During the prosecutor's plea for the death penalty, the continuing effects upon Nicholas due to the attack and the effects of the crimes upon the victim's family were mentioned. The jury sentenced Payne to death on each of the murder counts. Payne's contention that the admission of the grandmother's testimony and the state's closing argument violated his Eighth Amendment rights was rejected by the Tennessee State Supreme Court. Payne based his arguments on *Booth v. Maryland*, 482 U.S. 496 (1987) and *South Carolina v. Gathers*, 490 U.S. 805 (1989), which held that evidence and arguments relating to the victim and the impact of the victim's death on the victim's family are *per se* inadmissible in death penalty cases.

ISSUE: Does the Eighth Amendment prohibit the admission of victim impact evidence during the penalty phase of a capital trial? NO.

DECISION: The Eighth Amendment does not *per se* prohibit a capital sentencing jury from considering "victim impact" evidence relating to the victim's personal characteristics and the emotional impact of the murder on the victim's family, nor does it preclude a prosecutor from arguing such evidence at a capital sentencing hearing.

REASON: "There are numerous infirmities in the rule created by *Booth* and *Gathers*. Those cases were based on two premises: that evidence relating to a particular victim or to the harm caused a victim's family does not in general reflect on the defendant's 'blameworthiness,' and that only evidence of 'blameworthiness' is relevant to a capital sentencing decision. However, assessment of the harm caused by the defendant has long been an important factor in determining the appropriate punishment, and victim impact evidence is simply another method of informing the sentencing authority about such harm. In excluding such evidence, *Booth* misread the statement in *Woodson v. North Carolina*, 428 U.S. 280, 304, that the capital defendant must be treated as a 'uniquely individual human being.' As *Gregg v. Georgia*, 428 U.S. 153, 203-204, demonstrates, the *Woodson* language was not intended to describe a class of evidence that could not be received, but a class of evidence which must be received, i.e., any relevant, nonprejudicial material. *Booth*'s misreading of precedent has unfairly weighted the scales in a capital trial. Virtually no limits are placed on the relevant mitigating evidence a capital defendant may introduce concerning his own circumstances. The State has a legitimate interest in counteracting such evidence, but the *Booth* rule prevents it from doing so. Similarly, fairness to the prosecution requires rejection of *Gathers*' extension of the *Booth* rule to the prosecutor's argument, since, under the Eighth Amendment, this Court has given the capital defendant's attorney broad latitude to argue relevant mitigating evidence reflecting his client's individual personality. *Booth* also erred in reasoning that it would be difficult, if not impossible, for a capital defendant to rebut victim impact evidence without shifting the focus of the sentencing hearing away from the defendant to the victim. The mere fact that for tactical reasons it might not be prudent for the defense to rebut such evidence makes the case no different from others in which a party is faced with this sort of dilemma. Nor is there merit to the concern voiced in *Booth* that admission of such evidence permits a jury to find that defendants whose victims were assets to their communities are more deserving of punishment than those whose victims are perceived to be less worthy. Such evidence is not generally offered to encourage comparative judgments of this kind, but is designed to show instead each victim's uniqueness as an individual human being. In the event that victim impact evidence is introduced that is so unduly prejudicial that it renders the trial fundamentally unfair, the Fourteenth Amendment's due process clause provides a mechanism for relief. Thus, a State may properly conclude that for a jury to assess meaningfully the defendants' moral culpability and blameworthiness, it should have before it at the sentencing phase victim impact evidence."

CASE SIGNIFICANCE: This case virtually overrules *Booth v. Maryland*, 41 Cr. L. 3282 (1987), which held that victim impact statements (which typically describe a victim's characteristics and the effect of the crime on the victim's family) are not admissible in death penalty cases. The Court said that although the doctrine of *stare decisis* (adherence to decided cases) is usually the best policy, it is "not an inexorable command," particularly in cases in which the decisions are "unworkable or badly reasoned." Decided only four years earlier, the Court considered the rule in *Booth* to be unworkable and badly reasoned, and overruled that part of the decision. The Court said that the *Booth* decision was based on two premises: "that evidence relating to a particular victim or to the harm caused a victim's family does not in general reflect on the defendant's 'blameworthiness,' and that only evidence of 'blameworthiness' is relevant to the capital sentencing decision." The Court rejected these statements, saying that "assessment of the harm caused by the defendant has long been an important factor in determining the appropriate punishment, and victim impact evidence is simply another method of informing the sentencing authority about such harm."

Decided by a 6-3 vote, this decision reflects the definite imprint of a conservative Court that has shown willingness to allow into the sentencing phase evidence that previously was considered inadmissible. The Court rejected the concept that such evidence must be kept out of death penalty cases because a capital defendant must be treated as a "uniquely individual human being," saying that because there are virtually no limits placed on the relevant mitigating evidence that may be introduced for the defendant in a capital offense, the same should be true with aggravating circumstances as well. The Court seeks to place the prosecution and the defense on the same level in the introduction of evidence in the sentencing phase, even in death penalty cases.

Morgan v. Illinois
60 L.W. 4541 (1992)

CAPSULE: The defendant in death penalty cases must be allowed to ask a juror whether he or she would automatically vote to impose the death penalty upon conviction.

FACTS: In the state of Illinois, a capital trial is conducted in two phases, with the same jury determining both the defendant's guilt and whether the death penalty should be imposed. As required by state law, the trial court, rather than the attorneys, conducted the voir dire (the questioning of prospective jurors) to select the jury for Morgan's capital murder trial. The state requested, pursuant to *Witherspoon v. Illinois*, 319 U.S. 510 (1968), that inquiry be made to determine whether any potential juror would in all instances refuse to impose the death penalty upon conviction of the offense. The request was granted. However, when Morgan's attorney requested that the court ask if any juror would automatically vote to impose the death penalty regardless of the facts, the court refused. The court reasoned that it had "asked the question in a different vein substantially in that nature." Morgan was convicted and sentenced to death.

ISSUE: Is it constitutional for a trial court to refuse inquiry into whether a potential juror would automatically impose the death penalty upon conviction in a capital case? NO.

DECISION: A trial court's refusal to allow defendants to inquire whether potential jurors would automatically impose the death penalty upon conviction in a capital case is inconsistent with the due process clause of the Fourteenth Amendment, and therefore is unconstitutional.

REASON: "Due process demands that a jury provided to a capital defendant at the sentencing phase must stand impartial and indifferent to the extent commanded by the Sixth Amendment.

"Based on this impartiality requirement, a capital defendant may challenge for cause any prospective juror who will automatically vote for the death penalty. Such a juror will fail in good faith to consider the evidence of aggravating and mitigating circumstances as the instructions require.

"On voir dire a trial court must, at a defendant's request, inquire into the prospective jurors' views on capital punishment. Part of the guaranty of a defendant's right to an impartial jury is an adequate voir dire to identify unqualified jurors. Morgan could not exercise intelligently his challenge for cause against prospective jurors who would unwaveringly impose death after a finding of guilt unless he was given the opportunity to identify such persons by questioning them at voir dire about their views on the death penalty. Absent that opportunity, his right not to be tried by those who would always impose death, would be rendered as nugatory and meaningless as the State's right, in the absence of questioning, to strike those who never do so.

"A juror to whom mitigating evidence is irrelevant is plainly saying that such evidence is not worthy of consideration, a view which has long been rejected by this Court and which finds no basis in Illinois statutory or decisional law. Here, the instruction accords with the State's death penalty statute, which requires that the jury be instructed to consider any relevant aggravating and mitigating factors, lists certain relevant mitigating factors, and directs the jury to consider whether the mitigating factors are 'sufficient to preclude' the death penalty's imposition. Since the statute plainly indicates that a lesser sentence is available in every case where mitigating evidence exists, a juror who would invariably impose the death penalty would not give the mitigating evidence the consideration the statute contemplates."

CASE SIGNIFICANCE: In *Witherspoon v. Illinois*, 391 U.S. 510 (1968), the Court declared that in choosing juries to sentence defendants in capital cases, prosecutors (or in this case, the judge) may exclude for cause potential jurors who say that they are unwilling to vote for a death sentence under any circumstance. That ruling led to "death-qualified" juries. It should be noted, however, that mere opposition to the death penalty is not sufficient grounds for dismissal, rather, the juror must indicate that he or she would automatically vote against the death penalty regardless of the circumstances surrounding the case.

The *Witherspoon* decision has raised a similar issue for defendants. If the state can exclude for cause potential jurors unwilling to vote for a death sentence under any circumstances, then, should not the defense also have the opportunity to ask whether a potential juror would in all instances vote for the death penalty without regard to mitigating factors? It is that concern that the Court addressed in this case. The Court ruled that refusing to allow the defense in a capital case the opportunity to examine a potential juror's view on the automatic imposition of capital punishment violates the defendant's right to a fair and impartial hearing under the due process clause of the Fourteenth Amendment. The Court said:

> Part of the guaranty of a defendant's right to an impartial jury is an adequate voir dire to identify unqualified jurors. Morgan could not exercise intelligently his challenge for cause against prospective jurors who would unwaveringly impose death after a finding of guilt unless he was given the opportunity to identify such persons by questioning them at voir dire about their views on the death penalty. Absent that opportunity, his right not to be tried by those

who would always impose death would be rendered as nugatory and meaningless as the State's right, in the absence of questioning, to strike those who never do so.

This case, decided June 15, 1992, places the prosecution and the defense on the same level in death penalty cases as far as voir dire is concerned, in that it basically says that because the prosecution can ask whether a prospective juror would automatically vote against the death penalty no matter what the facts of the case are, the defense should also be allowed to ask whether any juror would automatically vote to impose the death penalty after conviction, regardless of the facts.

Graham v. Collins
52 Cr. L. 2114 (1993)

CAPSULE: The relief sought by the prisoner could not be granted because it would require the announcement of a new rule of constitutional law that could not be done in habeas corpus cases. Also, the Texas statute is constitutional because it adequately narrowed the class of murder defendants eligible for the death penalty and permitted the sentencing authority to consider the mitigating circumstances raised by the defendant.

FACTS: In 1981, Gary Graham approached Bobby Lambert in a grocery store parking lot and attempted to grab his wallet. Lambert resisted and Graham shot him to death. Graham was convicted of capital murder. During the sentencing phase of his trial, the state offered aggravating evidence that the murder was just the beginning of a week of violent attacks during which the 17-year-old Graham committed a series of robberies and assaults, and one rape. This evidence was not contested by the defense. The defense offered, in mitigation, testimony from Graham's stepfather and grandmother concerning his upbringing and positive character traits. The testimony included the fact that Graham had two children he was trying to support and that he had lived on and off with his grandmother during his childhood because his mother was periodically hospitalized for a "nervous condition." The grandmother also testified she had never known Graham to be violent and that he attended church regularly. In its closing argument to the jury, the defense described Graham's behavior as a moral lapse, an aberration, and urged the jury to consider Graham's youth in deciding his punishment. He was convicted and given the death penalty in accordance with the Texas capital sentencing statute. The statute required the jury to answer three special issues. If the jury responded in the affirmative to all three questions, then the death penalty could be imposed.

ISSUES:
1. Should the habeas corpus relief sought by the prisoner be granted? NO.
2. Did the Texas death penalty law, specifically the three questions asked during the sentencing phase, allow the jury to consider the mitigating factors of youth, family background, and positive character traits of the defendant? YES.

DECISIONS:
1. The relief sought by the prisoner should not be granted because it would require the announcement of a new rule of constitutional law that could not be done in habeas corpus cases.
2. The Texas statute is constitutional because it adequately narrowed the class of murder defendants eligible for the death penalty and permitted the sentencing authority to consider the mitigating circumstances raised by the defendant.

REASON: "Because this case is before us on Graham's petition for a writ of habeas corpus, 'we must determine, as a threshold matter, whether granting him the relief he seeks would create a "new rule" ' of constitutional law. 'Under *Teague*, new rules will not be applied or announced in cases on collateral review unless they fall into one of two exceptions.' This restriction on our review applies to capital cases as it does to those not involving the death penalty.

"A holding constitutes a 'new rule' within the meaning of *Teague* if it 'breaks new ground,' 'imposes a new obligation on the States or the Federal Government,' or was not '*dictated*' by precedent existing at the time the defendant's conviction became final. While there can be no dispute that a decision announces a new rule if it expressly overrules a prior decision, 'it is more difficult . . . to determine whether we announce a new rule when a decision extends the reasoning of our prior cases. Because of the leading purpose of federal habeas review is to 'ensur[e] that state courts conduct criminal proceedings in accordance with the Constitution as interpreted at the time of th[ose] proceedings,' ibid., we have held that '[t]he "new rule" principle . . . validates reasonable, good-faith interpretations of existing precedents made by state courts. This principle adheres even if those good-faith interpretations 'are shown to be contrary to later decisions.' Thus, unless reasonable jurists hearing petitioner's claim at the time his conviction became final 'would have felt compelled by existing precedent' to rule in his favor, we are barred from doing so now

"In the years since *Furman v. Georgia*, 408 U.S. 238 (1972), the Court has identified, and struggled to harmonize, two competing commandments of the Eighth Amendment. On one hand, as *Furman* itself emphasized, States must limit and channel the discretion of judges and juries to ensure that death sentences are not meted out 'wantonly' and 'freakishly.' *Id.*, at 310 (Stewart, J., concurring). On the other hand, as we have emphasized in subsequent cases, States must confer on the sentencer sufficient discretion to take account of the 'character and record of the individual offender' to ensure that 'death is the appropriate punishment in a specific case.'

"We cannot say that reasonable jurists considering petitioner's claim in 1984 would have felt that these cases *'dictated'* vacatur of petitioner's death sentence. To the contrary, to most readers at least, these cases reasonably would have been read as upholding the constitutional *validity* of Texas' capital-sentencing scheme with respect to mitigating evidence and otherwise. *Lockett* expressly embraced the *Jurek* holding, and *Eddings* signaled no retreat from that conclusion. It seems to us that reasonable jurists in 1984 would have found that, under our cases, the Texas statute satisfied the commands of the Eighth Amendment: it permitted petitioner to place before the jury whatever mitigating evidence revealed about the defendant's capacity for deliberation and prospects for rehabilitation."

CASE SIGNIFICANCE: The first issue in this case deals with the so-called *Teague* rule, mandated by the Court in the case of *Teague v. Lane*, decided by the Court earlier. In *Teague*, the Court said that new rules will not be applied or announced in cases on collateral review (such as a habeas corpus case) unless they fall into one of two exceptions. This case did not come under either exception and therefore the habeas corpus sought should be denied. The Court further said, however, that the Texas death penalty law was constitutional because it allowed the jury to consider the mitigating circumstances that should be taken into account in a death penalty case. The Court has consistently ruled that provisions should be made in the law for the jury to be allowed to consider mitigating circumstances when deciding on death penalty cases. The specific provision of the Texas law challenged in *Graham* were the three special issues where the jury had to answer yes before the jury could impose the death penalty. The Court said that these limiting provisions nonetheless allowed the jury to adequately consider mitigating factors and therefore the statute was constitutional.

Arave v. Creech
52 Cr. L. 2373 (1993)

CAPSULE: A capital sentencing provision that singles out first-degree murders committed with "utter disregard for human life" satisfies constitutional standards.

FACTS: In 1981, Thomas Creech beat and kicked to death a fellow inmate while both were incarcerated in the Idaho State Penitentiary. Creech pleaded guilty to first-degree murder and the judge sentenced him to death. One of the aggravating circumstances that served as partial basis for the sentence was that "[b]y the murder, or circumstances surrounding its commission, the defendant exhibited utter disregard for human life." In an earlier case, the Idaho Supreme Court identified a limiting construction of "utter disregard" to "be reflective of acts or circumstances surrounding the crime which exhibit the highest, the utmost, callous disregard for human life, i.e., the cold-blooded, pitiless slayer."

ISSUE: Does Idaho's "utter disregard" provision in its death penalty law sufficiently limit sentencing discretion as required by the Eighth and Fourteenth Amendments? YES.

DECISION: Because of the definition given the "utter disregard" provision by the Idaho Supreme Court, the Idaho law meets the constitutional requirements of the Eighth and Fourteenth amendments.

REASON: "This case is governed by the standards we articulated in *Walton, supra,* and *Lewis v. Jeffers,* 497 U.S. 764 (1990). In *Jeffers* we reaffirmed the fundamental principle that, to satisfy the Eighth and Fourteenth Amendments, a capital sentencing scheme must 'suitably direc[t] and limi[t]' the sentencer's discretion 'so as to minimize the risk of wholly arbitrary and capricious action.' The State must 'channel the sentencer's discretion by clear and objective standards that provide specific and detailed guidance, and that make rationally reviewable the process for imposing a sentence of death.'

"Unlike the Court of Appeals, we do not believe it is necessary to decide whether the statutory phrase 'utter disregard for human life' itself passes constitutional muster. The Idaho Supreme Court has adopted a limiting construction, and we believe that construction meets constitutional requirements."

CASE SIGNIFICANCE: This case once again addresses the issue of whether a state's death penalty law was so vague as to be unconstitutional. Idaho law provided that one of the aggravating circumstances that could be considered by the jury when deciding whether to impose the death penalty was that "by the murder, or circumstances surrounding its commission, the defendant exhibited utter disregard for human life." The issue on appeal was whether that phrase was so vague as to violate the due process provision of the Constitution. The Court answered no, saying that the Idaho Supreme Court, in *State v. Osborn,* 102 Idaho 405 (1981), interpreted "utter disregard" to mean "be reflective of acts or circumstances surrounding the crime which exhibit the highest, the utmost, callous disregard for human life . . ." This, said the Court, gave definite meaning to that phrase and therefore saved the Idaho law. This case is significant in that the Court, over the years, has continued to monitor state laws to ensure that death penalty statutes do not suffer from vagueness that can lead to an arbitrary application of the law. The Court also says, however, that vague legislation can be saved if given a more restrictive meaning by state court decision.

Johnson v. Texas
53 Cr. L. 2257 (1993)

CAPSULE: A special instruction advising a death penalty jury that it could consider age as a mitigating factor is not required.

FACTS: In 1986, Dorsie Johnson, then 19 years of age, and a companion, Amanda Miles, robbed a convenience store and killed the store clerk. They emptied the cash registers of $160 in cash, grabbed a carton of cigarettes, and fled the store.

Johnson was later found guilty of capital murder. A separate punishment phase of the proceedings was held to determine Johnson's sentence. Following the Texas capital sentencing statute then in effect, the trial judge instructed the sentencing jury to answer two special issues: (1) whether Johnson's conduct was committed deliberately and with the reasonable expectation that death would result, and (2) whether there was a probability that he would commit criminal acts of violence that would constitute a continuing threat to society (future dangerousness). The jury also received instructions that, in determining each of these issues, it could take into account all the evidence submitted to it, whether aggravating or mitigating, in either phase of the trial. The jury unanimously answered yes to both special issues and Johnson was sentenced to death, as required by Texas state law.

ISSUE: Does the Texas death penalty special issues provision allow a sentencing jury to give adequate mitigating effect to a defendant's youth? YES.

DECISION: The Texas death penalty special issues provision is consistent with The Eighth and Fourteenth Amendments in that there is room in the future dangerousness assessment of the law for a juror to take account of youth as a mitigating factor.

REASON: "The joint opinion determined that the Texas system satisfied the requirements of the Eighth and Fourteenth Amendments concerning the consideration of mitigating evidence: 'By authorizing the defense to bring before the jury at the separate sentencing hearing whatever mitigating circumstances relating to the individual defendant can be adduced, Texas has ensured that the sentencing jury will have adequate guidance to enable it to perform its sentencing function.'

"Today we are asked to take the step that would have been a new rule had we taken it in *Graham*. Like *Graham*, petitioner contends that the Texas sentencing system did not allow the jury to give adequate mitigating effect to the evidence of his youth. Unlike *Graham*, petitioner comes here on direct review, so *Teague* presents no bar to the rule he seeks. The force of *stare decisis*, though, which rests on considerations parallel in many respects to *Teague* is applicable here. The interests of the State of Texas, and those of the victims whose rights it must vindicate, ought not to be turned aside when the State relies upon an interpretation of the Eighth Amendment approved by this Court, absent demonstration that our earlier cases were themselves a misinterpretation of some constitutional command."

CASE SIGNIFICANCE: This case is a follow up of an earlier case, *Graham v. Collins*, 52 Cr. L. 2114 (1993), discussed earlier. The difference is that in this case, the defendant brought the case to the Court on direct review instead of through habeas corpus (a collateral proceeding) and so the *Teague* question that limited the decision in *Graham* was not a problem here. The Court said that "there is no dispute that a defendant's youth is a relevant mitigating circumstance that must be within the effective reach of a capital sentencing jury. . . ." It concluded, however that under the Texas statute, there was plenty of room for jurors to take into account youth as a mitigating factor. Said the Court: "By authorizing the defense to bring before the jury at the separate sentencing hearing whatever mitigating circumstances related to the individual defendant can be adduced," Texas ensured that the state could take into account defendant's age when determining the death penalty. This case, therefore, holds that age does not have to be mentioned by law as a mitigating factor in death penalty cases as long as the law is worded such that age is not excluded as a mitigating factor and can be considered by the jury in determining whether the death penalty should be imposed.

Simmons v. South Carolina
114 S. Ct. 2187 (1994)

CAPSULE: Death penalty defendants are entitled to a jury instruction informing the jury that a "life" sentence means life imprisonment without parole.

FACTS: In 1990, Jonathan Simmons beat Josie Lamb to death in her home. Ms. Lamb was an elderly woman. Prior to the start of his capital murder trial, Simmons pleaded guilty to first degree burglary and two counts of criminal sexual conduct in connection with two prior assaults on elderly women. Simmons was convicted of both violent offenses. The two violent offense convictions made him ineligible for parole if convicted for any other violent crime offense under South Carolina law. Prior to jury selection in the capital murder trial, the prosecutor was granted a motion by the trial judge barring the defense from making *any* mention of parole. The defense was expressly prohibited from questioning prospective jurors as to whether they understood the meaning of a "life" sentence under the state law. Simmons was convicted of the murder. During the penalty phase of the trial, the state argued that Simmons' future dangerousness was a factor the jury needed to consider when deciding whether to sentence him to death or life imprisonment. The defense pointed out that Simmons' future dangerousness was limited to elderly women and there was no reason to expect violent acts from him in prison. During jury instructions, the judge refused to point out to the jury that Simmons would be ineligible for parole under South Carolina law. At some point during the deliberation, the jury inquired whether life imprisonment carried the possibility of parole. The judge instructed the jury not to consider parole in reaching its verdict and that "the terms life imprisonment and death sentence were to be understood to have their plan [sic] and ordinary meaning." Simmons was given the death penalty.

ISSUE: Does the refusal to provide the jury with information regarding parole in a death penalty case violate the due process clause of the Fourteenth Amendment? YES.

DECISION: Due process requires that the sentencing jury be informed that the defendant is not eligible for parole where the defendant's future dangerousness is at issue, and state law prohibits the defendant's release on parole.

REASON: "In assessing future dangerousness, the actual duration of the defendant's prison sentence is indisputably relevant. Holding all other factors constant, it is entirely reasonable for a sentencing jury to view a defendant who is eligible for parole as a greater threat to society than a defendant who is not. Indeed, there may be no greater assurance of a defendant's future nondangerousness to the public than the fact that he will never be released on parole. The trial court's refusal to apprise the jury of information so crucial to its sentencing determination, particularly when the prosecution alluded to the defendant's future dangerousness in its argument to the jury, cannot be reconciled with our well established precedents interpreting the Due Process Clause.

"The Due Process Clause does not allow the execution of a person 'on the basis of information which he has no opportunity to deny or explain.' *Gardner v. Florida*, 430 U.S., at 362. In this case, the jury reasonably may have believed that petitioner could be released on parole if he were not executed. To the extent this misunderstanding pervaded the jury's deliberations, it had the effect of creating a false choice between sentencing petitioner to death and sentencing him to a limited period of incarceration. This grievous misperception was encouraged by the trial court's refusal to provide the jury with accurate information regarding petitioner's parole ineligibility, and by the State's repeated suggestion that petitioner would pose a future danger to society if he were not executed. Three times petitioner asked to inform the jury that in fact he was ineligible for parole under state law; three times his request was denied. The State thus succeeded in securing a death sentence on the ground, at least in part, of petitioner's future dangerousness, while at the same time concealing from the sentencing jury the true meaning of its non-capital sentencing alternative, namely, that life imprisonment meant life without parole. We think it clear that the State denied petitioner due process."

CASE SIGNIFICANCE: This case deals with an issue raised by an increasing number of state laws that prohibit release on parole for certain heinous offenses. South Carolina law provided that for the type of offense committed by the defendant in this case, imprisonment for life meant that the defendant could not be released on parole. This is important because jurors might not impose the death penalty and opt for life imprisonment if they are informed that life imprisonment for some defendants means that these defendants will never be released from prison. The assumption is that if life imprisonment can mean parole, jurors would rather impose the death penalty so that society may be protected from dangerous parolees. On the other hand, if jurors know that life imprisonment means that the defendant will never be released, then future danger to society does not become a consideration in imposing the penalty. The Court said that due process requires that the information on "life without parole" as an alternative to the death penalty in certain states be made available to the jury when determining the sentence to be imposed. It could make a difference in the punishment the jury ultimately imposes.

Tuilaepa v. California
55 Cr. L. 2244 (1994)

CAPSULE: Circumstances of the crime, the defendant's history of violent crimes, and the age of the defendant are constitutional as sentencing factors in death penalty cases.

FACTS: In California, a defendant is eligible for the death penalty when a jury finds him or her guilty of first-degree murder and finds one or more of the special circumstances listed in the California Penal Code Annotated, §190.2. Once the case is in the penalty phase, the jury is then instructed to consider numerous other factors listed in §190.3 in its decision whether to impose death.

California sought the death penalty against Paul Tuilaepa, charging him with murder and robbery. Tuilaepa was found guilty and the jury also found the special circumstance to be true. During the penalty phase, the trial judge instructed the jury to consider the relevant sentencing factors that were specified in §190.3. The jury unanimously sentenced Tuilaepa to death.

The death penalty was also brought against Proctor. He was charged with murder and a number of special circumstances under §190.2 of the California Penal Code, which included murder during the commission of a rape, murder during the commission of a burglary, and infliction of torture during a murder. Proctor was also found guilty of murder and the special circumstances were determined to be true. The trial judge instructed the jury to consider the sentencing factors specified in §190.3. Proctor received a unanimous verdict of death.

ISSUE: Are California's death penalty phase factors constitutional? YES.

DECISION: California's death penalty phase factors are not constitutionally vague and are not in violation of the Eighth Amendment.

REASON: "In our decisions holding a death sentence unconstitutional because of a vague sentencing factor, the State had presented a specific proposition that the sentencer had to find true or false (e.g., whether the crime was especially heinous, atrocious, or cruel). We have held, under certain sentencing schemes, that a vague propositional factor used in the sentencing decision creates an unacceptable risk of randomness, the mark of the arbitrary and capricious sentencing process prohibited by *Furman v. Georgia*, 408 U.S. 238 (1972). Those concerns are mitigated when a factor does not require a yes or a no answer to a specific question, but instead only points the sentencer to a subject matter. Both types of factors (and the distinction between the two is not always clear) have their utility. For purposes of vagueness analysis, however, in examining the propositional content of a factor, our concern is that the factor have some 'common-sense core of meaning . . . that criminal juries should be capable of understanding.'

"Petitioner's challenge to factor (a) is at some odds with settled principles, for our capital jurisprudence has established that the sentencer should consider the circumstances of the crime in deciding whether to impose the death penalty. We would be hard pressed to invalidate a jury instruction that implements what we have said the law requires. In any event, this California factor instructs the jury to consider a relevant subject matter and does so in understandable terms. The circumstances of the crime are a traditional subject for consideration by the sentencer, and an instruction to consider the circumstances is neither vague nor otherwise improper under our Eighth Amendment jurisprudence.

"Factor (b) is phrased in conventional and understandable terms and rests in large part on a determination whether certain events occurred, thus asking the jury to consider matters of historical fact. Under other sentencing schemes, in Texas for example, jurors may be asked to make a predictive judgment, such as 'whether there is a probability that the defendant would commit criminal acts of violence that would constitute a continuing threat to society.' See *Jurek, supra,* at 269. Both a backward-looking and a forward-looking inquiry are a permissible part of the sentencing process, however, and the States have considerable latitude in determining how to guide the sentencer's decision in this respect. Here, factor (b) is not vague.

"The factual inquiry is of the most rudimentary sort, and there is no suggestion that the term 'age' is vague. Petitioner contends, however, that the age factor is equivocal and that in the typical case the prosecution argues in favor of the death penalty based on the defendant's age, no matter how old or young he was at the time of the crime. It is neither surprising nor remarkable that the relevance of the defendant's age can pose a dilemma for the sentencer. But difficulty in application is not equivalent to vagueness. Both the prosecution and the defense may present valid arguments as to the significance of the defendant's age in a particular case. Competing arguments by adversary parties bring perspective to a problem, and thus serve to promote a more reasoned decision, providing guidance as to a factor jurors most likely would discuss in any event. We find no constitutional deficiency in factor (i)."

CASE SIGNIFICANCE: This case addresses again the issue of whether the factors listed by state law that the jury must consider during the sentencing phase of a death penalty case are so vague as to be unconstitutional. Under California law, the factors to be considered, among others, are: (a) "circumstances of the crime of which the defendant was convicted . . . and the existence of any special circumstances found to be true," (b) "the presence or absence of criminal activity involving the use or attempted use of force or violence or the express or implied threat to use force or violence," and (c) defendant's age at the time of the crime. The Court said that these factors are not vague and are constitutional. Once again, the Court demonstrates vigilance in ensuring that state laws governing the penalty phase of capital offenses do not suffer from vagueness as to be susceptible to arbitrary application by juries. Whether the specific provisions of a state law are vague or not is ultimately for the Court to decide in a specific case. This helps explain why, decades after the Court decided (in *Gregg v.*

Georgia, 428 U.S. 153 [1976]) that the death penalty is constitutional, a number of states have not as yet started executions. Their laws may be under challenge as unconstitutional. It also explains why, until now, many death penalty cases still reach the Court from the states.

Harris v. Alabama
56 Cr. L. 2152 (1995)

CAPSULE: A capital sentencing law that calls for the sentencing judge to consider an advisory jury verdict is not constitutionally required to specify the weight the judge must give the advisory verdicts.

FACTS: Louise Harris was having an affair with Lorenzo McCarter. McCarter was asked by Harris to find someone to kill her husband. Michael Stockwell and Alex Hood were each paid $100 by McCarter, with a vague promise of more money, upon completion of the crime. The victim was shot with a shotgun at point-blank range by Stockwell when he stopped his car at a stop sign. After Harris was arrested, McCarter agreed to testify against her in exchange for a promise by the prosecutor not to seek the death penalty against him. McCarter testified that Harris had asked him to kill her husband so they could share in his death benefits of $250,000.

Harris was convicted of capital murder in a jury trial. During the sentencing hearing, several witnesses testified to her good background and strong character. The jury heard that she was rearing seven children, held three jobs simultaneously, and participated actively in her church. It was recommended by the jury (in a 7-to-5 vote) that she receive life in prison without parole. In considering her sentence, the judge identified one aggravating circumstance (the murder was committed for pecuniary gain) and one statutory mitigating factor (Harris had no prior record). The judge also acknowledged as non-statutory mitigating circumstances that Harris was a hardworking, respected member of her church and community. The judge, however, noted that since Harris had planned and financed the commission of the crime and would have benefited the most from her husband's murder that the one statutory aggravating circumstance "far outweighs" any mitigating circumstances. Harris was sentenced to death.

ISSUE: Is a capital punishment sentencing scheme that requires a judge to only consider a sentencing jury's advisory verdict, but does not spell out the specific weight to be given to the jury's recommendation, a violation of the Eighth Amendment? NO.

DECISION: The Eighth Amendment's cruel and unusual punishment clause does not require a state's sentencing law to specify the weight the sentencing judge must give to the advisory verdicts.

REASON: "We have rejected the notion that 'a specific method for balancing mitigating and aggravating factors in a capital sentencing proceeding is constitutionally required.' Equally settled is the corollary that the Constitution does not require a State to ascribe any specific weight to particular factors, either in aggravation or mitigation, to be considered by the sentencer. To require that 'great weight' be given to the jury recommendation here, one of the criteria to be considered by the sentencer, would offend these established principles and place within constitutional ambit micromanagement tasks that properly rest within the State's discretion to administer its criminal justice system.

"The Constitution permits the trial judge, acting alone, to impose a capital sentence. It is thus not offended when a State further requires the sentencing judge to consider a jury's recommendation and trusts the judge to give it the proper weight."

CASE SIGNIFICANCE: In this case, the Court was asked whether a capital sentencing scheme that requires a judge to consider a sentencing jury's advisory verdict before imposing sentence but does not identify the specific weight to be given to that jury's recommendation was in violation of the Eighth Amendment's prohibition against cruel and unusual punishments. The Court held that it was not.

The Alabama statute is unique in that it stipulates that a capital sentencing jury is to return either a majority verdict of life imprisonment without parole or a strong majority verdict (at least 10 votes) of death. Here, the jury's recommendation was for life without parole but the judge imposed a death sentence without stating how much consideration he gave to the jury's recommendation. Harris argued that the absence of a specific standard allowed judges in Alabama to give varying degrees of consideration to the jury's recommendations and that this was against the Eighth Amendment's protection against arbitrariness in death penalty cases. The Court disagreed, stating that the different treatment of jury verdicts by different judges "simply reflects the fact that, in the subjective weighing process, the emphasis given to each decisional criterion must of necessity vary in order to account for the particular circumstances of each case."

The constitutionality of the Alabama capital sentencing scheme has been decided for the time being. This case was brought to the Court under the Eighth Amendment, however, and some justices suggested that variation in the consideration given to jury advisory verdicts may not hold up under the equal protection clause of the Fourteenth Amendment.

Chapter 5—Juvenile Justice

Haley v. Ohio, 68 S. Ct. 302 (1948)
Kent v. United States, 383 U.S. 541 (1966)
In re Gault, 387 U.S. 1 (1967)
In re Winship, 397 U.S. 358 (1970)
McKeiver v. Pennsylvania, 403 U.S. 528 (1971)
Davis v. Alaska, 415 U.S. 308 (1974)
Breed v. Jones, 421 U.S. 517 (1975)
Fare v. Michael C., 442 U.S. 707 (1979)
Smith v. Daily Publishing Co., 443 U.S. 97 (1979)
Schall v. Martin, 104 S. Ct. 2403 (1984)
New Jersey v. T.L.O., 469 U.S. 325 (1985)
Thompson v. Oklahoma, 487 U.S. 815 (1988)
Stanford v. Kentucky, 109 S. Ct. 2969 (1989)
Coy v. Iowa, 487 U.S. 1012 (1988)
Maryland v. Craig, 497 U.S. 836 (1990)

Haley v. Ohio
68 S. Ct. 302 (1948)

CAPSULE: **Coerced confessions are not admissible as evidence in a juvenile proceeding.**

FACTS: On October 14, 1945, a confectionery store was robbed; the owner of the store was shot and killed. Five days later, a 15-year-old juvenile named Haley was arrested for his alleged involvement in the crime. Beginning some time after midnight, Haley was questioned for five hours by the police. He was questioned in relays by various police officers or teams of police officers. At no time during this questioning was anyone present on Haley's behalf. After being shown alleged confessions of the other participants in the robbery, Haley confessed. At no time was Haley informed of his right to counsel. A statement appeared at the top of the written confession informing Haley that the document could be used against him and that he was giving his statement voluntarily. He was then held incommunicado for three days before being taken before a magistrate and formally charged. An attorney attempted to see him twice but was refused admission. His mother was not allowed to see him until five days after his arrest. At Haley's trial, the defense objected to the admission of the confession on the grounds that it violated Haley's rights under the Fourteenth Amendment. The judge admitted the confession into evidence and instructed the jury to disregard the confession if it believed that the confession was not given voluntarily and of free will. Haley was convicted of murder in the first degree and sentenced to life imprisonment.

ISSUE: Does the Fourteenth Amendment prohibit the use of coerced confessions in juvenile proceedings? YES.

DECISION: The due process clause of the Fourteenth Amendment prohibits the police from extracting involuntary or coerced confessions from adults and juveniles; any evidence obtained involuntarily cannot be used in court.

REASON: "We do not think the methods used in obtaining this confession can be squared with that due process of law which the Fourteenth Amendment commands.

"What transpired would make us pause for careful inquiry if a mature man was involved. And when, as here, a mere child—an easy victim of the law—is before us, special care in scrutinizing the record must be used. Age 15 is a tender and difficult age for a boy of any race. He cannot be judged by more exacting standards of maturity.

"No friend stood at the side of this 15-year-old boy as the police, working in relays, questioned him hour after hour, from midnight until dawn. No lawyer stood guard to make sure that the police went so far and no farther, to see that they stopped short of the point where he became the victim of coercion . . .

"This disregard of the standards of decency [is] underlined by the fact that he was held incommunicado for over three days during which the lawyer retained to represent him twice tried to see him and twice was refused admission. A photographer was admitted at once, but his closest friend—his mother—was not allowed to see him for over five days after his arrest. It is said that these events are not germane to the present problem because they happened after the confession was made. But they show such a callous attitude of the police towards the safeguards which respect for ordinary standards of human relationships compels that we take with a grain of salt their present apologia that the five-hour grilling of this boy was conducted in a fair and dispassionate manner.

"The age of the petitioner, the hours when he was grilled, the duration of his quizzing, the fact that he had no friend or counsel to advise him, the callous attitude of the police towards his rights combine to convince us that this was a confession wrung from a child by means which the law should not sanction. Neither man nor child can be allowed to stand condemned by methods which flout constitutional requirements of due process of law."

CASE SIGNIFICANCE: In this case, the Supreme Court for the first time suggested that, despite *parens patriae* (the doctrine stating that the state serves as the "parent" of juveniles), there are constitutional requirements that protect all accused persons, whether they be adults or juveniles. The Court was not willing to go so far as to say that juveniles have recognized constitutional rights, but it held that juveniles cannot be held to higher standards than adults. Juveniles stand a lesser chance of protecting themselves against police tactics, hence it is only reasonable that a juvenile be given the same, if not greater, protection against coercion than adults.

This decision is easy to accept today, but was not as easily reached in 1948 under the pure *parens patriae* philosophy. At present, the concept that juveniles deserve better protection than adults against possible police abuses is accepted. This was not the case in 1948, when *parens patriae* insulated police and courts from judicial scrutiny on the ground that these agencies were entitled to greater authority when dealing with juveniles.

Kent v. United States
383 U.S. 541 (1966)

CAPSULE: A juvenile must be given due process before being transferred from a juvenile court to an adult court.

FACTS: Kent, at age 16, was arrested and charged with housebreaking, robbery, and rape. Because of his age, he came under the jurisdiction of the District of Columbia Juvenile Court. That court, however, could waive jurisdiction after a "full investigation" (in accordance with District of Columbia law) and transferred him to the United States District Court for an adult criminal trial. Kent's attorney filed motions to have a hearing on the waiver. He also recommended that Kent be hospitalized for psychiatric observation and that he be allowed access to the file that the juvenile court had on his client. The juvenile court did not rule on these motions. Instead, the judge ordered that jurisdiction be transferred to the adult criminal court and stated that this finding was made after the required "full investigation." The judge held no hearing before his ruling and gave no reason for the waiver. Kent was convicted in criminal court on six counts of housebreaking and robbery, and was acquitted on two rape counts by reason of insanity.

ISSUE: Do juveniles have any due process rights in cases in which jurisdiction over a juvenile is transferred from a juvenile court to an adult court? YES.

DECISION: A transfer of jurisdiction in a juvenile hearing is a "critically important" stage in the juvenile process. Therefore, the juvenile is entitled to the following due process rights: (1) a hearing; (2) to be represented by counsel at such hearing; (3) to be given access to records considered by the juvenile court; and (4) to a statement of reasons in support of the waiver order.

REASON: "Because the State is supposed to proceed in respect of the child as *parens patriae* and not as adversary, courts have relied on the premise that the proceedings are 'civil' in nature and not criminal, and have asserted that the child cannot complain of the deprivation of important rights available in criminal cases. It has been asserted that he can claim only the fundamental due process right to fair treatment . . .

"While there can be no doubt of the original laudable purpose of juvenile courts, studies and critiques in recent years raise serious questions as to whether actual performance measures well enough against theoretical purpose to make tolerable the immunity of the process from the reach of constitutional guaranties applicable to adults. There is much evidence that some juvenile courts, including that of the District of Columbia, lack the personnel, facilities and techniques to perform adequately as representatives of the State in a *parens patriae* capacity, at least with respect to children charged with law violation. There is evidence, in fact, that there may be grounds for concern that the child receives the worst of both worlds: that he gets neither the protections accorded to adults nor the solicitous care and regenerative treatment postulated for children.

"It is clear beyond dispute that the waiver of jurisdiction is a 'critically important' action determining vitally important statutory rights of the juvenile. . . . The statutory scheme makes this plain. The Juvenile Court is vested with 'original and exclusive jurisdiction' of the child. This jurisdiction confers special rights and immunities. He is, as specified by the statute, shielded from publicity. He may be confined, but with rare exceptions he may not be jailed along with adults. He may be detained, but only until he is 21 years of age. The court is admonished by the statute to give preference to retaining the child in the custody of his parents 'unless his welfare and the safety and protection of the public can be adequately safeguarded without . . . removal.' The child is protected against consequences of adult conviction such as the loss of civil rights, the use of the adjudication against him in subsequent proceedings, and disqualification for public employment.

"The net, therefore, is that petitioner—then a boy of 16—was by statute entitled to certain procedures and benefits as a consequence of his statutory right to the 'exclusive' jurisdiction of the Juvenile Court. In these circumstances, considering particularly that decision as to waiver of jurisdiction and transfer of the matter to the District Court was potentially as important to petitioner as the difference between five years' confinement and a death sentence, we conclude that, as a condition to a valid waiver order, petitioner was entitled to a hearing, including access by his counsel to the social records and probation or similar reports which presumably are considered by the court, and to a statement of reasons for the Juvenile Court's decision. We believe that this result is required by the statute read in the context of constitutional principles relating to due process and the assistance of counsel."

CASE SIGNIFICANCE: Although not as significant as *In re Gault*, this case is important because it marks the first time that basic due process rights were extended to juveniles, thus heralding the demise of the pure *parens patriae* approach. The justification for this departure was stated by the Court when it said:

> There is much evidence that some juvenile courts, including that of the District of Columbia, lack the personnel, facilities and techniques to perform adequately as representatives of the State in a *parens patriae* capacity, at least with respect to children charged with law violation. There is evidence, in fact, that there may be grounds for concern that the child receives the worst of both worlds: that he gets neither the protections accorded to adults nor the solicitous care and regenerative treatment postulated for children.

Though limited in scope, these rights infused juvenile proceedings with due process guarantees. The Court said that the *parens patriae* philosophy "is not an invitation to procedural arbitrariness." It then added that "the waiver of jurisdiction is a 'critically important' action determining vitally important statutory rights of the juvenile."

The rights given in *Kent* are limited to waiver of jurisdiction hearings and are not extended to any other phase of the juvenile proceeding. While these rights, as well as others, were extended one year later to juvenile delinquency proceedings in cases in which the juvenile might be institutionalized (*In re Gault*, 387 U.S. 1 [1967]), they still do not apply constitutionally to all phases of juvenile proceedings. The Supreme Court based its decision in this case on the "critically important" nature of the waiver proceeding. Indeed, a waiver of jurisdiction (other terms used in various states are "transfer of jurisdiction," and "certification") carries far-reaching consequences for the juvenile. For example, instead of being kept in a juvenile institution and automatically released upon reaching adulthood, a juvenile tried in an adult criminal court is treated just like any other criminal and can be subjected to incarceration or a longer period of punishment. The consequences of juvenile proceedings are also vastly different from the effects of an adult conviction. In sum, the Court saw the serious consequences to the juvenile with such a transfer, and provided for due process rights before the transfer of jurisdiction could take place.

In re Gault
387 U.S. 1 (1967)

CAPSULE: Juveniles must be given four basic due process rights in adjudication proceedings that can result in confinement in an institution.

FACTS: On June 8, 1964, a 15-year-old named Gault and a friend were taken into custody as a result of a complaint that they had made lewd telephone calls. Gault's parents were not informed that he was in custody. The parents were never shown the complaint that was filed against their son. The complainant did not appear at any hearing and no written record was made at the hearings. Gault was committed to the State Industrial School as a delinquent until he reached majority, a total of six years from the date of the hearing. The maximum punishment for an adult found guilty of the same offense was a fine from $5 to $50, or imprisonment for a maximum of two months.

ISSUE: Is a juvenile entitled to procedural due process rights during the adjudication stage of a juvenile delinquency proceeding? YES.

DECISION: Juveniles are entitled to procedural due process rights in proceedings (such as adjudication of delinquency) that might result in commitment to an institution in which their freedom would be curtailed. These rights are:
1. Right to reasonable notice of the charges;
2. Right to counsel, his or her own, or appointed by the state if indigent;
3. Right to confront and cross-examine witnesses;
4. Privilege against self-incrimination, including the right to remain silent.

REASON: "The right of the state, as *parens patriae* to deny to the child procedural rights available to his elders was elaborated by the assertion that a child, unlike an adult, has a right 'not to liberty but to custody.' If his parents default in effectively performing their custodial functions—that is, if the child is 'delinquent'—the state may intervene. In doing so, it does not deprive the child of any rights, because he has none. It merely provides the 'custody' to which the child is entitled. On this basis, proceedings involving juveniles were described as 'civil' not 'criminal' and therefore not subject to the requirements which restrict the state when it seeks to deprive a person of his liberty.

"Accordingly, the highest motives and enlightened impulses led to a peculiar system for juveniles, unknown to our law in any comparable context. The constitutional and theoretical basis for this peculiar system is—to say the least—debatable. And in practice, as we remarked in the *Kent* case, *supra,* the results have not been entirely satisfactory. Juvenile Court history has again demonstrated that unbridled discretion, however benevolently motivated, is frequently a poor substitute for principle and procedure. . . . The absence of substantive standards has not necessarily meant that children receive careful, compassionate, individualized treatment. The absence of procedural rules based upon constitutional principles has not always produced fair, efficient, and effective procedures. Departures from established principles of due process have frequently resulted not in enlightened procedures, but in arbitrariness.

"Failure to observe the fundamental requirements of due process has resulted in instances, which might have been avoided, of unfairness to individuals and inadequate or inaccurate findings of fact and unfortunate prescriptions of remedy. Due process of law is the primary and indispensable foundation of individual freedom. It is the basic and essential term in the social compact which defines the rights of the individual and delimits the powers which the state may exercise . . .

". . . We do not mean by this to denigrate the juvenile court process or to suggest that there are not aspects of the juvenile system relating to offenders which are valuable. But the features of the juvenile system which its proponents have asserted are of unique benefit will not be impaired by constitutional domestication. For example, the commendable principles relating to the processing and treatment of juveniles separately from adults are in no way involved or affected by the procedural issues under discussion . . .

"Further, it is urged that the juvenile benefits from informal proceedings in the court. The early conception of the Juvenile Court proceeding was one in which a fatherly judge touched the heart and conscience of the erring youth by talking over his problems, by paternal advice and admonition, and in which, in extreme situations, benevolent and wise institutions of the State provided guidance and help 'to save him from a downward career.' Then, as now, goodwill and compassion were admirably prevalent. But recent studies have, with surprising unanimity, entered sharp dissent as to the validity of this gentle conception. They suggest that the appearance as well as the actuality of fairness, impartiality and orderliness—in short, the essentials of due process—may be a more impressive and more therapeutic attitude as far as the juvenile is concerned. . . . Of course, it is not suggested that juvenile court judges should fail appropriately to take account, in their demeanor and conduct, the emotional and psychological attitude of the juveniles with whom they are confronted. While due process requirements will, in some instances, introduce a degree of order and regularity to Juvenile Court proceedings to determine delinquency, and in contested cases will introduce some elements of the adversary system, nothing will require that the conception of the kindly juvenile judge will be replaced by its opposite, nor do we rule upon the question whether ordinary due process requirements must be observed with respect to hearings to determine the disposition of the delinquent child.

". . . it would be extraordinary if our Constitution did not require the procedural regularity and exercise of care implied in the phrase 'due process.' Under our Constitution, the condition of being a boy does not justify a kangaroo court."

CASE SIGNIFICANCE: *In re Gault* is the most important case ever to be decided by the Supreme Court on juvenile justice and is the most widely known case on the rights of juveniles. It basically says that juvenile proceedings, even though civil in nature, require due process protections that are afforded adults in criminal proceedings. Since the *Gault* case, the Court has decided other cases extending most constitutional rights to juvenile proceedings, such that at present the only rights not extended to juveniles are: (1) the right to a grand jury indictment, (2) the right to bail, (3) the right to a jury trial, and (4) the right to a public hearing. All other constitutional rights have gradually been given to juveniles by the Court in various cases.

This case represents a significant erosion of the pure *parens patriae* approach that characterized the role of the courts in juvenile proceedings since the founding of the first juvenile court in Chicago in 1899. *Gault* was decided in

1967, indicating that for a long time the Court respected the *parens patriae* approach and adopted a "hands-off" attitude in juvenile proceedings.

What led to the erosion of *parens patriae*? The answer lies in a footnote in the *Gault* case. Quoting an earlier case (*Kent v. United States*, 383 U.S. 541 [1966]), the Court said: "There is evidence . . . that there may be grounds for concern that the child receives the worst of both worlds: that he gets neither the protections accorded to adults nor the solicitous care and regenerative treatment postulated for children." In the face of this concern, the Court abandoned the pure *parens patriae* approach and injected due process into juvenile proceedings. Once that approach was taken, other constitutional rights for juveniles followed.

Gault must be understood in the proper context, which is: it applies only in proceedings that might result in the commitment of a juvenile to an institution in which his or her freedom would be curtailed. The rights given in *Gault* do not apply to every juvenile proceeding. For example, most CINS (Conduct In Need of Supervision), CHINS (Children In Need of Supervision), MINS (Minors In Need of Supervision), and PINS (Persons In Need of Supervision) proceedings need not give juveniles *In re Gault* rights if these proceedings, because of the provisions of state law or agency policy, do not result in the juvenile losing his or her freedom. What *Gault* says is that in adjudication proceedings that might result in institutionalization, a juvenile must be given basic due process rights. In a proceeding that will not result in institutionalization, the rights given to juveniles depend upon the provisions of state law.

In re Winship
397 U.S. 358 (1970)

CAPSULE: Proof beyond a reasonable doubt, not simply a preponderance of the evidence, is required in juvenile adjudication hearings in cases in which the act would have been a crime if it had been committed by an adult.

FACTS: During an adjudication hearing, a New York Family Court judge found that the juvenile involved, then a 12-year-old boy, had entered a locker and stolen $112 from a woman's purse. The petition, which charged the juvenile with delinquency, alleged that his act, "if done by an adult, would constitute the crime or crimes of larceny." The judge acknowledged that guilt might not have been established beyond a reasonable doubt but that the New York Family Court Act required that the verdict need only be based on a preponderance of the evidence. At the dispositional hearing (the equivalent of sentencing), the juvenile was ordered to be placed in training school for an initial period of 18 months, subject to annual extensions of his commitment until his eighteenth birthday.

ISSUE: Does the due process clause of the Fourteenth Amendment require proof beyond a reasonable doubt in a juvenile adjudication hearing? YES.

DECISION: Proof beyond a reasonable doubt, not simply a preponderance of the evidence, is required during the adjudicatory stage, if a juvenile is charged with an act that would constitute a crime if committed by an adult.

REASON: "The requirement of proof beyond a reasonable doubt has this vital role in our criminal procedure for cogent reasons. The accused during a criminal prosecution has at stake interests of immense importance, both because of the possibility that he may lose his liberty upon conviction and because of the certainty that he would be stigmatized by the conviction . . .

"We turn to the question whether juveniles, like adults, are constitutionally entitled to proof beyond a reasonable doubt when they are charged with a violation of a criminal law. The same considerations that demand extreme caution in factfinding to protect the innocent adult apply as well to the innocent child.

"Nor do we perceive any merit in the argument that to afford juveniles the protection of proof beyond a reasonable doubt would risk destruction of beneficial aspects of the juvenile process. Use of the reasonable-doubt standard during the adjudicatory hearing will not disturb New York's policies that a finding that a child has violated a criminal law does not constitute a criminal conviction, that such a finding does not deprive the child of his civil rights, and that the juvenile proceedings are confidential. Nor will there be any effect on the informality, flexibility, or speed of the hearing at which the factfinding takes place. And the opportunity during the post-adjudicatory or dispositional hearing for a wide-ranging review of the child's social history for his individualized treatment will remain unimpaired. Similarly, there is no effect on the procedures distinctive to juvenile proceedings that are employed prior to the adjudicatory hearing.

"Finally, we reject the Court of Appeals' suggestion that there is, in any event, only a 'tenuous difference' between the reasonable doubt and preponderance standards. The suggestion is singularly unpersuasive. In this very case, the trial judge's ability to distinguish between the two standards enabled him to make a finding of guilt that he conceded he might not have made under the standard of proof beyond a reasonable doubt. Indeed, the trial judge's action evidences the accuracy of the observation of commentators that 'the preponderance test is susceptible to the misinterpretation that it calls on the trier of fact merely to perform an abstract weighing of the evidence in order to determine which side has produced the greater quantum, without regard to its effect in convincing his mind of the truth of the proposition asserted.' "

CASE SIGNIFICANCE: Juvenile proceedings are civil proceedings and as such are decided by a "preponderance of the evidence" standard. In this case, the Supreme Court said that in juvenile cases in which a juvenile is charged with an act that would constitute a crime if committed by an adult, the standard of proof is not a preponderance of the evidence, but proof beyond a reasonable doubt. The implication is that although juvenile proceedings generally are considered civil proceedings, they are in fact treated like criminal proceedings in some instances. This gives credence to the assertion by some writers that juvenile proceedings are civil only in name and that in reality they are criminal proceedings and are considered as such by the United States Supreme Court.

This case does not hold that all juvenile proceedings require proof beyond a reasonable doubt. What it says is that all juvenile proceedings in which a juvenile "is charged with an act that would constitute a crime if committed by an adult" are subject to a higher standard of proof—proof beyond a reasonable doubt. Any juvenile proceeding that does not fall under this category is governed by the preponderance of the evidence standard. The reason for this distinction is the seriousness of the offense and possible punishment. Most cases in which a juvenile is charged with an act that would constitute a crime if committed by an adult constitute juvenile delinquency, which can result in institutionalization and therefore a deprivation of freedom. On the other hand, CINS, CHINS, MINS, or PINS cases (usually status or relatively minor offenses) result in probation or other forms of non-punitive rehabilitative sanctions and therefore are not subject to the proof beyond a reasonable doubt standard. The exception is if proof beyond a reasonable doubt is required by state law even for minor offenses or violations. In these cases, state law prevails.

McKeiver v. Pennsylvania
403 U.S. 528 (1971)

CAPSULE: Juveniles have no constitutional right to trial by jury in a delinquency proceeding.

FACTS: In 1968, 16-year-old McKeiver was charged with robbery, larceny, and receiving stolen goods, all acts of juvenile delinquency. Under Pennsylvania criminal law these offenses were felonies. McKeiver was represented by counsel at his adjudication hearing. He requested but was denied trial by jury. The judge ruled that McKeiver had violated a law of the Commonwealth and was adjudged a delinquent. He was placed on probation.

ISSUE: Do juveniles have a constitutional right to trial by jury in a delinquency proceeding? NO.

DECISION: Juveniles do not have a constitutional right to trial by jury in a juvenile adjudication hearing.

REASON: "All the litigants agree that the applicable due process standard in juvenile proceedings, as developed by *Gault* and *Winship*, is fundamental fairness. As that standard was applied in those two cases, we have an emphasis on factfinding procedures. The requirements of notice, counsel, confrontation, cross-examination, and standard of proof naturally flowed from this emphasis. But one cannot say that in our legal system the jury is a necessary component of accurate factfinding.

"There is the possibility, at least, that the jury trial, if required as a matter of constitutional precept, will remake the juvenile proceeding into a fully adversary process and will put an effective end to what has been the idealistic prospect of an intimate, informal protective proceeding.

"The imposition of the jury trial on the juvenile court system would not strengthen greatly, if at all, the factfinding function, and would, contrarily, provide an attrition of the juvenile court's assumed ability to function in a unique manner. It would not remedy the defects of the system. Meager as has been the hoped-for advance in the juvenile field, the alternative would be regressive, would lose what has been gained, and would tend once again to place the juvenile squarely in the routine of the criminal process.

"If the jury trial were to be injected into the juvenile court system as a matter of right, it would bring with it into that the traditional delay, the formality, and the clamor of the adversary system and, possibly, the public trial . . ."

CASE SIGNIFICANCE: Unlike other leading juvenile cases, this case does not give juveniles any constitutional rights. What it says instead is that juveniles are not entitled to a jury trial in an adjudication hearing (the equivalent of a trial) or at any stage of a juvenile proceeding. The Court gave a number of reasons for not extending the right to trial by jury to juvenile criminal proceedings. They are:

1. "Compelling a jury trial might remake the proceeding into a fully adversary process and effectively end the idealistic prospect of an intimate, informal protective proceeding;

2. "Imposing a jury trial on the juvenile court system would not remedy the system's defects and would not greatly strengthen the factfinding function;

3. "Jury trial would entail delay, formality, and clamor of the adversary system, and possibly a public trial; and

4.   "Equating the adjudicative phase of the juvenile proceeding with a criminal trial ignores the aspects of fairness, concern, sympathy, and paternal attention inherent in the juvenile court system."

The right to trial by jury is one of the few constitutional rights not enjoyed by juveniles. The other constitutional rights not extended to juveniles are: the right to a public trial, the right to bail, and the right to grand jury indictment. Note, however, that although the right to a jury trial is not constitutionally required, some states, by state law, give juveniles the right to a jury trial either during the adjudication process, the revocation process (if the juvenile is placed on probation), or both.

Davis v. Alaska
415 U.S. 308 (1974)

CAPSULE: Despite state confidentiality laws, the probation status of a juvenile witness may be brought out by the opposing lawyer on cross-examination.

FACTS: Davis was convicted of grand larceny and burglary in an Alaska court. A key prosecution witness during the trial was Richard Green, a juvenile. The trial court, on motion of the prosecuting attorney, issued a protective order prohibiting the defendant's attorney from questioning Green about his having been adjudicated as a juvenile delinquent because of a burglary he had committed and about his probation status at the time of the events about which he was to testify. The court's protective order was based on state law protecting the anonymity of juvenile offenders.

ISSUE: Does the confrontation clause of the Sixth Amendment allow a defendant in a criminal case to bring out the probation status of a juvenile witness on cross-examination even if state law protects the anonymity of juvenile offenders? YES.

DECISION: The accused in a criminal trial is entitled to confront and cross-examine witnesses under the Sixth and Fourteenth Amendments. This right prevails over a state policy protecting the anonymity of juvenile offenders.

REASON: "The Sixth Amendment to the Constitution guarantees the right of an accused in a criminal prosecution 'to be confronted with the witnesses against him.' This right is secured for defendants in state as well as federal proceedings under *Pointer v. Texas*, 380 U.S. 400 (1965). Confrontation means more than being allowed to confront the witness physically. 'Our cases construing the [confrontation] clause hold that a primary interest secured by it is the right to cross-examination' *Douglas v. Alabama*, 380 U.S. 415, 418 (1965).

"Cross-examination is the principal means by which the believability of a witness and the truth of his testimony are tested. Subject always to the broad discretion of a trial judge to preclude repetitive and unduly harassing interrogation, the cross-examiner is not only permitted to delve into the witness' story to test the witness' perceptions and memory, but the cross-examiner has traditionally been allowed to impeach, i.e. discredit, the witness. One way of discrediting the witness is to introduce evidence of a prior criminal conviction of that witness. By doing so the cross-examiner intends to afford the jury a basis to infer that the witness' character is such that he would be less likely than the average trustworthy citizen to be truthful in his testimony. The introduction of evidence of prior crime is thus a general attack on the credibility of the witness. A more particular attack on the witness' credibility is effected by means of cross-examination directed toward revealing possible biases, prejudices, or ulterior motives of the witness as they may relate directly to issues or personalities in the case at hand. The partiality of a witness is subject to exploration at trial, and is 'always relevant as discrediting the witness and affecting the weight of his testimony.' 3A J. Wigmore, *Evidence* [§] 940, p.775 (Chadbourn rev. 1970). We have recognized that the exposure of a witness' motivation in testifying is a proper and important function of the constitutionally protected right of cross-examination. *Greene v. McElroy*, 360 U.S. 474, 496 (1959).

"The State's policy interest in protecting the confidentiality of a juvenile offender's record cannot require yielding of so vital a constitutional right as the effective cross-examination for bias of an adverse witness. The State could have protected Greene from exposure of his juvenile adjudication in these circumstances by refraining from using him to make out its case; the State cannot, consistent with the right of confrontation, require the petitioner to bear the full burden of vindicating the State's interest in the secrecy of juvenile criminal records."

CASE SIGNIFICANCE: The message in this case is clear: the constitutional right of a criminal defendant to confrontation and cross-examination prevails over state policy, embodied in state law, that assures the anonymity of juvenile offenders.

In this case, the lawyer for the petitioner wanted to introduce Richard Green's juvenile record to show that at the time that Green was assisting the police in identifying the accused, Green was on probation for burglary and therefore Green acted out of fear or concern of possible revocation of probation if he did not provide the testimony needed by the police. The lawyer for the petitioner wanted to show that Green might have made a quick and faulty identification of the accused to shift suspicion away from himself as one of the possible perpetrators, and also that Green's identification of the accused may have been made out of fear of possible probation revocation, were Green found to be somehow involved in the crime. This attempt to make public, in court, Green's probation status was denied by the trial judge because of state law providing anonymity to juveniles. The Supreme Court disagreed with the trial judge's ruling and held that because Green was a key witness, his probation status could be disclosed.

What the Court did in this case was balance an accused's right to a fair trial and a juvenile's right, under state law, to anonymity. The Court concluded that "the right of confrontation is paramount to the State's policy of protecting a juvenile offender," adding that "whatever temporary embarrassment might result to Green or his family by disclosure of his juvenile record . . . is outweighed by petitioner's right to probe into the influence of possible bias in the testimony of a crucial identification witness." In sum, between an accused's constitutional right and a state policy to protect juveniles from disclosure of record, the accused's constitutional right prevails.

Breed v. Jones
421 U.S. 517 (1975)

CAPSULE: **Juveniles are entitled to the constitutional right against double jeopardy.**

FACTS: On February 9, 1971, a petition was filed in the Los Angeles County Juvenile Court, alleging that a 17-year-old male committed acts which, if committed by an adult, would constitute the crime of robbery with a deadly weapon. A detention hearing was held the following day and the accused was ordered to be detained pending a hearing on the petition. At the adjudicatory hearing (the equivalent of a trial), the juvenile court found the allegations against the accused to be true and ordered further detention. At the dispositional hearing (the equivalent of sentencing), the juvenile court said that it intended to find the juvenile offender unfit for the programs available through its juvenile facilities. The defense was not prepared for a fitness hearing and the matter was continued for one week. At the conclusion of the court's next hearing, it declared the offender unfit for treatment as a juvenile and ordered that he be prosecuted as an adult. The juvenile was subsequently found guilty of robbery in the first degree by the criminal court and it was ordered that he be committed to the California Youth Authority. The juvenile appealed, claiming a violation of his constitutional right against double jeopardy because he was adjudicated in the juvenile court and then tried by the criminal court.

ISSUE: Does the double jeopardy clause of the Fifth Amendment protect an individual from being prosecuted as an adult after undergoing adjudication proceedings in juvenile court? YES.

DECISION: A juvenile who has undergone adjudication proceedings in juvenile court cannot be tried on the same charge as an adult in a criminal court because such would constitute double jeopardy.

REASON: "Jeopardy denotes risk. In the constitutional sense, jeopardy describes the risk that is traditionally associated with a criminal prosecution . . .

"Although the juvenile-court system has its genesis in the desire to provide a distinctive procedure and setting to deal with the problems of youth, including those manifested by antisocial conduct, our decisions in recent years have recognized that there is a gap between the originally benign conception of the system and its realities. With the exception of *McKeiver v. Pennsylvania*, 403 U.S. 528 (1971), the Court's response to that perception has been to make applicable in juvenile proceedings constitutional guarantees associated with traditional criminal prosecutions. *In re Gault*, 387 U.S. 1 (1967); *In re Winship*, 397 U.S. 358 (1970).

"We believe it is simply too late in the day to conclude, as did the District Court in this case, that a juvenile is not put in jeopardy at a proceeding whose object is to determine whether he has committed acts that violate a criminal law and whose potential consequences include both the stigma inherent in such a determination and the deprivation of liberty for many years.

"In *In re Gault*, this Court concluded that, for purposes of the right to counsel, a 'proceeding where the issue is whether the child will be found to be "delinquent" and subjected to the loss of his liberty for years is comparable in seriousness to a felony prosecution . . .'

"Thus, in terms of potential consequences, there is little to distinguish an adjudicatory hearing such as was held in this case from a traditional criminal prosecution. For that reason, it engenders elements of 'anxiety and insecurity' in a juvenile, and imposes a 'heavy personal strain.'

"We deal here, not with the 'formalities of the criminal adjudicative process,' *McKeiver v. Pennsylvania*, 403 U.S., at 551, but with an analysis of an aspect of the juvenile-court system in terms of the kind of risk to which jeopardy refers. Under our decisions we can find no persuasive distinction in that regard between the proceeding conducted in this case and a criminal prosecution, each of which is designed 'to vindicate [the] very vital interest in enforcement of criminal laws.' We therefore conclude that respondent was put in jeopardy at the adjudicatory hearing. Jeopardy attached when respondent was 'put to trial before the trier of the facts,' 400 U.S. at 479, that is, when the Juvenile Court, as the trier of the facts, began to hear evidence."

CASE SIGNIFICANCE: This case is significant because: (1) it extended the double jeopardy protection to juvenile proceedings, and (2) it implies that juvenile proceedings, although considered civil proceedings, do in fact have penal consequences and are therefore tantamount to criminal trials. The juvenile in this case had been adjudicated, but the judge transferred jurisdiction to the adult criminal court because he found the juvenile "unfit for the programs available through its juvenile facilities." The juvenile was subsequently tried in an adult court and convicted. The Court concluded that there was double jeopardy, saying that "the Double Jeopardy Clause . . . is written in terms of potential or risk of trial and conviction, not punishment." The Court added: "Respondent was subjected to the burden of two trials for the same offense; he was twice put to the task of marshaling his resources against those of the State, twice subjected to the 'heavy personal strain' which such an experience represents."

Some scholars maintain that although juvenile proceedings are civil in nature, the Supreme Court considers the substance and effect of the proceedings to be criminal. This case validates that assertion. Double jeopardy is generally defined as successive prosecution for the same offense by the same jurisdiction. By definition, double jeopardy applies only to criminal, not civil, cases. Nonetheless, the Court in this case considered an adjudication as equivalent to a trial, and thus applied the double jeopardy prohibition. The giving of rights to juveniles in adjudication proceedings, as mandated in the *Gault* case (*In re Gault*, 387 U.S. 1, [1967]) further attests to the "criminalization" of juvenile proceedings.

The policy implication of this case is clear: if a juvenile is to be transferred to the adult criminal court for trial in connection with a criminal offense, such transfer (or "waiver" or "certification") must be made prior to the adjudicatory hearing, otherwise jeopardy attaches.

Fare v. Michael C.
442 U.S. 707 (1979)

CAPSULE: A request by a juvenile to see his probation officer is not equivalent to asking for a lawyer.

FACTS: Michael C., a juvenile, was taken into police custody under suspicion of murder. Prior to questioning by two police officers, Michael C. was advised of his *Miranda* rights. When asked if he wanted to waive his right to have an attorney present during questioning, he responded by asking for his probation officer. He was informed by the police that the probation officer would be contacted later, but that he could talk to the police if he wanted to. Michael C. agreed to talk and during questioning made statements and drew sketches that incriminated him. He was charged with murder in juvenile court. Michael C. moved to suppress the incriminating statements and sketches, alleging that they were obtained in violation of his *Miranda* rights and that his request to see his probation officer was, in effect, an assertion of his right to remain silent and that this was equivalent to his having requested an attorney.

ISSUE: Is the request by a probationer to see his probation officer during police questioning the same as the request for an attorney, thus invoking the Fifth Amendment right to remain silent, pursuant to *Miranda*? NO.

DECISION: The request by a juvenile probationer during police questioning to see his probation officer, after having been given the *Miranda* warnings by the police, is not equivalent to asking for a lawyer and therefore is not considered an assertion of the right to remain silent. Evidence voluntarily given by the juvenile probationer is therefore admissible in court in a subsequent criminal trial.

REASON: "A probation officer is not in the same posture [as is a lawyer] with regard to either the accused or the system of justice as a whole. Often he is not trained in the law, and so is not in a position to advise the accused as to his legal rights. Neither is he a trained advocate, skilled in the representation of the interests of his client before police and courts. He does not assume the power to act on behalf of his client by virtue of his status as advisor, nor are the communications of the accused to the probation officer shielded by the lawyer-client privilege.

"Moreover, the probation officer is the employee of the State which seeks to prosecute the alleged offender. He is a peace officer, and as such is allied, to a greater or lesser extent, with his fellow peace officers. He owes an obligation to the State notwithstanding the obligation he may also owe the juvenile under his supervision. In most cases, the probation officer is duty bound to report wrongdoing by the juvenile when it comes to his attention, even if by communication from the juvenile himself."

CASE SIGNIFICANCE: Although this case involved a juvenile probationer, the Court's decision should apply to adult probationers and parolees as well. In essence, the Court said that a probation officer does not perform the same function as a lawyer; therefore a request by a probationer to see his probation officer is not equivalent to a request to see a lawyer. The Court then proceeded to distinguish between a probation officer and a lawyer. First, the Court stated that the communications of the accused to the probation officer are not shielded by the lawyer-client privilege. This means that information given by a client to the probation officer may be disclosed in court, unlike information shared by a client with a lawyer. Second, the Court makes clear that a probation officer's loyalty and obligation is to the state, despite any obligation he or she may also have to the probationer. This means that despite an officer's feelings for or rapport with a client, there should be no question of where his or her loyalties lay. Professionalism requires that these two obligations not be confused and that it be made clear to the probationer and the officer, particularly in those situations in which confidences are shared, that the officer's loyalty is ultimately with the state, not with the probationer.

Smith v. Daily Publishing Co.
443 U.S. 97 (1979)

CAPSULE: A state law making it a crime to publish the name of a juvenile charged with a crime is unconstitutional.

FACTS: On February 9, 1978, a 15-year-old student was shot and killed at a junior high school. A 14-year-old classmate was identified by seven eyewitnesses as the assailant and was arrested soon after the incident. The *Charleston Daily Mail* and the *Charleston Gazette* routinely monitored the police band radio frequency and, upon learning of the shooting, dispatched reporters and photographers to the scene of the shooting. Both newspapers obtained the name of the alleged assailant from various witnesses, the police, and an assistant prosecuting attorney, who were at the school.

Both newspapers published articles about the incident. The *Daily Mail*'s first article did not mention the juvenile suspect's name because of a Virginia statute prohibiting such publication without prior court approval. The *Gazette* published both the juvenile's name and picture in its article. The name of the alleged attacker was also broadcast over at least three radio stations on the days the newspaper articles appeared. Because the juvenile's name had become public knowledge, the *Daily Mail* included the information in a subsequent article it printed. An indictment was brought against both papers alleging that each had knowingly published the name of the juvenile in violation of state statute.

ISSUE: Does a state statute that makes it a crime for a newspaper to publish, without written approval of the juvenile court, the name of any youth charged as a juvenile offender violate the First and Fourteenth Amendments to the Constitution? YES.

DECISION: The state cannot punish the truthful publication of an alleged juvenile delinquent's name lawfully obtained by a newspaper because to do so would be a violation of the First and Fourteenth Amendments. The state's interest in protecting the anonymity of the juvenile offender cannot justify the statute's imposition of criminal sanctions on the press for the publication of a juvenile's name when lawfully obtained by the press.

REASON: "The sole interest advanced by the State to justify its criminal statute is to protect the anonymity of the juvenile offender. It is asserted that confidentiality will further his rehabilitation because publication of the name may encourage further antisocial conduct and also may cause the juvenile to lose future employment or suffer other consequences for this single offense. In *Davis v. Alaska*, 415 U.S. 308 (1974), similar arguments were advanced by the State to justify not permitting a criminal defendant to impeach a prosecution witness on the basis of his juvenile record. We said there that '[w]e do not and need not challenge the State's interest as a matter of its own policy in the administration of criminal justice to seek to preserve the anonymity of a juvenile offender.' *Id.*, at 319. However, we concluded that the State's policy must be subordinated to the defendant's Sixth Amendment right of confrontation. The important rights created by the First Amendment must be considered along with the rights of defendants guaranteed by the Sixth Amendment. *See Nebraska Press Ass'n v. Stuart*, 427 U.S., at 581. Therefore, the reasoning of *Davis* that the constitutional right must prevail over the state's interest in protecting juveniles applies with equal force here.

"The magnitude of the State's interest in this statute is not sufficient to justify application of a criminal penalty to respondents. Moreover, the statute's approach does not satisfy constitutional requirements. The statute does not restrict the electronic media or any form of publication, except 'newspapers,' from printing the names of youths charged in a juvenile proceeding. . . . Thus, even assuming the statute served a state interest of the highest order, it does not accomplish its stated purpose.'

CASE SIGNIFICANCE: This case represents a classic confrontation between freedom of the press and a juvenile's right to anonymity in the name of rehabilitation. The Court said that freedom of the press prevails over the state's interest in protecting juveniles. Nonetheless, the Court emphasized that its decision in this case is narrow and must be so interpreted. It said: "At issue is simply the power of a state to punish the truthful publication of an alleged juvenile delinquent's name lawfully obtained by a newspaper. The asserted state interest cannot justify the statute's imposition of criminal sanctions on this type of publication."

What about prohibitions by the court, backed up by threats of judicial sanction, against the publication of names in a juvenile proceeding? Most states have such a rule, which is strictly enforced by judges. Such rules are constitutional although they infringe upon the freedom of the press. This is because such rules are not considered punitive actions taken as a form of prior restraint. What a judge does, instead, is use the judicial contempt power to enforce court-mandated rules in an effort to maintain anonymity. Citation for contempt is not equivalent to a penal sanction for a criminal offense, although both can result in imprisonment. Generally, a court's contempt power is subject to fewer constitutional restraints and is not viewed as penal in nature. In sum, what the legislature cannot do by statute, the judge can most likely do through the exercise of contempt powers.

Schall v. Martin
104 S. Ct. 2403 (1984)

CAPSULE: Preventive detention of juveniles is constitutional.

FACTS: Martin was arrested on December 13, 1977, and was charged with first-degree robbery, second-degree assault and criminal possession of a weapon. Martin was 14 years old at the time of arrest and therefore came under the jurisdiction of New York's Family Court. Martin's alleged offenses happened late at night and he lied to the police about where and with whom he lived. At the delinquency proceedings, the Family Court judge ordered Martin detained under New York statute, citing the possession of the loaded weapon, the false address given to the police, and the lateness of the hour, as evidence of lack of supervision. Five days later, a probable cause hearing was held and probable cause was found to exist for all charges against Martin. At the factfinding hearing, Martin was found guilty of robbery and criminal possession of a weapon. He was adjudicated a delinquent and placed on two years probation. Martin was detained a total of 15 days.

The New York law challenged by Martin in this case contained the following provisions: it authorized the pretrial detention of an accused juvenile delinquent on the basis of a finding, preceded by notice and a hearing and supported by a statement of reasons and fact, of a "serious risk" that the child "may before the return date commit an act which if committed by an adult would constitute a crime," and provided for a more formal hearing within at least 17 days if detention was ordered.

ISSUE: Does the due process clause of the Fourteenth Amendment prohibit the preventive detention of accused juveniles? NO.

DECISION: Preventive detention is constitutional because it serves to protect both the juvenile and society from the hazards of pretrial crime. This objective is compatible with the "fundamental fairness" requirement of the due process clause in juvenile proceedings.

REASON: "There is no doubt that the Due Process Clause of the Fourteenth Amendment is applicable to juvenile proceedings. . . . We have held that certain basic constitutional protections enjoyed by adults accused of crimes also apply to juveniles. But the Constitution does not mandate elimination of all differences in the treatment of juveniles. See, e.g., *McKeiver v. Pennsylvania*, 403 U.S. 528 (1971) (no right to a jury trial). The state has a 'parens patriae interest in preserving and protecting the welfare of the child.' *Santosky v. Kramer*, 455 U.S. 745, 766 (1982) which makes a juvenile proceeding fundamentally different from an adult criminal trial. We have tried to strike a balance—to respect the 'informality' and 'flexibility' that characterize juvenile proceedings and yet to ensure that such proceedings comport with the 'fundamental fairness' demanded by the Due Process Clause.

In *Bell v. Wolfish*, "we left open the question whether any governmental objective other than ensuring a detainee's presence at trial may constitutionally justify pretrial detention. As an initial matter, therefore, we must decide whether, in the context of the juvenile system, the combined interest in protecting both the community and the juvenile himself from consequence of future criminal conduct is sufficient to justify such detention.

"The 'legitimate and compelling state interest' in protecting the community from crime cannot be doubted. *De Veau v. Braisted*, 363 U.S. 144 (1960) . . . The harm suffered by the victim of a crime is not dependent upon the age of the perpetrator. And the harm to society generally may even be greater in this context given the high rate of recidivism among juveniles.

"The juvenile's countervailing interest in freedom from institutional restraints, even for a brief time involved here, is undoubtedly substantial as well. But that interest must be qualified by the recognition that juveniles, unlike adults, are always in some form of custody. Children, by definition are not assumed to have the capacity to take care of themselves. They are assumed to be subject to the control of their parents, and if parental control falters, the State must play its part as *parens patriae*. In this respect, the juvenile's liberty interest may, in appropriate circumstances, be subordinated to the State's '*parens patriae* interest in preserving and promoting the welfare of the child.' *Santosky v. Kramer, supra*, at 766."

CASE SIGNIFICANCE: This case is important because, for the first time, the Supreme Court recognized the constitutionality of preventive detention of juveniles, an issue hitherto unresolved. Preventive detention is defined as detention for the purpose of preventing the juvenile from committing crimes in the future. It is questionable because of the presumption of innocence and because it punishes a juvenile for crimes he or she has not yet committed.

The Court held that while a juvenile's constitutional interests must be protected, the interests of the State and society must also be considered. When these interests appear to conflict, it is the Court's duty to weigh and balance these interests and rule in favor of the more compelling interest. The type of preventive detention used in New York has the best interests of both the child and the community in mind. Under the New York law, the juvenile is held only as long as necessary to process the case and these proceedings are bound by time requirements. What little harm may be done to the juvenile while being detained does not outweigh the harm that conceivably could be inflicted on community members by an unsupervised juvenile.

This decision does not say that unlimited preventive detention is constitutional. The New York law that was upheld in this case provided for preventive detention on the basis of a finding, preceded by notice and a hearing, and supported by a statement of reasons and facts of a serious risk that the child "may before the return date commit an act which if committed by an adult would constitute a crime." The law also provided for a more formal hearing within at least 17 days if detention was ordered. These provisions of the New York law were deemed constitutional. What this means is that any state statute with provisions for preventive detention similar to New York's would also be upheld as constitutional. Those with different provisions, particularly if they are more arbitrary, might not merit the Court's approval. State juvenile detention laws will be decided by the Court on a case-by-case basis. The closer the provisions of these laws are to the New York statute, the greater are their chances of being declared constitutional.

New Jersey v. T.L.O.
469 U.S. 325 (1985)

CAPSULE: Public school officials need only have "reasonable grounds" to search; they do not need a warrant or probable cause.

FACTS: A 14-year-old girl was discovered smoking a cigarette in a high school lavatory in violation of school rules. She was taken to the principal's office by a teacher. When the student denied that she had been smoking, the assistant vice principal demanded to see her purse. Inside the purse, a pack of cigarettes and a package of cigarette rolling papers, commonly associated with the use of marijuana, were discovered. The assistant vice principal then proceeded to search the purse thoroughly and found marijuana, a pipe, plastic bags, a substantial amount of money, an index card containing a list of names of students who owed her money, and two letters that implicated her in marijuana dealing. The state brought delinquency charges against the student in juvenile court. She moved to have the evidence found in her purse suppressed, alleging that the search was illegal.

ISSUES:
1. Does the Fourth Amendment prohibition against unreasonable searches and seizures apply to high school officials? YES.
2. Does the warrant requirement apply to searches performed by high school officials? NO.

DECISIONS:
1. The Fourth Amendment prohibition against unreasonable searches and seizures applies to searches conducted by high school officials, but the school's legitimate need to maintain a learning environment requires some easing of the Fourth Amendment restrictions.
2. Public school officials do not need a warrant or probable cause before conducting a search. For a search to be valid, all they need are "reasonable grounds" to suspect that the search will produce evidence that the student has violated or is violating either the law or the rules of the school.

REASON: "In determining whether the search at issue in this case violated the Fourth Amendment, we are faced initially with the question whether that Amendment's prohibition on unreasonable searches and seizures applies to searches conducted by public school officials. We hold that it does.

"It is now beyond dispute that 'the Federal Constitution, by virtue of the Fourteenth Amendment, prohibits unreasonable searches and seizures by state officers.' *Elkins v. United States*, 364 U.S. 206, 213 (1960). . . . Equally indisputable is the proposition that the Fourteenth Amendment protects the rights of students against encroachment by public school officials . . .

"These two propositions—that the Fourth Amendment applies to the States through the Fourteenth Amendment, and that the actions of public school officials are subject to the limits placed on state action by the Fourth Amendment—might appear sufficient to answer the suggestion that the Fourth Amendment does not proscribe unreasonable searches by school officials. On reargument, the State of New Jersey has argued that the history of the Fourth Amendment indicates that the Amendment was intended to regulate only searches and seizures carried out by law enforcement officials; accordingly, although public school officials are concededly state agents for purposes of the Fourteenth Amendment, the Fourth Amendment creates no rights enforceable against them.

". . . this Court has never limited the Amendment's prohibition on unreasonable searches and seizures to operations conducted by the police. Rather, the Court has long spoken of the Fourth Amendment's strictures as restraints imposed upon 'governmental action'—that is, 'upon the activities of sovereign authority.' *Burdeau v. McDowell*, 256 U.S. 465, 475 (1921). Accordingly, we have held the Fourth Amendment applicable to the activities of civil as well as criminal authorities: building inspectors . . . and even firemen entering privately owned premises to battle a fire . . . all are subject to the restraints imposed by the Fourth Amendment . . .

"To hold that the Fourth Amendment applies to searches conducted by school authorities is only to begin the inquiry into the standards governing such searches. Although the underlying command of the Fourth Amendment is always that searches and seizures be reasonable, what is reasonable depends on the context within which a search takes place. The determination of the standard of reasonableness governing any specific class of searches requires 'balancing the need to search against the invasion which the search entails.' *Camara v. Municipal Court, supra*, at 536-537. On one side of the balance are arrayed the individual's legitimate expectations of privacy and personal security; on the other, the government's need for effective methods to deal with breaches of public order.

"The school setting also requires some modification of the level of suspicion of illicit activity needed to justify a search. Ordinarily, a search—even one that may permissibly be carried out without a warrant—must be based on 'probable cause' to believe that a violation of the law has occurred . . . However, 'probable cause' is not an irreducible requirement of a valid search. The fundamental command of the Fourth Amendment is that searches and seizures be reasonable, and although 'both the concept of probable cause and the requirement of a warrant bear on the reasonableness of a search, . . . in certain limited circumstances neither is required.' *Almeida-Sanchez v. United States* [413 U.S. 266 (1973)] at 277."

CASE SIGNIFICANCE: This case clarifies the issue of whether public school officials must obtain a warrant before conducting a search, and what degree of certainty is needed for a valid search by public school officials. The Court said that public school officials are representatives of the state and as such are limited by the provisions of the Fourth Amendment. But the Court also recognized that in order to maintain an environment in which learning can take place, some restrictions placed on public authorities by the Fourth Amendment had to be eased. Therefore, the Court ruled that public school officials: (1) need not obtain a warrant before conducting a search, and (2) do not need probable cause to justify a search; they only need reasonable grounds—a lower standard of certainty.

Whether the ruling applies to college students or to high school students in private schools was not addressed by the Court. It would be reasonable to assume, however, that this ruling would also apply to public elementary school students. On the other hand, lower court decisions have usually held that college students, regardless of age, are considered adults and therefore this case probably does not apply to college students or campuses. It is noted that this case applies to high school teachers and administrators who are conducting a search. It does not apply to police officers who are bound by the "probable cause" requirement even in school searches. The only possible exception might be if the officers are to perform the search at the request of public school authorities.

Thompson v. Oklahoma
487 U.S. 815 (1988)

CAPSULE: It is cruel and unusual punishment to impose the death penalty on a juvenile who commits an offense at age 15 or younger.

FACTS: Thompson, at age 15, actively participated in the brutal murder of his brother-in-law. Although considered a child under Oklahoma law, the district attorney sought to have him tried as an adult. Thompson was tried as an adult and was found guilty of the murder. Due to the heinous nature of the crime, Thompson was sentenced to death.

ISSUE: Is the death penalty cruel and unusual punishment for a crime committed by a 15-year-old? YES.

DECISION: The execution of a person who was under 16 years of age at the time of the offense is cruel and unusual punishment and therefore is prohibited by the Eighth and Fourteenth Amendments.

REASON: "In determining whether the categorical Eighth Amendment prohibition applies, this Court must be guided by the 'evolving standards of decency that mark the progress of a maturing society,' *Trop v. Dulles*, 356 U.S. 86, 101, and, in doing so must review relevant legislative enactments and jury determinations and consider the reasons why a civilized society may accept or reject the death penalty for a person less than 16 years old at the time of the crime.

"Relevant state statutes—particularly those of the 18 states that have expressly considered the question of a minimum age for imposition of the death penalty, and have uniformly required that the defendant have attained at least the age of 16 at the time of the capital offense—support the conclusion that it would offend civilized standards of decency to execute a person who was less than 16 years old at the time of his or her offense.

"The juvenile's reduced culpability, and the fact that the application of the death penalty to this class of offenders does not measurably contribute to the essential purposes underlying the penalty, also support the conclusion that the imposition of the penalty on persons under the age of 16 constitutes unconstitutional punishment."

CASE SIGNIFICANCE: Under this ruling, any offender who was 15 years old or younger at the time the offense was committed could not be given the death penalty, regardless of the nature or heinousness of the offense. The Court took into account the fact that the statutes of approximately 18 states require that the defendant be at least 16 years old at the time of the commission of the offense for the death penalty to be imposed, saying that "it would offend civilized standards of decency to execute a person who was less than 16 years old at the time of his or her offense." In a concurring opinion, however, Justice O'Connor noted that "the Federal Government and 19 States have authorized capital punishment without setting any minimum age, and have also provided for some 15-year-olds to be prosecuted as adults." This indicates, she said, that there was no consensus about whether 15-year-olds should be executed.

What this decision did not say was whether juveniles could be executed at all. Is 15 the minimum age, or would juvenile status be a better determinant of whether the offender should be executed? Opponents of the Oklahoma law wanted the Court to declare any execution of a juvenile to be unconstitutional. The Court did not go that far; however, the issue of the absolute age when an execution could take place was decided by the Court one year later in the case of *Stanford v. Kentucky*, 109 S. Ct. 2969 (1989).

Stanford v. Kentucky
109 S. Ct. 2969 (1989)

CAPSULE: It is not cruel and unusual punishment to impose the death penalty on a juvenile who commits an offense at age 16 or older.

FACTS: Stanford was charged with capital murder. He was 17 years old when the crime was committed. He was transferred to adult court after a juvenile hearing under state statute. Stanford was convicted, and because of the heinousness of the crime, was sentenced to death.

ISSUE: Does the imposition of the death penalty for a crime committed at age 16 or 17 years old constitute cruel and unusual punishment? NO.

DECISION: It is not cruel and unusual punishment to impose capital punishment on an offender who was 16 or 17 years old at the time the crime was committed.

REASON: "Whether a particular punishment violates the Eighth Amendment depends on whether it constitutes one of 'those modes or acts of punishment . . . considered cruel and unusual at the time the Bill of Rights was adopted.' *Ford v. Wainright*, 477 U.S. 399, 405, or is contrary to the 'evolving standards of decency that mark the progress of a maturing society, *Trop v. Dulles*, 356 U.S. 86, 101. Petitioners have not alleged that their sentences would have been considered cruel and unusual in the 18th century, and could not support such a contention, since, at that time, the common law set the rebuttable presumption of incapacity to commit felonies (which were punishable by death) at the age of 14.

"In determining whether a punishment violates evolving standards of decency, this Court looks not to its own subjective conceptions, but, rather, to the conceptions of modern American society as reflected by objective evidence. E.g., *Coker v. Georgia*, 433 U.S. 584, 592. The primary and most reliable evidence of national consensus—the pattern of federal and state laws—fails to meet petitioner's heavy burden of proving a settled consensus against the execution of 16- and 17-year-old offenders."

CASE SIGNIFICANCE: This case resolves an issue that the Court refused to address the previous year in *Thompson v. Oklahoma*, 487 U.S. 815 (1988)—whether a defendant who was of juvenile age (either 16 or 17) at the time the offense was committed could be given the death penalty. The Court's ruling here is unequivocal, stating that "the imposition of capital punishment on an individual for a crime committed at 16 or 17 years of age does not constitute cruel and unusual punishment under the Eighth Amendment." Thus the Court set the minimum age at 16 if the state is to impose the death penalty. Juveniles who are age 15 or younger during the commission of the offense cannot be given the death penalty.

In reaching that conclusion, the Court relied on "evolving standards of decency that mark the progress of a maturing society." It then concluded that there was no consensus against the execution of 16- and 17-year-olds, stating that "of the 37 States that permit capital punishment, 15 states decline to impose it on 16-year-olds and 12 on 17-year-olds." The Court said that "this does not establish the degree of national agreement this Court has previously thought sufficient to label a punishment cruel and unusual."

Thus the issue is settled, at least for now: executing 15-year-olds is cruel and unusual punishment, hence unconstitutional; executing juveniles who are 16 years old or older is constitutional. It must be stressed, however, that there must be state or federal law authorizing the imposition of the death penalty before that form of punishment can be carried out in a particular jurisdiction.

Coy v. Iowa
487 U.S. 1012 (1988)

CAPSULE: Placing a screen between the complaining witnesses and the defendant during a criminal trial violates a defendant's right to confront witnesses and is unconstitutional.

FACTS: Defendant Coy was arrested and charged with sexually assaulting two 13-year-old girls while they were camping out in the backyard of the house next door to him. According to the girls, the assailant entered the tent after the girls fell asleep. He was wearing a stocking over his head, shined a flashlight in their eyes, and warned the girls not to look at him. Neither girl was able to describe his face. At the beginning of Coy's trial, the prosecutor filed a motion to allow the complaining witnesses to testify either via closed-circuit television or behind a screen. The trial court approved the use of a large screen to be placed between Coy and the witness stand during the girls' testimony. The screen enabled Coy to dimly perceive the witnesses, but the witnesses were not able to see Coy at all. Coy objected to the use of the screen on constitutional grounds but the trial judge rejected his claims. The jury was instructed to draw no inference of guilt from the screen. Coy was convicted of two counts of lascivious acts with a child.

ISSUE: Is placing a screen between a complaining witness and the defendant during a criminal trial constitutional? NO.

DECISION: The confrontation clause of the Sixth Amendment provides the defendant with the right to confront witnesses giving testimony against him face-to-face.

REASON: "The perception that confrontation is essential to fairness has persisted over the centuries because there is much truth to it. A witness 'may feel quite differently when he has to repeat his story looking at the man whom he will harm greatly by distorting or mistaking the facts. He can now understand what sort of human being that man is. It is always more difficult to tell a lie about a person 'to his face' than 'behind his back.' In the former context, even if the lie is told, it will often be told less convincingly. The Confrontation Clause does not, of course, compel the witness to fix his eyes upon the defendant; he may studiously look elsewhere, but the trier of fact will draw its own conclusions. Thus the right to face-to-face confrontation serves much the same purpose as a less explicit component of the Confrontation Clause that we have had more frequent occasion to discuss—the right to cross-examine the accuser; both 'ensur[e] the integrity of the factfinding process. The State can hardly gainsay the profound effect upon a witness of standing in the presence of the person the witness accuses, since that is the very phenomenon it relies upon to establish the potential 'trauma' that allegedly justified the extraordinary procedure in the present case. That face-to-face presence may, unfortunately, upset the truthful rape victim or abused child; but by the same token it may confound and undo the false accuser, or reveal the child coached by a malevolent adult. It is a truism that constitutional protections have costs.

"The remaining question is whether the right of confrontation was in fact violated in this case. The screen at issue was specifically designed to enable the complaining witnesses to avoid viewing appellant as they gave their testimony, and the record indicates that it was successful in this objective. App. 10-11. It is difficult to imagine a more obvious or damaging violation of the defendant's right to face-to-face encounter."

CASE SIGNIFICANCE: This was the first of two cases (the other being *Maryland v. Craig*, 497 U.S. 836 [1990]) decided by the Court in a span of two years on the defendant's right to confrontation. The Court said that the use of a big screen to be placed between the defendant and the witness stand during the girl-victims' testimony violated defendant's constitutional right, saying that "we have never doubted that the Confrontation Clause guarantees the defendant a face-to-face meeting with witnesses appearing before the trier of fact." The Court said that defendant's right to confrontation is fundamental and prevails over the state's power to protect the child. This decision, however, was modified two years later in *Maryland v. Craig*, 497 U.S. 836 (1990), wherein the Court held that the right to confrontation is not absolute and could be limited by the state.

Maryland v. Craig
497 U.S. 836 (1990)

CAPSULE: A criminal defendant does not have an absolute right to face-to-face confrontation of witnesses.

FACTS: In 1986, Sandra Craig was charged with child abuse, first and second degree sexual offenses, perverted sexual practice, assault, and battery of a six-year-old child that attended the kindergarten and child care center that was owned and operated by Craig. Before the trial began, the State of Maryland sought the use of a procedure that permitted the judge to receive, via one-way closed circuit television, the testimony of the alleged child abuse victim. The prosecution said that the child's courtroom testimony would result in serious emotional distress and the child not being able to reasonably communicate. When the procedure is used, the child, prosecutor, and defense counsel withdraw to another room where the child is examined and cross-examined; the judge, jury, and defendant remain in the courtroom where the testimony is given. Although the child cannot see the defendant, the defendant remains in electronic communication with counsel, and objections can be made and ruled on as if the witness were in the courtroom. Craig objected to the procedure claiming constitutional violation.

ISSUE: Does the confrontation clause of the Sixth Amendment categorically prohibit a witness from testifying against a defendant at trial outside the defendant's physical presence? NO.

DECISION: The confrontation clause does not guarantee criminal defendants an absolute right to a face-to-face meeting with the witnesses against them at trial. The right to confront accusatory witnesses may be satisfied despite the absence of a physical, face-to-face confrontation at trial if denial of such confrontation is necessary to further an important public policy and if the testimony's reliability is otherwise assured.

REASON: "In sum, our precedents establish that 'the Confrontation Clause reflects a *preference* for a face-to-face confrontation at trial,' *Roberts, supra*, at 63 (emphasis added; footnote omitted), a preference that 'must occasionally give way to considerations of public policy and necessities of the case.'. . . '[W]e have attempted to harmonize the goal of the Clause—placing limits on the kind of evidence that may be received against a defendant—with a societal interest in accurate factfinding, which may require consideration of out-of-court statements.' We have accordingly interpreted the Confrontation Clause in a manner sensitive to its purposes and sensitive to the necessities of trial and the adversary process.

"That the face-to-face confrontation requirement is not absolute does not, of course, mean that it may easily be dispensed with. As we suggested in *Coy*, our precedents confirm that a defendant's right to confront accusatory witnesses may be satisfied absent a physical, face-to-face confrontation at trial only where denial of such confrontation is necessary to further an important public policy and only where the reliability of the testimony is otherwise assured.

"We likewise conclude today that a State's interest in the psychological well-being of child abuse victims may be sufficiently important to outweigh, at least in some cases, a defendant's right to face his or her accusers in court. That a significant majority of States have enacted statutes to protect child witnesses from the trauma of giving testimony in child abuse cases attests to the widespread belief in the importance of such a public policy."

CASE SIGNIFICANCE: *Craig* is not really a juvenile justice case; instead, it is a case involving children. As in *Coy*, the defendant in this case maintained that she had a constitutional right to a face-to-face confrontation with the victim-witness, a child. She maintained that the Maryland procedure that permitted the judge to receive, via one-way closed circuit television, the testimony of the alleged child abuse victim was unconstitutional as a violation of the defendant's right to cross-examine witnesses. The prosecution justified the procedure by saying that the child's courtroom testimony would result in serious emotional distress and not being able to reasonably communicate. The Court upheld the prosecutor's contention and declared the procedure constitutional, saying that "we have never held . . . that the Confrontation Clause guarantees criminal defendants the absolute right to a face-to-face meeting with witnesses against them at trial." This means that in this clash between the constitutional right of the accused to confrontation and the power of the state to protect juveniles, the interest of the juvenile prevails and the power of the state is upheld. How far the Court will go to allow procedures that protect child witnesses in criminal trials is difficult to tell. What is important to realize is that the defendant's right to confrontation is not absolute and that, given proper safeguards, the interest of children can and should be upheld.

Chapter 6—Sentencing

Weems v. United States
217 U.S. 349 (1910)

CAPSULE: A sentence that is disproportionate to the offense constitutes cruel and unusual punishment.

FACTS: Weems, a U.S. government officer stationed in the Philippine Islands, was charged with falsifying a "public and official document." The complaint charged that while Weems was acting as the disbursing officer of the Bureau of Coast Guard and Transportation of the United States government of the Philippine Islands, he sought to deceive and defraud the United States government of the Philippine Islands and its officials. The falsification was committed by entering into the cashbook as paid out, wages to lighthouse employees in the amounts of 204 pesos and 408 pesos, Philippine currency. Weems was convicted and sentenced to 15 years at hard labor, the wearing of chains, the lifelong loss of certain rights, and the payment of a fine of 4,000 pesos and court costs.

ISSUE: Does a sentence that is disproportionate to the offense committed violate the Eighth Amendment? YES.

DECISION: A sentence that is disproportionate to the offense violates the Eighth Amendment ban against cruel and unusual punishment.

REASON: "By other provisions of the Code we find that there are only two degrees of punishment higher in scale than cadena temporal—death, and cadena perpetua. The punishment of cadena temporal is from twelve years and one day to twenty years which 'shall be served' in certain 'penal institutions.' And it is provided that 'those sentenced to cadena perpetua shall labor for the benefit of the state. They shall always carry a chain at the ankle, hanging from the wrists; they shall be employed at hard and painful labor, and shall receive no assistance whatsoever from without the institution.' There are, besides, certain accessory penalties imposed, which are defined to be: (1) civil interdiction; (2) perpetual absolute disqualification; (3) subjection to surveillance during life.

"These provisions are attacked as infringing that provision of the Bill of Rights of the islands which forbids the infliction of cruel and unusual punishment . . . Let us confine it to the minimum degree of the law, for it is with the law that we are most concerned. Its minimum degree is confinement in a penal institution for twelve years and one day, a chain at the ankle and wrist of the offender, hard and painful labor, no assistance from friend or relative, no marital authority or parental rights or rights of property, no participation even in the family council. These parts of his penalty endure for the term of imprisonment. From other parts there is no intermission. His prison bars and chains are removed, it is true, after twelve years, but he goes from them to a perpetual limitation of his liberty. He is forever kept under the shadow of his crime, forever kept within voice and view of the criminal magistrate, not being able to change his domicile without notice to the 'authority in charge of his surveillance,' and without permission in writing. He may not seek, even in other scenes and among other people, to retrieve his fall from rectitude. Even that hope is taken from him, and he is subject to tormenting regulations that, if not so tangible as iron bars and stone walls, oppress as much by their continuity, and deprive of essential liberty. No circumstance of degradation is omitted. It may be even the cruelty of pain is not omitted. He must bear a chain night and day. He is condemned to painful as well as hard labor. What painful labor may mean we have no exact measure. It must be something more than hard labor. It may be hard labor pressed to the point of pain. Such penalties for such offenses amaze those who have formed their conception of the relation of a state to even its offending citizens from the practice of the American commonwealths, and believe that it is a precept of justice that punishment for crime should be graduated and proportioned to offense."

CASE SIGNIFICANCE: This is perhaps the earliest case decided by the Supreme Court under the Eighth Amendment protection against cruel and unusual punishment as it applied to sentencing. In essence it says that a sentence that is disproportionate to the offense violates the Eighth Amendment. The Court stated that the punishment here was more severe than the crime warranted, and therefore was unconstitutional. The Court pointed out that there were only two degrees of punishment for this particular crime in the Philippine Islands, neither of which fit the plaintiff's case. The Court therefore simply chose something in between. But more important to the Court than the arbitrary manner in which the punishment was chosen was the statute itself. The punishments for fraud of any degree were extreme. Even after an offender had served sentence at hard and "painful" labor, punishment did not cease. The offender faced losing rights of family and property for life. The Court stated that the Constitution prohibited punishment that is cruel and unusual and Weem's sentence was both. (Note: Although this case took place in the Philippines, the provisions of the U.S. Constitution applied because at that time the Philippines was a United States colony.)

Trop v. Dulles
356 U.S. 86 (1958)

CAPSULE: Loss of American citizenship constitutes cruel and unusual punishment.

FACTS: In 1944, Trop, a native-born American, was a private in the United States Army, serving in French Morocco. On May 22, he escaped from the stockade at Casablanca, where he had been confined due to a breach of discipline. The next day, Trop and a companion were walking along a road in the general direction back to Casablanca when an Army truck approached and stopped. A witness testified that Trop boarded the truck willingly and that no words were spoken. Trop was turned over to military police. Trop's "desertion" lasted less than one day and he willingly surrendered to an Army officer while walking back toward his base. He testified that before the Army vehicle appeared, he and his companion had decided to return to the stockade. He stated they had no money, nowhere to go, and they were cold and hungry. A general court-martial convicted Trop of desertion and sentenced him to three years at hard labor, forfeiture of all pay and allowances, and a dishonorable discharge. In 1952, Trop applied for a passport. His application was denied on the ground that under the provisions of §401(g) of the Nationality Act of 1940, he had lost his citizenship because of his conviction and dishonorable discharge for wartime desertion.

ISSUE: Is loss of citizenship as punishment for desertion cruel and unusual, in violation of the Eighth Amendment? YES.

DECISION: Citizenship is not subject to the general powers of the national government and therefore cannot be divested in the exercise of those powers. Even if citizenship could be divested in the exercise of some governmental power, §401(g) violates the Eighth Amendment because it is penal in nature and prescribes a "cruel and unusual" form of punishment.

REASON: "Citizenship is not a license that expires upon misbehavior. The duties of citizenship are numerous, and the discharge of many of these obligations is essential to the security and well-being of the Nation. The citizen who fails to pay his taxes or to abide by the laws safeguarding the integrity of elections deals a dangerous blow to his country. But could a citizen be deprived of his nationality for evading these basic responsibilities of citizenship? In time of war the citizen's duties include not only the military defense of the Nation but also full participation in the manifold activities of the civilian ranks. Failure to perform any of these obligations may cause the Nation serious injury, and in appropriate circumstances, the punishing power is available to deal with derelictions of duty. But citizenship is not lost every time a duty of citizenship is shirked. And the deprivation of citizenship is not a weapon that the government may use to express its displeasure at a citizen's conduct, however reprehensible that conduct may be. As long as a person does not voluntarily renounce or abandon his citizenship, and this petitioner has done neither, I believe his fundamental right of citizenship is secure. On this ground alone the judgment in this case should be reversed.

"Section 401(g) is a penal law, and we must face the question whether the Constitution permits the Congress to take away citizenship as a punishment for crime. If it is assumed that the power of Congress extends to divestment of citizenship, the problem still remains as to this statute whether denationalization is a cruel and unusual punishment within the meaning of the Eighth Amendment. Since wartime desertion is punishable by death, there can be no argument that the punishment of denationalization is excessive in relation to the gravity of the crime. The question is whether this penalty subjects the individual to a fate forbidden by the principle of civilized treatment guaranteed by the Eighth Amendment.

". . . The basic concept underlying the Eighth Amendment is nothing less than the dignity of man. While the State has the power to punish, the Amendment stands to assure that this power be exercised within the limits of civilized standards. Fines, imprisonment and even execution may be imposed depending upon the enormity of the crime, but any technique outside the bounds of these traditional penalties is constitutionally suspect. This Court has had little occasion to give precise content to the Eighth Amendment, and, in an enlightened democracy such as ours, this is not surprising. But when the Court was confronted with a punishment of 12 years in irons at hard and painful labor imposed for the crime of falsifying public records, it did not hesitate to declare that the penalty was cruel in its excessiveness and unusual in its character. *Weems v. United States*, 217 U.S. 349. The Court recognized in that case that the words of the Amendment are not precise, and that their scope is not static. The Amendment must draw its meaning from the evolving standards of decency that mark the progress of a maturing society.

"We believe, as did Chief Judge Clark in the court below, that use of denationalization as a punishment is barred by the Eighth Amendment. There may be involved no physical mistreatment, no primitive torture. There is instead the total destruction of the individual's status in organized society. It is a form of punishment more primitive than torture, for it destroys for the individual the political existence that was centuries in the development. The punishment strips the citizen of his status in the national and international political community. His very existence is at the sufferance of the country in which he happens to find himself. While any one country may accord him some rights, and presumably as long as he remained in this country he would enjoy the limited rights of an alien, no country need do so because he is stateless. Furthermore, his enjoyment of even the limited rights of an alien might be subject to termination at any time by reason of deportation. In short, the expatriate has lost the right to have rights."

CASE SIGNIFICANCE: This is one of the few cases decided by the Supreme Court on the Eighth Amendment ban against cruel and unusual punishment in a non-criminal law context. Although the Court considered the stripping of citizenship penal in nature, this case denied a passport on grounds that the applicant was no longer a citizen because he was stripped of citizenship as a result of desertion. In essence, the Court said that denationalization as a form of punishment is barred by the Eighth Amendment. The Court stated:

> There may be involved no physical mistreatment, no primitive torture. There is instead the total destruction of the individual's status in organized society. It is a form of punishment more primitive than torture, for it destroys for the individual the political existence that was centuries in the development. The punishment strips the citizen of his status in the national and international political community.

The Court added that "this punishment is offensive to cardinal principles for which the Constitution stands." What this decision says is that the cruel and unusual punishment provision of the Constitution applies not only to physical forms of punishment, but to psychological forms as well—as exemplified in the deprivation of citizenship. The Court said that a denationalized person "knows not what discriminations may be established against him, what proscriptions may be directed against him, and when and for what cause his existence in his native land may be terminated." The Court also considered practices in other countries to determine whether a form of punishment is proscribed by the Constitution, saying that "the civilized nations of the world are in virtual unanimity that statelessness is not to be imposed as punishment for crime."

North Carolina v. Pearce
395 U.S. 711 (1969)

CAPSULE: Full credit must be given upon reconviction to time already served in prison for the same offense. Judges may impose a higher sentence on reconviction.

FACTS: Pearce was convicted in North Carolina of assault with intent to commit rape. He was given a prison sentence of 12 to 15 years by the trial judge. His conviction was later reversed. Pearce was retried, convicted, and sentenced. The term he received on reconviction, added to the time that Pearce had already served in prison, amounted to a longer total sentence than that originally imposed.

ISSUES:
1. Must full credit be given for time already served when a second sentence for a new conviction of the same offense is imposed? YES.
2. May a judge, upon reconviction, impose a longer prison sentence than the defendant originally received? YES.

DECISIONS:
1. The double jeopardy clause of the Fifth Amendment is violated when punishment already exacted for an offense is not fully "credited" in imposing sentence upon a new conviction for the same offense.
2. Neither the double jeopardy clause nor the equal protection clause imposes an absolute bar to a more severe sentence upon reconviction.

REASONS:
1. "We hold that the constitutional guarantee against multiple punishments for the same offense absolutely requires that punishment already exacted be fully 'credited' in imposing sentence upon a new conviction for the same offense. If, upon a new trial, the defendant is acquitted, there is no way the years he spent in prison can be returned to him. But if he is reconvicted, those years can and must be returned—by subtracting them from whatever new sentence is imposed.
2. "Long-established constitutional doctrine makes clear that, beyond the requirement already discussed, the guarantee against double jeopardy imposes no restriction upon the length of a sentence imposed upon reconviction. At least since 1896, when *United States v. Ball*, 163 U.S. 662, was decided, it has been settled that this constitutional guarantee imposes no limitations whatever upon the power to retry a defendant who has succeeded in getting his first conviction set aside.

"The other argument advanced in support of the proposition that the Constitution absolutely forbids the imposition of a more severe sentence upon retrial is grounded upon the Equal Protection Clause of the Fourteenth Amendment. The theory advanced is that, since convicts who do not seek new trials cannot have their sentences increased, it creates an invidious classification to impose that risk only upon those who succeed in getting their original convictions set aside. The argument, while not lacking in ingenuity, cannot withstand close examination.

"To say that there exists no absolute constitutional bar to the imposition of a more severe sentence upon retrial is not, however, to end the inquiry. There remains for consideration the impact of the Due Process Clause of the Fourteenth Amendment. It can hardly be doubted that it would be a flagrant violation of the Fourteenth Amendment for a state trial court to follow an announced practice of imposing a heavier sentence upon every reconvicted defendant for the explicit purpose of punishing the defendant for his having succeeded in getting his original conviction set aside.

"Due process of law, then, requires that vindictiveness against a defendant for having successfully attacked his first conviction must play no part in the sentence he receives after a new trial. And since the fear of such vindictiveness may unconstitutionally deter a defendant's exercise of the right to appeal or collaterally attack his first conviction, due process also requires that a defendant be freed of apprehension of such a retaliatory motivation on the part of the sentencing judge."

CASE SIGNIFICANCE: This case clarifies two previously murky issues in the sentencing process: whether time served for the first sentence in a previous trial should be given full credit if the defendant is retried and reconvicted for the same offense, and whether a more severe penalty can be imposed in a second trial for the same offense. The Supreme Court resolved both issues affirmatively, saying that full credit must be given for the previous time served for the same offense and that a higher sentence could be imposed for the same offense upon a second conviction resulting from a new trial.

On the first issue, the Court wrote: "We hold that the constitutional guarantee against multiple punishments for the same offense absolutely requires that punishments already exacted be fully 'credited' in imposing sentences upon a new conviction for the same offense. If, upon a new trial, the defendant is acquitted, there is no way the years spent in prison can be returned to him. But if he is reconvicted, those years can and must be returned—by subtracting them from whatever new sentence is imposed." In short, justice requires full credit for prior time served.

On the second issue, the Court justified allowing a new sentence, whether greater or less than the original sentence, "in light of events subsequent to the first trial that may have thrown new light upon the defendant's life, health, habits, conduct, and mental and moral propensities." Such information, the Court added, may come from various sources, including the new presentence investigation, the defendant's prison record, or possibly from other sources. Courts have a great deal of discretion, therefore, in imposing a new sentence. The Court issued this caution, however, which limits a judge's discretion: "Due process of law . . . requires that vindictiveness against a defendant for having successfully attacked his first conviction must play no part in the sentence he receives after a new trial." A higher sentence must be based on factors other than anger on the part of the judge due to the defendant's success in obtaining a second trial.

Williams v. Illinois
399 U.S. 235 (1970)

CAPSULE: A state law that requires "work off" for indigents beyond the maximum sentence is unconstitutional.

FACTS: Williams was convicted of petty theft and given the maximum sentence allowed by Illinois law—one year imprisonment and a fine of $500. He was also assessed $5 in court costs. State law provided that after serving the one year if the defendant defaulted the payment of the fine and court costs, he would remain in jail to "work off" his monetary obligation at a rate of $5 per day. The result was that, whereas the maximum term of imprisonment for petty theft was one year, the effect of the sentence imposed required Williams to be confined for 101 days beyond the maximum period of confinement fixed by the statute because he could not pay the fine and costs of $505.

ISSUE: Is a state law that imposes imprisonment plus a fine, and provides that if the fine is not paid the prisoner must remain in jail longer than the prescribed maximum sentence to "work off" the unpaid fine constitutional? NO.

DECISION: A state law that imposes imprisonment plus a fine and provides that if the fine is not paid, the prisoner must remain in jail longer than the prescribed maximum sentence to "work off" the unpaid fine is unconstitutional because it violates the equal protection clause of the Fourteenth Amendment.

REASON: "A State has wide latitude in fixing the punishment for state crimes. Thus, appellant does not assert that Illinois could not have appropriately fixed the penalty, in the first instance, at one year and 101 days. Nor has the claim been advanced that the sentence imposed was excessive in light of the circumstances of the commission of this particular offense. However, once the State has defined the outer limits of incarceration necessary to satisfy its penological interests and policies, it may not then subject a certain class of convicted defendants to a period of imprisonment beyond the maximum solely by reason of their indigency.

"It is clear, of course, that the sentence was not imposed upon appellant because of his indigency but because he had committed a crime. And the Illinois statutory scheme does not distinguish between defendants on the basis of ability to pay fines. But, as we said in *Griffin v. Illinois, supra,* 'a law nondiscriminatory on its face may be grossly discriminatory in its operation.' *Id.*, at 17 n. 11. Here the Illinois law as applied to Williams works an invidious discrimination solely because he is unable to pay the fine.

"A statute permitting a sentence of both imprisonment and fine cannot be parlayed into a longer term of imprisonment than is fixed by the statute since to do so would be to accomplish indirectly as to an indigent that which cannot be done directly. We have no occasion to reach the question whether a State is precluded in any other circumstances from holding an indigent accountable for a fine by use of a penal sanction. We hold only that the Equal Protection Clause of the Fourteenth Amendment requires that the statutory ceiling placed on imprisonment for any substantive offense be the same for all defendants irrespective of their economic status."

CASE SIGNIFICANCE: This case establishes the principle that defendants are entitled to equal protection in the sentencing phase of a criminal trial. Its bedrock is a statement made by the Court in an earlier case (*Griffin v. Illinois*, 351 U.S. 12 [1956]) to the effect that "there can be no equal justice where the kind of trial a man gets depends on the amount of money he has." In this case, if Williams had been able to pay the fine and court costs, he would not have spent more time in jail.

The *Williams* case was the precedent for a similar case, *Tate v. Short*, 401 U.S. 395 (1970). In *Tate* the Court said the Texas law that provided for only a fine for traffic offenses but converted the fine to imprisonment if the defendant was unable to pay the fine, also violated the equal protection clause. Together, these cases stand for the proposition that there can be no equal justice where the poor go to prison primarily because they do not have the money to pay a fine. It must be stressed, however, that the Court itself said that the holding in *Williams* "does not deal with a judgment of confinement or nonpayment of a fine in the familiar pattern of alternative sentence of $30 or 30 days." This distinction means that a defendant in court who does not have $30 to pay his or her fine during sentencing may instead be validly sent to jail for 30 days.

The key to understanding the *Williams* case is to realize that the "work-off" arrangement exceeded the maximum allowed by law for the offense. Note that a distinction must be made between inability to pay a fine because of indigency and refusal to pay a fine. A defendant may be sent to prison any time if, being able to do so, he or she refuses to pay a fine for any reason.

Tate v. Short
401 U.S. 395 (1971)

CAPSULE: A state law that automatically converts a fine to imprisonment if an indigent defendant cannot pay is unconstitutional.

FACTS: The defendant, an indigent, was fined a total of $425 upon conviction of nine traffic offenses. Under Texas law, only fines could be imposed for such offenses. The law, however, also required that persons unable to pay must be incarcerated until the fines are satisfied, at a rate of $5 per day. In this defendant's case this meant being in jail for 85 days.

ISSUE: Is a law that automatically converts a fine to imprisonment, if an indigent defendant cannot pay, constitutional? NO.

DECISION: It is a violation of the equal protection clause of the Fourteenth Amendment to limit punishment to payment of a fine for those who are able to pay but to convert the fine to imprisonment for those unable to pay.

REASON: "In *Morris v. Schoenfield*, 399 U.S. 508, 509 (1970), four members of the Court anticipated the problem of this case and stated the view, which we now adopt, that:

> the same constitutional defect condemned in *Williams* also inheres in jailing an indigent for failing to make immediate payment of any fine, whether or not the fine is accompanied by a jail term and whether or not the jail term of the indigent extends beyond the maximum term that may be imposed on a person willing and able to pay a fine. In each case, the Constitution prohibits the State from imposing a fine as a sentence and then automatically converting it into a jail term solely because the defendant is indigent and cannot forthwith pay the fine in full.

"Our opinion in *Williams* stated the premise of this conclusion in saying that 'the Equal Protection Clause of the Fourteenth Amendment requires that the statutory ceiling placed on imprisonment for any substantive offense be the same for all defendants irrespective of their economic status.' 399 U.S., at 244. Since Texas has legislated a 'fines only' policy for traffic offenses, that statutory ceiling cannot, consistently with the Equal Protection Clause, limit the punishment to payment of the fine if one is able to pay it, yet convert the fine into a prison term for an indigent defendant without the means to pay his fine. Imprisonment in such a case is not imposed to further any penal objective of the State. It is imposed to augment the State's revenues but obviously does not serve that purpose; the defendant cannot pay because he is indigent and his imprisonment, rather than aiding collection of revenue, saddles the State with the cost of feeding and housing him for the period of his imprisonment.

"We emphasize that our holding today does not suggest any constitutional infirmity in imprisonment of a defendant with the means to pay a fine who refuses or neglects to do so. Nor is our decision to be understood as precluding imprisonment as an enforcement method when alternative means are unsuccessful despite the defendant's reasonable efforts to satisfy the fines by those means; the determination of the constitutionality of imprisonment in that circumstance must await the presentation of a concrete case."

CASE SIGNIFICANCE: This case was decided on the basis of the precedent set by the Supreme Court in *Williams v. Illinois*, 399 U.S. 235 (1970). In *Williams*, the Court said that a state may not, under the equal protection clause, subject a certain class of convicted defendants to a period of imprisonment beyond the maximum set by state law if the reason for non-payment is indigency. Said the Court: "Since Texas has legislated a 'fines only' policy for traffic offenses, that statutory ceiling cannot, consistently with the Equal Protection Clause, limit the punishment to payment of the fine if one is able to pay it, yet convert the fine into a prison term for an indigent defendant without the means to pay his fine." The Court added: "We emphasize that our holding today does not suggest any constitutional infirmity in imprisonment of a defendant with the means to pay a fine who refuses or neglects to do so." This means that a person who is indigent and cannot pay a fine cannot be sent to prison for non-payment, whereas one who refuses to pay a fine or neglects to do so can be given a jail or prison term. The question arises: who bears the burden of proof? In many jurisdictions indigency is an affirmative defense, meaning it must be raised and proved by the defendant instead of the government having to prove that defendant can pay. There is no constitutional requirement that the state bear the burden of proving that the defendant is not in fact indigent. The fact that a defendant cannot pay because of indigency must be raised and proved by the defendant.

Harmelin v. Michigan
59 L.W. 4839 (1991)

CAPSULE: Mandatory and disproportionate sentences are not necessarily unconstitutional.

FACTS: Harmelin was convicted of possessing 672 grams of cocaine and was sentenced to a mandatory term of life in prison without possibility of parole.

The Michigan State Court of Appeals rejected his argument that the sentence was "cruel and unusual" within the meaning of the Eighth Amendment. Harmelin claimed that the sentence was cruel and unusual because it was "significantly disproportionate" to the crime he committed. He also asserted that the sentencing judge was statutorily required to impose the sentence without taking into account the particular characteristics of the crime or the criminal.

ISSUES:
1. Is a sentence that requires a mandatory term of life in prison without possibility of parole for an offense such as that committed by the defendant constitutional even if it does not take into account the particularized circumstances of the crime and the criminal? YES.
2. Is a disproportionate sentence cruel and unusual punishment in violation of the Eighth Amendment? NO.

DECISIONS:
1. The sentence here is not unconstitutional merely because its mandatory nature precludes judicial inquiry into whatever mitigating factors may exist; an "individualized" determination of whether a particular sentence is appropriate punishment is necessary only in death penalty cases.
2. The Eighth Amendment contains no proportionality guarantee; therefore, the sentence cannot be considered unconstitutionally disproportional. For crimes concededly classified and classifiable as felonies—i.e., as punishable by significant terms of imprisonment in a state penitentiary—the length of the sentence actually imposed is purely a legislative prerogative.

REASONS:
1. "That the Americans who adopted the Eighth Amendment intended its Cruel and Unusual Punishments Clause as a check on the ability of the Legislature to authorize particular modes of punishment—i.e., cruel methods of punishment that are not regularly or customarily employed—rather than as a guarantee against disproportionate sentences is demonstrated by the available evidence of contemporary understanding, including the context of adoption, the debates of the state ratifying conventions and the First Congress, and early commentary and judicial decisions. It is particularly telling that those who framed and approved the Federal Constitution chose not to include within it the explicit guarantee against disproportionate sentences that some State Constitutions contained.

"There are no adequate textual or historical standards to enable judges to determine whether a particular penalty is disproportional. The first two of the factors that *Solem* found relevant—the inherent gravity of the defendant's offense and the sentences imposed for similarly grave offenses in some jurisdictions—fail for lack of an objective standard of gravity. Since, as the statutes Americans have enacted in different times and places demonstrate there is enormous variation of opinion as to what offenses are serious, the proportionality principle is an invitation for judges to impose their own subjective values. Moreover, although the third *Solem* factor—the character of the sentences imposed by the other States for the same crime—can be applied with clarity and ease, it is irrelevant to the Eighth Amendment. Traditional notions of federalism entitle States to treat like situations differently in light of local needs, concerns, and social conditions.

"Although this Court's 20th-century jurisprudence has not remained entirely in accord with the proposition that there is no Eighth Amendment proportionality requirement, it has not departed to the extent that *Solem* suggests. While *Weems v. United States*, 217 U.S. 349—which was cited by *Solem, supra,* at 287, as the 'leading case'—did contain language suggesting that mere disproportionality might make a punishment cruel and unusual, 217 U.S., at 366-367, it also contained statements indicating that the unique punishment there at issue was unconstitutional because it was unknown to Anglo-American tradition, id., at 377. It is hard to view *Weems* as announcing a constitutional proportionality requirement, given that it did not produce a decision implementing such a requirement, either in this Court or the lower federal courts for six decades. This Court's first such opinion, *Coker v. Georgia*, 433 U.S. 584, 592, was a death penalty case. The *Coker* line of authority should not be treated as a generalized aspect of Eighth Amendment law, since proportionality review is one of several respects in which 'death is different,' requiring protections that the Constitution nowhere else provides.

2.   ". . . Harmelin's claim that his sentence is unconstitutional because it is mandatory in nature, allowing the sentencer no opportunity to consider 'mitigating factors,' has no support in the Eighth Amendment's text and history. Severe, mandatory penalties may be cruel, but they are not unusual in the constitutional sense, having been employed in various forms throughout the Nation's history. Although Harmelin's claim finds some support in the so-called 'individualized capital sentencing doctrine' of this Court's death penalty jurisprudence, *see, e.g., Woodson v. North Carolina*, 428 U.S. 280, that doctrine may not be extended outside the capital context because of the qualitative differences between death and all other penalties."

CASE SIGNIFICANCE: This is the latest case decided by the Court on the cruel and unusual punishment clause of the Eighth Amendment. The defendant argued that the sentence was unconstitutional because of its mandatory nature (Michigan law provided that for a crime like this the sentencing judge is statutorily required to impose the prescribed sentence without taking into account the peculiar circumstances of the crime and criminal), and because the sentence was significantly disproportionate to the offense for which he was convicted. In a 5-4 split, the Court rejected the defendant's argument, saying that the concept of "individualized sentencing" (in which the court must consider mitigating factors) is limited only to cases in which the death penalty is imposed and not to other types of sentences. As for the proportionality argument, the Court could not agree on it. Justice Scalia (who wrote the opinion) and Chief Justice Rehnquist maintained that the Eighth Amendment contains no proportionality guarantee, hence Harmelin's sentence could not be considered unconstitutional. In contrast, Justices Kennedy, O'Connor, and Souter concluded that the Eighth Amendment does not require strict proportionality between crime and sentence; however, it forbids extreme sentences that are "grossly disproportionate" to the crime, adding that "although a sentence of life imprisonment without parole is the second most severe penalty permitted by law, it is not grossly disproportionate to Harmelin's crime of possessing more than 650 grams of cocaine." The dissenting justices, led by Justice White, disagreed, saying that "the language of the Amendment does not refer to proportionality in so many words, but it does forbid 'excessive' fines, a restraint that suggests that a determination of excessiveness should be based at least in part on whether the fine imposed is disproportionate to the crime committed."

Given the disagreement among the justices, it must be concluded that the issue of whether the Eighth Amendment ban against cruel and unusual punishment means that the sentence imposed must be proportionate to the crime committed is still unresolved by the Court. Two justices opined that the Eighth Amendment does not require proportionality, three justices said that it proscribes sentences that are "grossly disproportionate' to the offense, while the four dissenters maintained that sentences must be proportionate to the offense otherwise they can run afoul of the Constitution. It is to be noted, however, that in death penalty cases, the Court requires that mitigating factors be taken into account in sentencing. This is because, as the Court says, "death is different."

Nichols v. United States
114 S. Ct. 1921 (1994)

CAPSULE: Because an uncounseled misdemeanor conviction is valid as long as no term of imprisonment is imposed, a prior misdemeanor conviction obtained in the absence of counsel may be used for sentence enhancement for another offense.

FACTS: In 1990, Kenneth Nichols pleaded guilty to conspiracy to possess cocaine with intent to distribute, in violation of federal law. Under the federal sentencing guidelines, Nichols was given three criminal history points for a

1983 federal felony drug conviction. He was also given one criminal history point for a 1983 state misdemeanor conviction for driving under the influence (DUI). He received a fine of $250 but was not incarcerated for that conviction. The additional criminal history point increased Nichols' Criminal History Category from category II to category III, which resulted in his sentencing range increasing from 168-210 months to 188-235 months. Nichols argued that his DUI misdemeanor should not be included in his criminal history score because he had not been represented by counsel.

ISSUE: Does the Sixth Amendment prohibit a sentencing court from considering a defendant's previous uncounseled misdemeanor conviction when sentencing him for a subsequent offense? NO.

DECISION: A sentencing court may constitutionally consider a defendant's previous uncounseled misdemeanor conviction in sentencing him for a subsequent offense as long as the previous uncounseled misdemeanor conviction did not result in a sentence of imprisonment.

REASON: "Reliance on such a conviction is also consistent with the traditional understanding of the sentencing process, which we have often recognized as less exacting than the process of establishing guilt. As a general proposition, a sentencing judge 'may appropriately conduct an inquiry broad in scope, largely unlimited either as to the kind of information he may consider, or the source from which it may come. 'Traditionally, sentencing judges have considered a wide variety of factors in addition to evidence of guilt in determining what sentence to impose on a convicted defendant.' One such important factor, as recognized by state recidivism statutes and the criminal history component of the Sentencing Guidelines, is a defendant's prior convictions. Sentencing courts have not only taken into consideration a defendant's prior convictions, but have also considered a defendant's past criminal behavior, even if no conviction resulted from that behavior. We have upheld the constitutionality of considering such previous conduct in *Williams v. New York*, 337 U.S. 241 (1949). We have also upheld the consideration of such conduct, in connection with the offense presently charged, in *McMillan v. Pennsylvania*, 477 U.S. 79 (1986). There we held that the state could consider, as a sentence enhancement factor, visible possession of a firearm during the felonies of which defendant was found guilty.

"Thus, consistently with due process, petitioner in the present case could have been sentenced more severely based simply on evidence of the underlying conduct which gave rise to the previous DUI offense. And the state need prove such conduct only by a preponderance of the evidence. *Id.*, at 91. Surely, then, it must be constitutionally permissible to consider a prior uncounseled misdemeanor conviction based on the same conduct where that conduct must be proven beyond a reasonable doubt."

CASE SIGNIFICANCE: In *Scott v. Illinois*, 440 U.S. 367 (1979), the Court held that a defendant charged with a misdemeanor on whom no sentence of imprisonment was imposed had no constitutional right to counsel, and therefore the trial held without a lawyer was valid. A year later, in *Baldasar v. Illinois*, 446 U.S. 222 (1980), the Court ruled that a misdemeanor conviction without a lawyer could not be used to convert a second misdemeanor conviction into a felony under the state's sentencing enhancement statute. *Nichols* says that a misdemeanor conviction obtained in the absence of a lawyer may be used in a sentence enhancement for another offense. Significantly, the Court said that it agreed with the dissent in *Baldasar* that "a logical consequence of the holding is that an uncounseled conviction valid under *Scott* may be relied upon to enhance the sentence for a subsequent offense, even though that sentence entails imprisonment." In effect, the Court said that the ruling in *Baldasar* (decided in 1980 on a 5-4 vote) would most likely be different if the case were decided today.

Koon v. United States
64 L.W. 4512 (1996)

CAPSULE: An appellate court should not review *de novo* (meaning afresh or anew) a decision to depart from the Federal Sentencing Guidelines. Instead, the question to be asked is whether the sentencing court abused its discretion.

FACTS: Stacey Koon and Laurence Powell, two Los Angeles police officers, were acquitted on state charges of assault and excessive use of force in the beating of Rodney King during an arrest. They were later convicted under 18 U.S.C. §242 of violating King's constitutional rights under color of law. The United States Sentencing Guidelines indicated that they should be imprisoned for 70 to 87 months. The District Court granted them two downward departures from that range. The judge reasoned that King's misconduct during the arrest contributed significantly to provoking the offense and was the basis for the first departure from the guideline range. The second departure was based on a combination of four factors: (1) that Koon and Powell were unusually susceptible to abuse in prison; (2) that they would lose their jobs and be precluded from employment in law enforcement; (3) that they had been subject to successive state and federal prosecutions; and (4) that they posed a low risk of recidivism. The resulting sentencing range was 30 to 37 months, and both Koon and Powell received a sentence of 30 months. The Ninth Circuit reviewed the departure decisions *de novo* and rejected all of them.

ISSUE: Is *de novo* (afresh or anew) the proper standard by which departures from the United States Sentencing Guidelines should be reviewed? NO.

DECISION: An appellate court should not review *de novo* a decision to depart from the Federal Sentencing Guidelines. Instead, the question that should be asked is whether the sentencing court abused its discretion.

REASON: "A district court's decision to depart from the Guidelines, by contrast, will in most cases be due substantial deference, for it embodies the traditional exercise of discretion by a sentencing court. See *Mistretta*, 488 U.S., at 367 (noting that although the Act makes the Guidelines binding on sentencing courts, 'it preserves for the judge the discretion to depart from the guideline applicable to a particular case'). Before a departure is permitted, certain aspects of the case must be found unusual enough for it to fall outside the heartland of cases in the Guidelines. To resolve this question, the district court must make a refined assessment of the many facts bearing on the outcome, informed by its vantage point and day-to-day experience in criminal sentencing. Whether a given factor is present to a degree not adequately considered by the Commission, or whether a discouraged factor nonetheless justifies departure because it is present in some unusual or exceptional way, are matters determined in large part by comparison with the facts of other Guideline cases. District courts have an institutional advantage over appellate courts in making these sorts of determinations, especially as they see so many more Guidelines cases than appellate courts do.

"Considerations like these persuaded us to adopt the abuse-of-discretion standard in *Cooter & Gell v. Hartmarx Corp.*, 496 U.S. 384 (1990), which involved review of a district court's imposition of Rule 11 sanctions, and in *Pierce v. Underwood*, 487 U.S. 552 (1988), which involved review of a district court's determination under the Equal Access to Justice Act, 28 U.S.C. §2412(d), that the position of the United States was 'substantially justified,' thereby precluding an award of attorney's fees against the Government. There, as here, we noted that deference was owed to the 'judicial actor . . . better positioned than another to decide the issue in question.' Furthermore, we adopted deferential review to afford 'the district court the necessary flexibility to resolve questions involving multifarious, fleeting, special, narrow facts that utterly resist generalization.' 496 U.S., at 404 (quoting *Pierce, supra,* at 561-562). Like the questions involved in those cases, a district court's departure decision involves 'the consideration of unique factors that are 'little susceptible . . . of useful generalization,'

496 U.S., at 404, and as a consequence, *de novo* review is 'unlikely to establish clear guidelines for lower courts,' *id.*, at 405."

CASE SIGNIFICANCE: This case involved two of the Los Angeles police officers who were involved in the Rodney King beating in Los Angeles. In the first criminal trial, in Simi Valley, all of the officers were acquitted. In the second trial, in Los Angeles, two of the officers were convicted, including Stacey Koon. The Federal Sentencing Guidelines indicated that the officers should be imprisoned for 70 to 87 months. The sentencing judge departed from that range and gave a much lower sentence of 30 to 37 months, saying that there were factors that justified two downward departures from the usual sentencing range. The government appealed. The Supreme Court ruled that the departures were proper and that the standard for review by an appellate court of a sentence imposed was not a *de novo* determination of the case, but whether the sentencing judge abused his or her discretion. This case is significant because despite the Federal Sentencing Guidelines, which was passed by the U.S. Congress to control the discretion of federal judges, the appellate court has limited power to review the sentence imposed by a federal court judge. That power to review is limited to determining whether the sentencing judge abused discretion when imposing the sentence. In this case, the sentence imposed by the trial court did not represent judicial abuse and therefore the sentence was upheld.

Index